CW01559187

The African Union

The African Union

The First Ten Years

Ambassador Omar Alieu Touray

ROWMAN & LITTLEFIELD
Lanham • Boulder • New York • London

Published by Rowman & Littlefield
A wholly owned subsidiary of The Rowman & Littlefield Publishing Group, Inc.
4501 Forbes Boulevard, Suite 200, Lanham, Maryland 20706
www.rowman.com

Unit A, Whitacre Mews, 26-34 Stannary Street, London SE11 4AB

British Library Cataloguing in Publication Information Available

Library of Congress Cataloging-in-Publication Data Available

ISBN 978-1-4422-6897-5 (cloth : alk.paper)
ISBN 978-1-4422-6898-2 (electronic)

∞™ The paper used in this publication meets the minimum requirements of American National Standard for Information Sciences—Permanence of Paper for Printed Library Materials, ANSI/NISO Z39.48-1992.

Printed in the United States of America

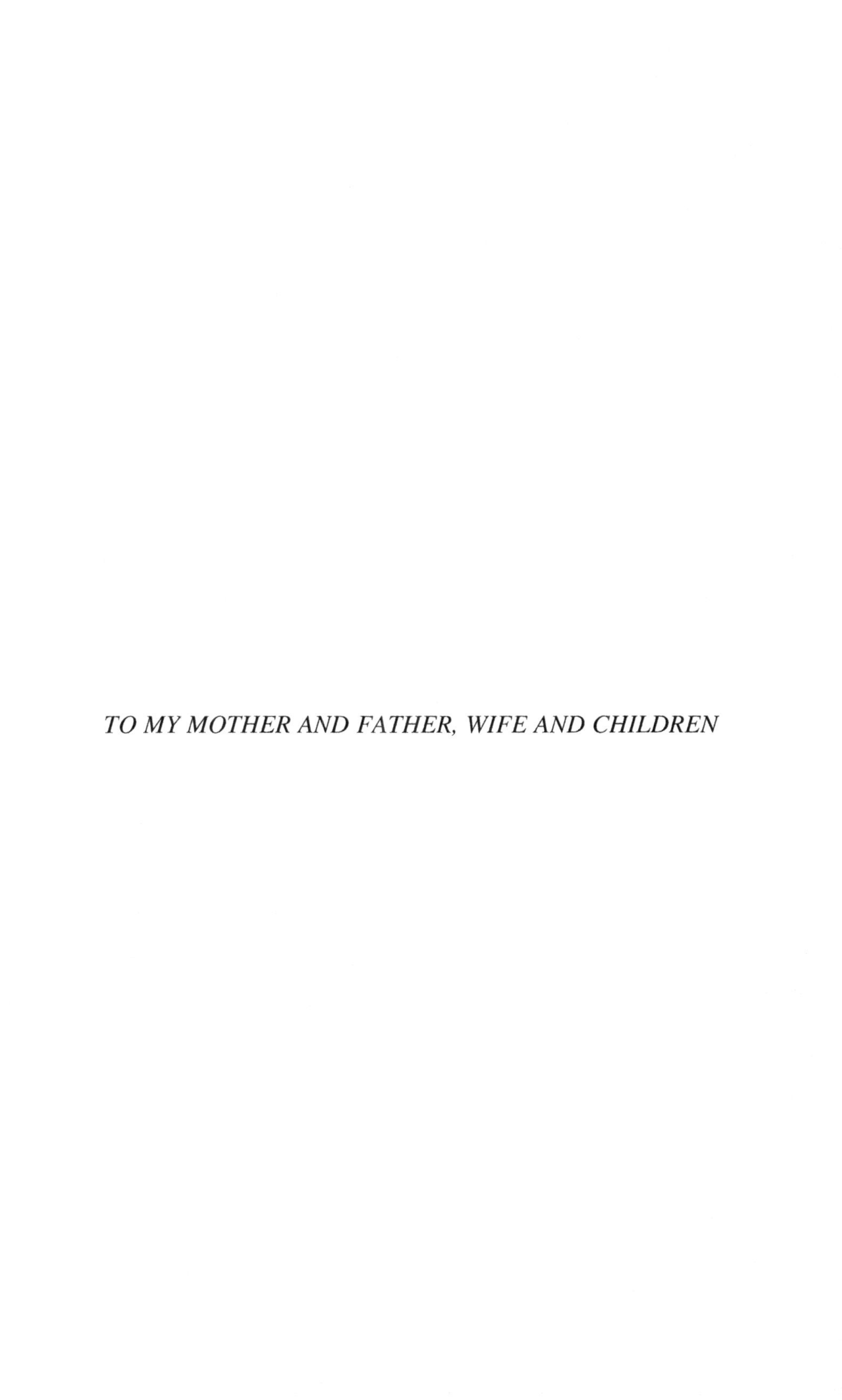

TO MY MOTHER AND FATHER, WIFE AND CHILDREN

Contents

List of Figures and Tables

FIGURES

TABLES

List of Abbreviations

AAP	Africa Action Plan
AAU	Association of African Universities
ACA	Advisory Council on Ageing
ACERWC	African Committee of Experts on the Rights and Welfare of the Child
ACHPR	African Commission on Human and People's Right
ACRT	African Crises Response Initiative
ADB	African Development Bank
ADEA	Association for the Development of Education in Africa
ADF	African Development Forum
ADPD	African Decade for Persons with Disability
AEC	African Economic Community
AGOA	African Growth and Opportunities Act
AHG	African Heads of Government
AIR	African Institute for Remittances
AMIB	African Mission in Burundi
AMIS	African Mission in Sudan
AMISOM	African Union Mission in Somalia
ANC	Africa National Congress
ANWFZT	African Nuclear Weapons Free Zone Treaty
APRM	African Peer Review Mechanism
APTSP	African Peace Keeping Training Support Programme
ASF	African Standby Force
AU	African Union
AUC	African Union Commission
CA	Constitutive Act

CAADP	Comprehensive African Agriculture Development Programme
CADSP	Common African Defence and Security Policy
CARMMA	Campaign for the Accelerated Reduction of Maternal, Infant, and Child Mortality in Africa
CDCA / CDAC	Central African Development Community
CDS	Chiefs of Defence Staff
CEMAC	Communauté Economique et Monétaire de l'Afrique Centrale
CEN-SAD	Community of Sahara and Sahelian States
CERGL / ECGLR	Communauté Economique de la région des Grands Lacs
CEWS	Continental Early Warning System
CMCA	Committee on Mediation, Conciliation and Arbitration
CO	Central Organ
COMEDAF	Conference of Ministers of Education
COMESA	Common Market for Eastern and Southern Africa Cooperation
COREPER	Comité des Représentants Permanents
CSSDCA	Conference on Security, Stability, Development and Cooperation in Africa
DAC	Development Assistance Committee
DDA	Doha Development Agenda
EAC	East African Community
EC	European Communities
ECOSOC	Economic and Social Council
ECOWAS	Economic Community of West African States
ECSC	European Coal and Steel Community
EEC	European Economic Community
EMIS	Education Management Information System
EU	European Union
EWM	Early Warning Mechanism
FAO	Food and Agriculture Organization
FDI	Foreign Direct Investment
FTA	Free-Trade Area
G8	Group of Eight Industrial Nations
GDP	Gross Domestic Product
GNI	Gross National Index
HCTs	High Commission Territories
HDI	Human Development Index
HIPC	Heavily Indebted Poor Country
IDPs	Internally Displaced Persons
IGAD	Intergovernmental Authority on Development

ILO	International Labour Organization
IMF	International Monetary Fund
IOC	Indian Ocean Commission
LDC	Least Developed Countries
MDG	Millennium Development Goals
MEP	Member of the European Parliament
MINEDAF	African Ministers of Education
MIP	Minimum Integration Programme
MRU	Mano River Union
NATO	North Atlantic Treaty Organization
NEPAD	New Partnership for Africa's Development
OAU	Organization of African Unity
OECD	Organization for Economic Cooperation and Development
ORID	Other Related Infectious Diseases
PAP	Pan African Parliament
PAU	Pan African University
PCRD	Post Conflict Reconstruction and Development
PLANELM	Planning Element
PLWHA	People Living with HIV and AIDS
PRC	Permanent Representatives Committee
PSC	Peace and Security Council
RECAMP	Renforcement des Capacités Africaines de Maintien de la Paix
RECs	Regional Economic Communities
RM	Regional Mechanism
SACU	Southern African Customs Union
SADC	Southern African Development Community
SALW	Small Arms and Lights Weapon
SDGEA	Solemn Declaration on Gender Equality in Africa
TB	Tuberculosis
TRIPS	Trade-Related Intellectual Property Rights
UEMOA	Union Economique et monétaire de l'Ouest Afrique
UMA	Union de Maghreb Arabe
UN	United Nations
UNDP	United Nations Development Programme
UNECA / ECA	United Nations Economic Commission for Africa
UNESCO	United Nations Educational, Scientific and Cultural Organization
UNIP	United National Independence Party of Zambia
WHO	World Health Organization
WTO	World Trade Organization

Preface

When the OAU began operations in 1963, it had only 32 member states. By the time the organization was transformed into the African Union 40 years later, its membership had grown to 53 states. By the end of 2012, the majority of member states had accredited full-fledged permanent missions to the African Union Commission, in compliance with the provisions of the Constitutive Act of the Union. This alone shows the measure of seriousness with which African governments have come to take the African Union. Nothing, however, points to the potential and the considerable promise that the African union holds than the decision of the non-African states to be associated with the African Union, not only by funding the activities of the organization but also by closely working with the Commission. By the end of 2012, over 60 non-African countries and a dozen of international organizations and UN agencies had accredited representatives to the African Union in Addis Ababa.

The hope that African leaders and ordinary citizens have had in the organization and the interest it has generated outside the continent is sufficient to justify an enterprise such as this book. By and large the study seeks to unravel the mechanics of the organization as well as the challenges it faced during its first ten years.

Such an ambitious enterprise could not have been possible without the invaluable support and cooperation of family members, colleagues, individuals and organizations. At the outset, I would like to express gratitude to my wife, Sally, and children, Basiru, Alieu and Zahra. My gratitude also goes to anonymous readers and referees for their painstaking review of the manuscript and for their invaluable suggestions. Colleagues in the diplomatic and development fields who have contributed to this enterprise either directly or indirectly are too many to name here. I am grateful to all of them as well as to the staff of the African Union Commission for their exemplary cooperation both during my tour of duty in Addis Ababa and during other assignments I undertook subsequently. While I recognize the role of the very many people and institutions in the present enterprise, I alone remain responsible for all its shortcomings. And, needless to say, the views expressed here are mine and do not in any way represent the views of my present and past employers.

O.A. Touray
Jeddah, April 2016

Chapter 1

Introduction

In his concise study, Colin Legum identified three distinctive epochs in the contemporary political history of Africa.[1] The period leading up to and immediately following independence (1950–1970) was essentially the "romantic period." This was the period of optimism and high hopes for Africa. But the romanticism soon faded and was eclipsed by the hard reality of nation building. The arrival of military and single-party regimes on the continent's public space further precipitated the end of the romantic era. Running roughly from 1970 to the mid-1980s, the second period was marked by a hopeless decline in almost all spheres of life on the continent. It was the attempt to arrest this decline and raise hopes on the continent that marked the third period (mid-1980s to mid-1990s). No doubt the miscarriage of the decolonization process[2] continued into the 1990s, but hope came with the demise of the Cold War and the relative retreat of the external political interest in the continent. Weakened by the flight of external backing and threatened by the mounting demands from within their national frontiers, Africa's military and single-party regimes crumbled under the increasing weight of domestic demand for good economic and political governance. The result is that by the mid-1990s African political landscape changed considerably – with more democratically elected governments and fewer military and single-party authoritarian regimes being installed in most countries.

The momentum generated by domestic reforms went beyond national frontiers. At the continental level, it triggered a chorus of voices calling for the reform of the continental organization, the Organization of African Unity (OAU). It turned out that the OAU did not need reform, it needed a complete overhaul. This exigency gave birth to the new continental body, the African Union (AU).

Since its establishment, the African Union has attracted unparalleled interest both within and outside the continent. Much of this interest was borne largely by the expectation that the Union would address the difficulties, which, according to critics, evaded the erstwhile Organization of African Unity. The sizeable body of literature on the Union shows that the academic community has also had considerable interest in the African Union. Key areas of academic focus include the rationale and origins of the AU,[3] peace and security,[4] human rights, democracy and good governance,[5] and development.[6]

The present study builds on the existing work and offers in a single volume a comprehensive assessment of the African Union during the first ten years on the basis of first-hand knowledge and primary sources that might not readily be available to many students of the continental organization.

A subject like the African Union can be approached from various perspectives. It can be assessed as an extension of pan-Africanism – the latest incarnation of pan-Africanism, as Murithi has put it.[7] It can also be looked at as an international organization.[8] In my view, however, the African Union is about the integration of the African continent. It is therefore best assessed within the framework of integration theories. Thus, in addition to offering a comprehensive examination of the first ten years of the African Union, the study seeks to have a bearing on the existing academic debate on international integration. Although an exhaustive assessment of the bulky literature on integration is neither the objective nor is it practically feasible within the confines of this chapter, I have provided in the following few pages an outline of the existing arguments as a context within which my own thesis is to be situated.

INTEGRATION: CONTENDING PERSPECTIVES

The move towards a more systematic study of social sciences in the United States since the 1950s has given rise to a multiplicity of theories and analytical frameworks that seek to explain the behaviour of states in international affairs. Few subfields of international relations have been the subject of such theorization more than integration. Since the inception of the European Coal and Steel Community (which blossomed into present-day European Union), academic interest in integration has grown to such an extent that the theoretical literature has become too bulky for any single study to exhaust. For this purpose, therefore, I will limit my analysis to an overview of key schools of thought that have strongly influenced the study of integration. They are the Functionalists and Neofunctionalists, Liberal Intergovernmentalists, Institutionalists,[9] and Constructivists.

Functionalists, who are considered pioneers in the field, see integration as a gradual and self-sustaining process that is largely spurred and nurtured by groups of technical experts working outside the confines of the state.[10] The habit of cooperation that these experts build eventually spills over into cooperation in political and military affairs, as experts lose their close identification with the state and develop new sets of allegiance to like-minded individuals within the Community. Functionalists maintain that the European Union has followed such a route. The European Coal and Steel Community, for example, was a forum for cooperation in non-political issues. Cooperation in that area eventually spilled over to cooperation in trade and labour matters, which led to the progressive reduction of tariffs and duties between member states and to the removal of restrictions on the movement of labour.

Liberal Intergovernmentalism, as developed and later fine-tuned by Andrew Moravcsik, represents a serious challenge to functionalism and its subsequent variant, neofuntionalism.[11]

Essentially, *Liberal Intergovernmentalists* posit that integration is an intergovernmental process that involves two sequential processes: preference formation and international bargaining.[12] The first process involves national leaders sounding and registering the interest of their domestic constituency (including their own interest) and articulating national preferences. In the second process, national governments bring their preferences to the intergovernmental bargaining table, where agreements reflect the relative power of each member state. When Liberal Intergovernmentalism was initially developed, its proponents saw little causal role for supranational organizations in the intergovernmental process.[13]

Just like their functionalist and neofunctionalist rivals, Liberal Intergovernmentalists also came under severe criticism. First, they were criticized for overlooking endogenous factors as well as the impact of the identity of national elites in the process of preference formation.[14]

Second, Liberal Intergovernmentalism was rejected by students who advanced the theory of "multi-level governance," where an individual member government of an international organization is seen as one among many sub-national and supranational actors in a complex and unique system of governance.[15]

Third, the social movement theorists, on their part, argue that social movements are not confined to having their interests articulated by national governments, but like regional governments they do in fact influence decision-making directly or eschew the institutions of government in favour of direct action by transnational civil society.[16]

The most sweeping, though constructive, criticism came from institutional theorists, who came under various strains including *Historical Institutionalists, Sociological Institutionalists* and *Rational Choice Institutionalists.* On the whole, the institutionalists agree with the basic assumptions of the Liberal Intergovernmentalist about preference formation, but dispute the exclusive role of the state and national leaders in this process. They maintain that Liberal Intergovernmentalists fail to capture how supranational institutions shape and constrain intergovernmental policymaking process.[17] Based on empirical evidence, Institutionalists argue that invariably integration decisions get *locked in* and become difficult for members of government to change even if they wish to do so.[18]

Institutionalists also examined among other things the question of supranational delegation and agency and the agenda-setting role of institutions such as the European Parliament. They sought to determine why and under what conditions principals (e.g., members of an organization) might delegate powers to agents (secretariat or administration of an organization). They also sought to determine what happens if an agent behaves in a way that diverges from the preferences of the principal.[19] Their conclusion is that it is the administrative procedures that enable the principals to define *ex ante* the scope of the agency's activities as well as the oversight procedures. Applying this principal–agency analysis to the European Union, they concluded that agency autonomy is likely to vary across issues and over time, depending on the preferences of member states, the amount of information that the principal and agent have, and the rule governing the application of sanctions or the adoption of new legislation.[20]

Indeed, Institutionalist scholars have advanced the debate in several ways. First they have refocused attention to institutions in a way that both functionalists and intergovernmentalists failed to do initially. Second, they, more than any other contending school of thought, have also prompted the reappraisal of intergovernmental thesis by its chief architect, Moravcsik, who in his later work considered *institutional choice* as an additional dimension to his intergovernmental argument, thereby drawing the core assumptions of the Intergovernmentalists closer to that of their Institutionalist rivals.[21] According to Moravcsik, states choose to pool and delegate sovereignty to international organizations as a means of controlling each other, especially in areas where unilateral efforts are ineffective.[22] Thus, in a bid to advance their preferences, states act rationally by aggregating interest and selecting institutions that are designed to maximize their utility.[23] While this development established a major common ground between Liberal Intergovernmentalists and Institutionalists, it had a limited effect on the apparent schism between Institutionalists and another school generally referred to as *Constructivists*.

Although they share a major assumption – that institutions matter – institutionalists and constructivists differ on the nature of institution and how institutions matter. For Institutionalists, institutions are formal and non-formal rules of the game that provide an incentive for rational actors to follow a certain course of action in the pursuit of their preferences. Constructivists, on the other hand, see institutions as formal norms, general understandings and formal rules that shape both the preference and identity of national actors. It is these transformational effects that Constructivists consider to have been lost on Institutionalists.[24] In response, Institutionalists maintain that the Constructivist thesis is void of any empirical evidence as its proponents have failed to place their claims at the risk of empirical disconfirmation.[25] According to Pollack:

> If constructivism and rationalism[26] have emerged as the defining poles of international relations in general and integration studies in particular, and if these two approaches have different assumptions about the nature of agency and social interaction, then the logical course of action is subject their hypothesis to the test of empirical evidence as the ultimate and indeed the only standard of what constitutes "good work" and what determines support for one or the other approach.[27]

Indeed, the logical course of action may consist in subjecting the various hypotheses to the test of empirical evidence as a way of determining "what constitutes good work." It may also entail testing the claims against empirical evidence from the periphery or non-Western context to determine the universality that proponents ascribe to their various positions.[28] The latter constitutes an objective of the present study. In the following section, I articulate in detail how I intend to pursue that objective.

TOWARDS AN INTEGRATED FRAMEWORK – "FUSIONISM?"

A closer assessment of the various schools of thoughts reveals that their assumptions are closer than they appear at first sight. The centrality of institutions in the theses of both institutionalists and constructivists renders the difference between the two traditions superficial. Constructivists do not only accept that institutions matter, they also insist that institutions have transformational effects on leaders. In my view, therefore, Constructivists are just another strain of Institutionalists, just as historical, sociological and rational choice Institutionalists are. Thus, throughout this study, the term Institutionalists will be used broadly to refer to both the traditional strains of the institutionalist school of thought (historical institutionalists, sociological institutionalists and rational choice advocates) as well as Constructivists.

Although Intergovernmentalists also acknowledge (albeit in a later stage) the importance of institutions, their core thesis – that integration is an intergovernmental process – sets them apart from Institutionalists who argue that state and national leaders do not have exclusive monopoly in the process of integration. It is these diametrically opposed views that make it difficult to put the two frameworks in the same category. Thus, Functionalism, Intergovernmentalism and Institutionalism are the three distinct theoretical frameworks around which the present study is framed.

The question that arises immediately is: does the empirical evidence offered by the African Union support the claims that the three analytical traditions have made? In other words, how applicable are these frameworks to a non-European model such as the African Union? The following section offer some responses.

Despite their weight in the theoretical literature, Functionalists are largely Eurocentric. Much of their argument is supported by the European Union, whose origins can be traced to the European Coal and Steel Community (ECSC) and to cooperation in other functional sectors. Applying their argument to non-European contexts immediately shows the limitation of Functionalist framework. In the case of the African Union, there was hardly any evidence of functional cooperation that has spilled over to the ongoing political integration agenda. From the onset, the African Union and the OAU were driven by governments of member states. Although the Charter of the OAU and the Constitutive Act of the African Union provided for Specialized Technical Commissions,[29] and for a role for the private sector and the civil society in the continental integration process,[30] there is hardly any major impact of these actors on AU's agenda for much of the period under consideration. The Specialized Technical Committees (STCs) and the Economic and Social Councils (ECOSOC), which according to the functionalist thesis should have driven the integration agenda, remained dominated by governments and government-selected functionaries, and the outcome of their deliberations required endorsement by the Council of Foreign Ministers before they could be adopted by the heads of state. It is therefore difficult to find any empirical evidence in the African Union that supports the Functionalist thesis.

By contrast, Intergovernmentalist and Institutionalist frameworks offer valuable insights into the Africa Union. However, these too have limitations that, though I cannot assess in detail, need to be highlighted from the onset. On their own, these frameworks cannot explain the African Union in an exhaustive manner. For example, the intergovernmentalist thesis can help us understand the intergovernmental processes that led to the establishment of the African Union and the OAU, and that remained the hallmark of the Africa's integration efforts. But the framework offers little explanation of the factors that influence the intergovernmental processes. Similarly, Intergovernmentalists argue that preference formation takes place at the local and national levels before it is taken to the international negotiation table. This too may tell us the level at which preferences are formed, but says little about the factors that shape preferences.

Institutionalists and other critics have attempted to provide answers to some of the questions that Intergovernmentalists have left unanswered. They posit that the intergovernmental processes are influenced by institutions that "lock in" governments in the process and makes it hard for them to get out even if they wish to do so.[31] They further contend that institutions shape preferences. While these responses have a lot of merit, they are hardly sufficient.

Empirical evidence provided by both African Union and the OAU suggests that the main factors that influence both intergovernmental processes and leaders' preferences in Africa include history, geography, politics, and socio-economic realities of African countries as well as the idiosyncrasies of individual leaders. Beyond identifying these internal determinants of processes and preferences, there is also the need to clarify the role of institutions. A closer assessment of the African Union will confirm the importance that Institutionalists have given to institutions. But institutions exercise influence only after they are created, not before. Thus, determining *when* institutions exercise influence is important.

These limitations suggest that on their own Liberal Intergovernmentalists and Institutionalists cannot offer an exhaustive explanation of integration. However, reappraising and fusing the two traditions into a single framework will not only enable us to understand integration better, it will also show that the two complement each other more than what has been so far recognized.

It is this complementarity on the one hand of the various strains of Institutionalists (including Constructivists) and, on the other hand, between them and Intergovernmentalists that account for our proposal for "Fusionism," not à la Meyer,[32] but more as an integrated framework. The core trait of the proposed Fusionism is a reformulation and integration of the Intergovernmentalists' and Institutionalists' theses into a single analytical framework, according to which

1. integration is generally an intergovernmental process;
2. the intergovernmental process involves the formation and pursuit of preferences;
3. preferences are formed at various levels and shaped by institutions and other determinants such as geography, politics, history and socio-economic realities of states as well as the idiosyncrasies of national leaders;
4. states act rationally by aggregating interest and selecting institutions that are designed to maximize their utility in a bid to advance their preferences;
5. the intergovernmental process does not only involve the formation and pursuit of preferences, it also creates institutions. Once created, institutions take on a life of their own. Over time, they have a transformational influence on leaders at various levels, shape intergovernmental policymaking

and lock in decision-makers in a manner that makes it difficult for member governments to change even if they wish to;

6. institutions also promote and regulate relationships between principals (members of the organization) and agency (administration of the organization). They enable principals to define ex ante the scope of the agency's activity as well as the oversight procedure. They also determine the level of agency autonomy with respect to various issues.

It will be recognized that, as proposed here, Fusionism has a major similarity with the New Regionalism Approach (NRA). They both recognize the multidimensional nature of regionalism. However, while the integrated framework endorses the centrality of intergovernmental processes in integration, the NRA places a lot of emphasis on transnational cooperation and cross-border flows, just like the functionalists have done.[33]

In the preceding pages, I have tried to situate the study within the main theoretical approaches to regional integration. I have indicated that whereas functionalists can hardly explain the African Union, Liberal Intergovernmentalist and Institutionalists offer valuables insights. However, on their own, the two frameworks cannot explain the African Union in an exhaustive manner. I have therefore proposed "Fusionism," which consists in the reappraisal, reformulation, and fusion of Intergovernmentalist and Institutionalist frameworks into a single framework that can help understand the African Union in a comprehensive manner.

In the remainder of the study, I will demonstrate how the Fusionist framework can explain the African Union. It will be shown that contrary to popular belief, the African Union was not the pet project of the former Libyan leader Colonel Muammar Ghaddafi. Although the Libyan leader invested considerable energy in the formation of the African Union, he did not dictate the text of the Constitutive Act of the Union. The African Union was a product of lengthy intergovernmental processes that lasted for several years, and for most member states the Union constituted an aggregate of interests and a rational means of pursuing collective preferences. Over the years, some of the preferences were redefined, whereas others were replaced altogether.

In the immediate aftermath of independence, the most pressing preference of African leaders was the political liberation of the entire continent. President Nkrumah's well-publicized statement that "the independence of Ghana is meaningless unless it is linked up with the total Liberation of Africa" reflects his worldview. But most importantly, it shows the importance that African leaders attach to the liberation of a continent that was, with the exception of Ethiopia and Liberia, carved out among European powers at the 1886 Berlin Conference. By many counts, the organization succeeded on this score. At the founding conference of the organization in 1963, 31 states were in attendance; by the launch of the AU in 2002, the membership of the continental body increased to 53 countries. It is undisputable that the increase was due to one historical factor alone – the decolonization of the continent – and the role of the OAU in that process ought to be fully recognized. With the independence of South Africa in 1991, decolonization was removed from the list of African leaders' preferences.

While decolonization remained a priority of African leaders during the period between the 1950s and the 1990s, it was pursued simultaneously with other important preferences such as socio-economic development. But if Africa was successful on the decolonization front, the continent remained faced with daunting political and socio-economic challenges. As outlined below,[34] Africa not only accounted for the bulk of the world's intrastate conflicts, but the continent started the twenty-first century as the poorest, the most indebted and the most marginalized region of the world. Yet the OAU's inability to forge ahead in these areas does not offer sufficient justification for the sweeping claim that the organization had actually failed. The organization was endowed and structured in a manner that best served its mandate. Additional mandates such as intrastate conflict resolution, socio-economic development, and good political and economic governance require greater autonomy in the form of additional resources and mandates. But these were not forthcoming largely because of the lack of political will on the part of African governments themselves, limited financial resources of member states as well as the Cold War and Realist politics that characterized much of the period of OAU's existence.[35]

The end of the Cold War was celebrated for reviving idealism in international affairs.[36] In Africa, the idealistic undercurrent found expression in renewed interest in African institutions and in finding African solutions to African problems. Thus, the changed global environment, coupled with the new political dispensation and the limited individual capacity of African states, made a collective approach to common challenges a more realistic and feasible project. This consideration accounts for the decision to replace the erstwhile OAU with the AU and to give the new organization a broader mandate in the area of peace and security, as well as in governance and socio-economic development. To a large extent therefore, the African Union and the OAU were aggregates of national interests and constituted a rational means of advancing national utility in the face of limited individual capacity. However, the study will show that as an agent the AU's autonomy varied across issues, and that this variation accounts for the relative success in some areas and failure in others.

With regard to the determinants of the preferences, the study will show that the preferences of the national leaders in Africa were determined largely by both domestic and external factors. Among the domestic factors were the idiosyncrasies of the leaders, geography, politics, historical experiences and socio-economic realities of African states. This consideration, especially African leaders' experience of colonialism, apartheid and racism, accounts for the different Western and African perceptions of and approaches to various questions, including the land reform programmes in Southern Africa.

I will also show that although further research is required to determine the extent to which institutions transform national elites (as Institutionalists assert), there is sufficient evidence to suggest that African Union institutions had some transformational effect on African civilian and military elites, especially in the area of governance.[37] For many years, non-interference in each other's domestic affairs constituted a key preference of African leaders, and often cited as justification for OAU's inaction in several instances. But over time, that policy changed and gave way to what is referred to as the "right to intervene."[38] This, together with other instruments on governance, played a decisive role in the demise of coups d'etat on the continent and represented an enhancing factor in the continent's experiment with democratic pluralism.

In sum, the study will show that: integration is generally an intergovernmental process that involves the formation and pursuit of preferences; preferences are formed at various levels and shaped by institutions and various other internal determinants; preferences are pursued through an aggregation of interests and institutions that are designed to maximize members' utility; the intergovernmental process also creates institutions that exercise transformational influence on leaders at various levels; and institutions also promote and regulate principal–agency relationship and determine the level of agency autonomy with respect to various issues.

SOURCES

The study is based on primary sources as constituted by African Union official and semi-official documents. Secondary sources in the form of existing scholarly works have been used extensively both as a means to situate my thesis in a proper context and as a foundation on which the present study builds. But most importantly, the study is largely based on the author's own experience as an African Union insider and an active participant in the various AU processes for several years. It has also benefited from the insights of various other insiders, including representatives of AU member states, staff of the Commission of the African Union, other governmental and intergovernmental and non-governmental officials. Because a lot about the Union, just like similar bodies elsewhere, remains unwritten, the insights offered by these people are invaluable to our attempt to understand the African Union.

STRUCTURE

The 12 chapters of the book are divided into three parts: chapters 1–3 anchor the book in a theoretical framework, as well as in Africa's history and various challenges. Chapters 4–8 chronicle the OAU's success in supporting the total emancipation for all of Africa and provide an overview of the substantive issue areas AU tried to collectively address. Chapters 9–11 assess the AU's actual moving policy parts and how they work. What follows is an outline of the individual chapters.

Chapter 1 sets out the problem, states the main research question, indicates the sources and outlines the structure of the study.

Chapter 2 looks at the variables that determine the preferences of national leaders. It examines the political and socio-economic context that shaped the preferences of African leaders and within which the new African Union was established and had to operate. This context was not only characterized by political goodwill on the part of the African leaders, but also by considerable political and socio-economic difficulties. These constitute the challenges to which the new continental organization had to rise.

Chapter 3 demonstrates that preferences shift and that institutions are selected rationally as a means of maximizing individual and collective utility. More specifically, it shows that contrary to popular belief, the African Union was not the pet project of the former Libyan leader Colonel Muammar Ghaddafi. Although the Libyan leader iplayed an important role in the formation of the African Union, he did not dictate the text of the Constitutive Act. The African Union was a product of lengthy intergovernmental processes that lasted for several years. The former presidents of South Africa and Nigeria, Thabo Mbeki and Olusegun Obasanjo respectively played pivotal roles in these processes. For these two leaders, the African Union represented an appropriate foreign policy instrument. For the entire membership, however, the AU constituted an aggregate of interests and a rational means of maximizing the individual countries' utility.

Chapter 4 shows how decolonization and stability represented the most pressing collective preference of African leaders from the 1960s up to the independence of South Africa in 1991; it outlines the manner in which the OAU managed its mandate in these areas. The chapter concludes that the OAU succeeded in its decolonization struggle because the organization was properly mandated and equipped to attain that objective. To some extent, the organization also succeeded in reducing interstate conflicts. However, the OAU was less successful in managing civil wars and in addressing socio-economic problems of its members because it had limited autonomy in these areas.

Chapter 5 assesses how poverty and underdevelopment that African states found themselves in at independence made socio-economic development a key preference. Besides decolonization, collective effort was geared toward economic development. The chapter looks at the various continental initiatives that constituted the African Union's mandate in the area of socio-economic development. Particular attention has been given to the Abuja Treaty of 1991 that focuses on development through regional integration, and the New Partnership for Africa's Development (NEPAD). Although it is built on the Abuja prescriptions, NEPAD added the dimension of international partnership and political accountability through its African Peer Review Mechanism (APRM). The chapter concludes that NEPAD and other development blueprints suffered from poor funding from member states and over-reliance on external support that was not forthcoming. As a result, they remained, for the most part, just blueprints on paper.

Chapter 6 extends the examination of AU's preferences by focusing on social questions, especially the challenges facing the Union, as well as its mandate in the areas of health, education, gender and population. The chapter argues that, by and large, the African Union had little to its credit in these areas other than a few legal instruments, and limited autonomy that accounts for OAU's limited success in addressing civil wars also accounts for AU's ineffectiveness in the area of human development on the continent.

Chapter 7 shows that peace and security remained a key preference of African leaders in the post-independence period, it was only in the aftermath of the Cold War that the OAU and the AU began to look at collective peace support operations more seriously, as demonstrated by the number of legal frameworks on peace and security that the continent adopted and the peace support activities undertaken. The study argues that despite the multiplicity of legal frameworks and peace support activities, the Union's peace and security agenda consisted of two main components: *preventive diplomacy* and *peacekeeping*. Although considerable advances were made in these areas, the implementation of the continental peace and security agenda continued to face many challenges, including those associated with *limited agency autonomy* and the problematic application of the principle of *subsidiarity*.

Chapter 8 looks at governance on the continent and shows how political preferences shift and how institutions exercise transformational influence on leaders at various levels. More specifically, the chapter shows how military and single-party regimes that dominated African political scene before the 1990s quickly gave way to democratically elected governments. This development is attributable to various factors including key continental instruments such as The African Charter on Human and People's Rights, the Conference on Stability, Security, Development and Cooperation in Africa (CSSDCA), The New Partnership for Africa's Development (NEPAD), the

Declaration on Democratic Elections, and the African Charter on Democracy, Elections and Governance. Together these instruments constitute the African Union's governance architecture. It is shown that despite considerable improvement in governance on the continent, only a handful of African countries had reached a point where the peaceful transfer of power through elections was routine.

Chapter 9 is the first of three chapters that examine the AU's policy organs. The chapter focuses on organs composed principally of governments: the Assembly of heads of state and government, the Executive Council of Foreign Ministers, and the Committee of Permanent Representatives.

Chapter 10 looks at the composition, the powers and the rules of procedure of a key institution of the Union: the Pan African Parliament. Most importantly, the chapter assesses the prospects of the parliament against the limitations it faced, including funding constraints and member states' unwillingness to cede legislative authority to the body. It shows that despite the fact that it is supposed to be the voice of the people, the PAP made little inroads in the decision-making of the Assembly of heads of state and the Council of Ministers, thereby reinforcing the argument that integration is largely an intergovernmental affairs.

Chapter 11 examines AU Commission's composition, statutes and rules of procedure. It also looks at the mechanics of this giant body as well as some of the challenges that emerged during the first ten years of the commission, including administrative and financial difficulties. Most importantly, the chapter highlights the tension that characterized the relationship between the Permanent Representatives Committee (PRC) and the AU Commission, providing an example of the delicate nature of principal–agent relationship.

Chapter 12 sums up the main findings of the study and relates it to the existing theoretical traditions on integration. It also raises signposts to some of the challenges that further research into the history of the African Union after the first ten years must necessarily examine.

NOTES

1. Colin Legum, *Africa since Independence* (Bloomington and Indianapolis: Indiana University Press 1999).

2. For an interesting characterization of the failure of the African development efforts, see Sabelo J Ndlovu-Gatsheni, *Coloniality of Power in Post-Colonial Africa: Myth of Decolonization* (Dakar, CODESRIA, 2013), p. 240.

3. Geer La Porte and James Mackie (editors), "Building the African Union: An Assessment of Past Progress and Future Prospects for the African Union's Institutional Architecture," Policy and Management Report 18, Nordic Africa and

ECDPM, October 2010; Thomas Kwasi Tieku, "Explaining the Clash and Accommodation of Interests of Major Actors in the Creation of the African Union," *African Affairs,* 103 (2004), pp. 246–47; Corinne A. A. Parker and Donald Rukare, "The New African Union and its Constitutive Act," *American Journal of International Law*, 92, 2 (2002), pp. 365–78; Naldi Gino, "The African Union: a New Dawn for Africa?," *The International and Comparative Law Quarterly*, Vol. 51 (2002), pp. 415–25; Nsongurua J. Udombaba, "The Institutional Structure of the African Union: A Legal Analysis," *California Western International Law Journal,* Vol. 33 (2002), pp. 49–135; Ahmed Iyane Sow, "L'Union Africaine," *Revue Internationale de Droit Africain*, 49 (2001), pp. 7–28; Tuyanjana Maluwa, "The Constitutive Act of the Africa Union and Institution-building in Post-Colonial Africa," *Leiden Journal of International Law,* 16, 1 (2003), pp. 157–70; Tiyanjana Maluwa, "Re-imaging African Unity: Some Preliminary Reflections on the Constitutive Act of the African Union," *African Yearbook of International Law,* Vol. 9 (2001), pp. 3–38; Suleyman, Bula-Bula, "Les fondements de l'union africaine," *African Yearbook of International Law*, Vol.9 (2001), pp. 39–74; Michael Cowling, 'The African Union: an Evaluation,' in *South African Yearbook of International Law*, Vol. 27 (2002), pp. 193–205; Kathryn Sturman, "The Rise of Libya as a Regional Player" *African Security Review* vol. 12, No 2 (2003), pp. 109–12.

4. See Issaka K. Souaré, "The African Union as a 'Norm Entrepreneur' on Coups D'Etat in Africa, 1952–2012: An Empirical Assessment," *Journal of Modern African Studies*, Vol 52, 1 (2014): 69–94. F. Söderbaum and R. Tavares (eds), *Regional Organizations in African Security*, London: Routledge 2010; Paul D. Williams, *The African Union's Conflict Management Capabilities*, Working Paper (Washington DC: Council on Foreign Relations 2011); Langer Johannes, "The Responsibility to Protect: Kenya's Post-Electoral Crises," *Journal of International Service* (Fall 2011) available at www.american.educ/sis. Rupiya Martin, A review of the African Union's experience in facilitating peaceful power transfers: Zimbabwe, Ivory Coast, Libya and Sudan: Are there Prospects for Reform, *Africa Journal of Conflict Prevention*, 12, 2 (2012): 161–83; Freear, M. and de Coning, C. Lessons from the African Union Mission for Somalia (AMISOM) for Peace Operations in Mali. *Stability: International Journal of Security and Development.* (2013). 2(2), p.Art. 23. DOI: http://doi.org/10.5334/sta.bj; Paul. D. William, "The Peace and Security Council of the African Union: Evaluating and Embryonic International Institution," *Journal of Modern African Studies*, Vol 47, 4 (2009), pp. 603–23; P. D. Williams, "From Non-intervention to Non-interference: The Origins and Development of the African Union's Security Culture," *African Affairs*, Vol. 106, 423 (2007), pp. 253–79; Ulf Engel and J. Porto, editors, *Africa's New Peace and Security Architecture : Promoting norms, Institutionalizing Solutions,* (Farnham: Ashgate 2010); Eki Yemisi Omorogbe, "Can African Union Deliver Peace and Security," *Journal of Conflict and Law*, vol. 16, 1 (2011); Eki Yemisi Omorogbe, "A Club of Incumbents? The African Union and Coups D'Etat," *Venderbilt Journal of Transnational Law*, Vol. 44, 123 (2008), pp. 123–54 pp. 35–62; Omar A. Touray, "The Common African Defence and Security Policy," *African Affairs*, Vol. 104, No.417 (2005), pp. 635–54; Abdul Mohammed, Paulos Testagiorgis and Alex de Waal, "Peace and Security Dimension of the African Union,"

Document Presented at the African Development Forum III (Addis Ababa: ECA 2003), James W. Swigert, "Challenges of Peace Keeping in Africa," *The DISARM Journal* (Winter 2004–2005), pp. 37–39; Ademola Abass, Mashood A. Baderin, "Towards Effective Collective Security and Human Rights Protections in Africa: An Assessment of the Constitutive Act of the New African Union," *Netherlands International Law Review*, Vol. 49 (2002) pp. 1–38; T. A. Imobighe, *The OAU (AU) and OAS in Regional Conflict Management: A Comparative Assessment* (Lagos: Spectrum 2003); Ben Kioko, "The Right of Intervention under the African Union Constitutive Act: From Non-interference to Non-intervention," *International Review of the Red Cross*, Vol 85 (2003), pp. 807–25; Jeremy I. Levitt, "The Peace and Security Council of the African Union: the Known Unknowns," *Transnational Law and Contemporary Problems*, Vol. 13, 1 (2003), pp. 109–37; John S. Moolakkatu, "The Role of the African Union in the Continental Peace and Security Governance," *India Quarterly*, Vol. 66 2, (2009), pp 151–65; Dominique Bangura, "Les nouvelles institutions africaines en matière de sécurité," in Pierre Pascallon, *La Politique de sécurité de la France en Afrique* (Paris: Harmattan, 2004); Albrecht Schnabel and David Carment, eds, *Conflict Prevention: From Rhetoric to Reality* (Lexington Books 2004). Tom Keeting and W. Andy Knight, eds., *Building Sustainable Peace* (United Nations University Press 2004). Jeremy I. Levitt, "The Peace and Security Council of the African Union: the Known Unknowns," *Transnational Law and Contemporary Problems*, vol. 13, 1 (2003), pp. 109–37; United States Department of Defense, "African Union," Summary of the 2005–2006 *Quadrennial Defense Review* (May 2006), pp. 1–9; Christopher Landsberg, "The Fifth Wave of Pan-Africanism," in Adekeye Adebajo and Ismail Rasheed, eds, *West Africa's Security Challenges: Building Peace in a Troubled Region* (Boulder: Rienner 2004), Alex Ramsbotham, Alhaji M. S. Bah and Fanny Calder, "Enhancing African Peace and Security Capacity: A Useful Role for the UK and the G8," *International Affairs*, 81:2 (March 2005), pp. 325–28.

5. See Stef Vandeginste, "The African Union: Constitutionalism and Power Sharing," *Journal of International law* (2013) pp. 1–28; Nathan Laurie, "Mediating in Madagascar by Bypassing the AU Ban on Coup Legitimization," *Kujega Amani*, 5 November 2013, available at www.ssrc.org; Konstantinos D. Magliveras: The Sanctioning System of the African Union: Part Success, Part Failure, 2011 available at /http://www.academia.edu/1103678; Ernest Harsch, "Africa Defends Democratic Rule," *African Renewal*, April 2010; Kelley, Judith. "Watching the Watchmen: The Role of Election Observers in Africa," available at www.thinkafricapress.com May 2013. Election Institute of Southern Africa, "Two Decades of Elections Observation in Africa: Lessons Learned, Role, Performance and Impact on Democracy Building," available at www.eisa.org/event/symposium 2.htm ; Ogune, H. "Appraising Election Monitoring and Observation in Africa: The Case of the Democratic Republic of Congo's 2011 Presidential Elections," sited in www.eisa.org.za; M. C. Houngnikpo, *Guarding the Guardians: Civil Military Relations and Democratic Governance in Africa* (Farnham: Ashgate 2010) Ademola Abass, Mashood A. Baderin, "Towards Effective Collective Security and Human Rights Protections in Africa," in John Akokpari, "Policing and Preventing Human Rights Abuses in Africa: the OAU, the AU and the NEPAD Peer Review," *International Journal of Legal Information*,

32, 2, (2004), pp. 461–73; Rachel Murray, *Human Rights in Africa, From the OAU to the African Union* (Cambridge University Press, 2004). John Akokpari, "Policing and Preventing Human Rights Abuses in Africa: the OAU, the AU and the NEPAD Peer Review," *International Journal of Legal Information*, 32, 2, (2004), pp. 461–73. Abdalla Bujra and Said Adejumob, *Breaking Barriers, Creating New Hopes: Democracy, Civil Society and Good Governance in Africa* (New Jersey: Africa World Press 2004); Adrien Katherine Wing and Tyler Murray Smith, "The New African Union and the Women's Right," *Transnational Law and Contemporary Problems* Vol. 13 (2003), pp. 33–81; Evarist Baimu, "The African Union: Hope for Better Protection of Human Rights in Africa," *African Human Rights Law Journal*, Vol. 1, 2 (2001), pp. 299–314; Nsongurua J. Udombaba, "Can the Leopard Change its Spots?: The African Union Treaty and Human Rights," *American University International Law Review*, Vol. 17 (2002) pp.1177–95;

6. Said Adejumobi and Adebayo Olukoshi, The African Union and New Strategies for Development in Africa, (Amherst, New York: Cambria Press 2014); Amanda Lucey and Sibongila Gida, *Enhancing South Africa's Post-Conflict Development Role in the African Union,* ISS Paper 256 (Pretoria: ISS, 2014); Mark Paterson, Rapporteur, *The African Union at Ten: Problems, Progress and Prospects*, Report of the International Colloguium (Berlin Friedrich Ebert Stiftung 2012); Barry Carin, The African Union and the Post 2015 Development Agenda, Policy Brief No45 (Waterloo, Ontario: Centre For the International Governance Innovation, 2014); Abayomi Azikiwe: 51st Anniversary: The African Union and the illusive Promise of Unity, (Global Research 2014); Tim Murithi, The African Union: Pan Africanism, Peace Building and Development (Lanharm: Ashgate 2005); Pau Masson and Catherine Pattillo, A single Currency for Africa? *Finance and Development* (2004) pp. 9–15; Nsongurua J. Udombana, "A Harmony or Cacophony?: The Music of Integration in the African Union Treaty and the New Partnership for Africa's Development," *Indiana International and Comparative Law Review*, 13, 1 (2002), pp. 185–236; Adebayo O. Olukoshi, *Governing the African Developmental Process: The New Challenge of the New Partnership for Africa's Development (NEPAD)*, Occasional Paper (Copenhagen: Centre of African Studies 2002). Keith Gottschalk and Siegmar Schmidt, "The African Union and the New Partnership for Africa's Development: Strong Institutions for Weak States?" *IPG* Vol. 4 (2004), pp. 138–58; P. Chabal, "The Quest for Good Governance and Development in Africa: Is NEPAD the Answer?," *International Affairs* 78, 3 (2002): pp. 447–62;

7. Tim Murithi, "From Pan Africanism to the African Union," Global Policy Forum, available at https://www.globalpolicy.org/component/content/article/173/30537.html; See also Thomas Tieku, "Pan Africanism as International Relations Theory: Agency and Constructivism in African Politics," Social Science Research Network, 2013 available at http://papers.ssrn.com/sol3/papers.cfm?abstract_id=2274254.

8. See Christopher Balding and Daniel Wehrenfennig, "An Organizational Theory of International Institutions," available at http://journal-iostudies.org/sites/journal-iostudies.org /files/JIOS201121 final. pdf; Hurd, Ian, *International Organizations: Politics, Law, Practice.* (Cambridge: Cambridge University Press, 2011),

pp. 1–14. Ruggie, John Gerard "Multilateralism: The Anatomy of an Institution," *International Organization*, 46(3) (Summer 1992), pp. 561–98.

9. The term "Institutionalists" is used to cover the various strains of institutionalist school of thought including the rational choice advocates.

10. For more on Functionalism in International Relations, see Ernst B. Haas, *Beyond the Nation-State: Functionalism in International Organizations* (Republished by ECPR 2008), chapter 2.

11. See Andrew Moravcsik, "Negotiating the Single European Act," in Robert O. Keohane and Stanley Hoffman, eds. *The New European Community* (Boulder: West View Press, 1991), pp. 41–84; Andrew Moravcsik, "Preferences and Power in the European Community: A Liberal Intergovernmentalist Approach," *Journal of Common Market Studies* Vol. 31 (1993), pp. 473–524; Andrew Moravcsik, "Liberal Intergovernmentalism and Integration: A Rejoinder," *Journal of Common Market Studies*, Vol. 33 (1995), pp. 611–28; Andrew Moravcsik, *The Choice for Europe: Social Purpose and State Power from Messina to Maastricht* (Ithaca: Cornell University Press, 1998); Andrew Moravcsik, "A New Statecraft? Supranational Entrepreneurs and International Cooperation," *International Organization*, Vol. 53 (1999) 227–306.

12. For this section, the author draws liberally on the review article by Mark Pollack, *International Relations Theory and European Integration*, EUI Working Paper RSC No. 2000/55 (Sab Domenico, Italy: The European University Institute, 2000).

13. This view was subsequently reviewed, as shown infra, pp. 8–9

14. See J. Lewis, "Constructing Interests: EU Membership, COREPER and the Constitutive Processes of National Preference Formation," Paper Presented at the 5th Biennial International Conference of the European Community Studies Association, Washington, Seattle, 1997, cited in Mark Pollack, *International Relations Theory*, p. 5.

15. See, for example, J. Peterson, "Decision-Making in the European Union: Towards a Framework for Analysis," Journal of European Public Policy, vol. 2 (1995), pp. 69–93; J. Peterson, "Policy Networks and European Union Policy-Making: A Reply to Kassim," *West European Politics*, Vol. 18 (1995), pp. 389–407.

16. Mark Pollack, *International Relations Theory*, p. 6, and Margaret Keck and Cathryn Sikkink, Activists Beyond Borders: Advocacy Networks in International Relations (Ithaca: Cornell University Press, 1998).

17. For more on this, see Paul Pierson, "The Path to European Integration: A Historical Institutional Analysis," *Comparative Political Studies*, Vol. 29 (1996), pp. 123–63; and also Mark Pollack, *International Relations Theory*, p. 6.

18. Various definitions of institutions exist. Rational Choice theorists define institutions as formal rules of the game; sociological institutionalists much more broadly to include informal norms and as well as formal rules. The Constructivists add subjective understandings to the definition given by the Sociological Institutionalists; Mark Pollack, *International Relations Theory*, p. 7.

19. For more on this, see Pollack, *International Relations Theory,* p. 8.

20. Mark Pollack, "Delegation, Agency and Agenda-setting in the European Community," *International Organization*, Vol. 5 (1997), pp. 99–135.

21. Moravcsik, "The Choice for Europe: Social Purpose and State Power from Messina to Maastricht" (Ithaca, Cornell University Press 1998), and Moravcsik, "A New Statecraft: Supranational Entrepreneurs and International Cooperation," *International Organization*, Vol 53 (1999), pp. 227–306.

22. Moravcsik, The Choice for Europe, p. 9.

23. Ibid. Also Pollack, *International Relations Theory*, p. 13.

24. See Thomas Christiansen, Knud Erik Jorgensen and Antje Wiener, "The Social Constitution of Europe," *Journal of European Public Policy*, Vol. 6 (1999), pp. 528–44.

25. Andrew Moravcsik, "Is Something Rotten in the State of Denmark? Constructivism and the European Integration," *Journal of European Public Policy*, vol 6 (1999), pp. 669–81.

26. It should be recalled that Rationalism is a strain of Institutionalism, as explained above, pp. 2–5.

27. Pollack, *International Relations Theory*.

28. Many attempts have been made in this regard, but in most cases, Africa has been left out. See, for example, Fin Laursen (editor), *Comparative Regional Integration* (Larnham: Ashgate 2010); Academy of Global Governance, Regional Integration Beyond the European Experience: Latin America and Asia, 3–5 October 2012, available at http://globalgovernanceprogramme.eui.eu/executive-training/2011-2012-executive-training-seminars/regional-integration-beyond-the-european-experience-latin-america-and-asia/; Fraser Cameron, *The European Union as a Model for Regional Integration*, Council on Foreign Relations 2010, available at http://www.cfr.org/world/european-union-model-regional-integration/p22935; James Caporaso, "Regional Integration and Domestic Institutional Homogeneity: A Comparative Analysis of Regional Integration in the America's, Pacific Asia and Western Europe," *Review of International Political Economy*, Vol 10, 2 (2003); Georgios Karras, "Economic Integration and Convergence: Lessons from Asia, Europe and Latin America," *Journal of Economic Integration* Vol 12, 4 (1997), pp. 419–52.

29. Articles 5 and 14 of the Constitutive Act of the African Union, and Article 20 of the Charter of the OAU.

30. Article 22 of the Constitutive Act; for more on the limited role of the civil society in the AU processes, see, "Civil Society Exclusions Dampen Mood at the African Union Summit," *The Guardian* 28 May 2013, available at http://www.theguardian.com/global-development/2013/may/28/civil-society-exclusions-african-union.

31. Paul Pierson, "The Path to European Integration," pp. 123–63

32. The term "fusionism" is used in this study loosely to refer to the study of integration on the basis of an aggregate of frameworks that in isolation only offer partial explanation of the complex nature of integration. As such it is different from classic "fusionism" as popularized in the early 1960s by William F. Buckley and Frank S. Meyer of *the National Review,* and which refers to the philosophical and political combination or "fusion" of traditionalist and social conservatism with political and economic right-libertarianism. For more on the classical "fusionism," see Clark Ruper, "The Death of Fusinism," *Cato Un Bound: Journal of Debate*, May 2013, available at http://www.cato-unbound.org/2013/05/10/clark-ruper/death-fusionism.

33. Bjorn Hettne and Fredrik Soderbaum, "The New Regionalism Approach," *Ploiteia* Vol. 17, 3 (1998), available at http//ssm.com/abstract+2399180.

34. See Chapters 2 and 5.

35. Realists see the international system as being anarchical, that is, there is no central authority to order relations between states. They are bound only by forcible coercion or their own consent. For an introduction to realism and other theories of International Relations, see Karen Mingst and Ivan M. Arreguin-Toft, *Essentials of International Relations,* 5th edition (New York: W.W. Norton & Co., 2010), especially pp. 60–75.

36. Idealism is generally seen as the opposite of Realism. Whereas Realists consider the world to be an anarchical space where states are engaged in a power struggle, Idealists believe in the existence of the common good and the possibility of states promoting their common good through international norms and organizations such as the United Nations. For more on Idealism, see Karen Mingst and Ivan M Arreguin-Toft, *Essentials of International Relations.*

37. Chapter 8.

38. For more on this, see Ben Kioko, "The Right of Intervention under the African Union Constitutive Act."

Chapter 2

The Context

Africa on the Eve of the Twenty-first Century

In the previous chapter, I outlined my proposal for fusionism, an integrated framework that seeks to explain international integration on the basis of an amalgamation of Intergovernmentalist and Institutionalist analytical traditions. In the following few chapters, I will demonstrate the utility of my proposal by analysing different aspects of the African Union on the basis of these fused analytical frameworks. In this chapter, I will show that while liberal Intergovernmentalists are right in maintaining that integration is essentially an intergovernmental process that involves preference formation and bargaining, they tell us little about how those preferences are made and what shapes particular preferences. The answer institutionalists provide in this regard – that institutions shape preferences – is hardly sufficient. Our own position, supported by empirical evidence, is that among the determinants of state preferences are the socio-economic realities, geography, politics, history and the idiosyncrasies of individual leaders. Thus, in order to understand the African Union's preferences, we need to understand the political and socio-economic context within which the organization was formed and operated, and which gave rise to the various preferences that African leaders pursued collectively.

The challenges facing Africa at the dawn of the twenty-first century have been the subject of many reports by the World Bank, the IMF, the African Development Bank, the United Nations, the OECD and several other institutions. They have equally been catalogued in the NEPAD basic policy document.[1] The intention in this chapter is therefore limited solely to providing a bird's eye view of these challenges as they characterize the context within which the new African Union was established and to which the continental body must rise. For the sake of simplification, this chapter examines these issues under three broad categories: (a) political flux, including threats to peace and security; (b) economic underdevelopment; and (c) deteriorating social condition. I have taken this path while being clearly aware of the pitfalls of overstatement or understatement inherent in such an approach. It is up to the reader to determine the dangers into which I have fallen.

POLITICAL CHANGE

Two years before the African Union was established, *The Economist* published two articles that have been paraphrased and summed up as follows:

> Africans had lived in small communities in the past. Bitter experience in mastering a volatile climate and unusually poor soils taught them a hardy conservatism. The Atlantic demand for labour that accompanied Europe's first global expansion had set these communities at each other's throat, under slave-catching warlords. Western colonialism, later, proceeded to undermine African's self-confidence. Worse still, in the middle of the twentieth century, departing white rulers had bequeathed unreformed, authoritarian power to tiny successor elites. Their new states lacked the long histories of nation-building and external wars that had, at great cost, provoked the rise of critically patriotic politics in Europe. African regimes had, therefore, to rule by manipulating "tribal affiliation" for want of consent. History condemned them to manage two-faced states. These had to appear to meet western expectation of public probity, but their real business was private gratification. There administration shells were outer show. Within "hidden networks" of kin and client manufactured the trust that all states need but Africa's lacked. Until a more civic trust created a public opinion alert to the abuses of power, Africa would never escape its crises and the whole world might just give up on the entire continent.[2]

This bleak view of Africa, though challenged and refuted in several instances,[3] shows the persistence of Afro-pessimism in many quarters. But the progress that most African countries made in the decade following the *Economist*'s publication was sufficiently encouraging to prompt the die-hard Afro-pessimists to think again. African Renaissance might have overblown, but it was real. The introduction of good governance into Africa's body politic, though a timid step by many counts, was perhaps the single most important factor that accounted for the continent's renaissance.[4] Since the early 1990s, single-party states and military dictatorships had given way to political pluralism and greater accountability in the majority of African countries. The emergence of vocal civil societies led to greater decentralization and popular participation in the development process. Yet, much of the rebirth remained largely in the domain of political pluralism. On the eve of the twenty-first century, Africa accounted for the bulk of the world's intra-state conflicts; of the 53 member states of the African Union, 12 were experiencing intrastate conflict, two were involved in border disputes, and three had just emerged from conflict. As a result, Africa accounted for a large part of the war-induced deaths in the world.[5] The continent also accounted for 24.4 per cent of the world refugee population of 20.7 million.[6] Although considerable progress was registered from the mid-1990s, about one-third of African states were classified as fragile in 2012.

The link between violent conflict and development has been well established. Beyond the tragic direct effects such as deaths, injuries and displacement, violent conflicts also endanger economic and infrastructure collapse, with their attendant toll on human lives. Conflicts do not only impose heavy social and economic costs on the countries in which they occur, they also impose costs on neighbouring countries by generating refugee flows, increasing military spending, impeding key communication routes and reducing both domestic and foreign trade and investment. A World Bank report produced on the eve of the twenty-first century estimated resources diverted from development uses by conflict at US$1 billion in Central Africa and more than US$800 million in West Africa. Added to this was the cost of refugee assistance, estimated at more than US$500 million in Central Africa alone.[7] These estimates do not include the costs of environmental degradation occasioned by the disruptive movement of large numbers of people.

The first challenge of the African Union in this area was understanding the nature and the causes of the conflict before it could deal with them. From the academic point of view, efforts have been made to identify the causes of conflict, and a number of conflict prevention and resolution scenarios have been suggested.[8]

Too often, ethnicity, or ethnic diversity, was blamed for the high incidence of civil wars in Africa because the majority of rebel movements often identify with a particular ethnic group. However, studies have revealed that although ethnicity plays a crucial role in African internal conflicts, its pre-eminence is often overblown. African conflicts conform to a pattern observed in other regions and that they are accounted for largely by political and economic factors as well as ethnic, cultural and religious diversity.

Thus, in order to understand African conflict, attention should be paid to the possible factors, particularly the economic and the political causes. First, it is evident that civil wars are less likely when youth unemployment is low.[9] Second, having extensive natural resources is the desire of all developing and developed countries, but these resources are associated with high risk of war. And third, political repression and the lack of political rights are factors associated with civil wars. These considerations explain why Africa was so prone to civil wars. African countries were dependent on natural resources, and resources provide a convenient way to sustain "justice-seeking" rebel movements, and are easily lootable assets that can encourage loot-seeking rebellion. They can also help governments fund armies or buy popular support. Although the presence of natural resources is not in itself a sufficient condition, it increases the risk of civil wars when combined with low income. Poverty, unemployment and rampant illiteracy among the youth make this group ready recruits to rebel causes. The ILO estimated that the average unemployment rate on the continent stood at 10.9 per cent of the 271 million work force in 2003. Of those who were employed, 140 million lived on less than one dollar a day. These were the working poor who were unable to provide their families with decent living conditions. Unemployment and under employment of the young people were a compelling problem in most parts of Africa. Estimates show that unemployment rate for the 15–24 age group was about 21 per cent in 2003, twice as high as the overall African unemployment rate of 10.9 per cent, and among the highest youth unemployment rates in the world. And young men and women account for the bulk of the working poor, concentrated in the informal sector in both the rural and urban areas. The lack of political rights and other political conditions in several African countries had also played an important role in increasing the continents' civil war propensity. Until the 1990s, single-party civilian regimes and military dictatorships in several countries made coups d'état and attendant violence the only means through which transfer of power could be achieved. This is not to justify coups d'état and violence; the conditions that create them are the subject of the analysis. As the World Bank has summed up, for Africa to give its back to civil wars the continent would need combination of greater political rights, improved standard of living and diversified economies.[10]

ECONOMIC DECLINE

Africa's economic challenges were equally daunting. The continent started the twenty-first century as the poorest, the most technologically backward, the most debt distressed and the most marginalized region in the world. It accounted for 12.5 per cent of the world's populations but produced only 3.7 per cent of global GDP, and accounted for less than 2 per cent global trade in goods and services. In 1998, Africa's 778 million people produced goods and services worth US$537 billion at 1990 prices. This amounted to a per capita income of 691 a year or US$58 a month, ranging from a high of US$5,975 for Seychelles to a low of US$92 for Mozambique.[11] Disaggregating the data reveals that at the sub-regional level, North Africa accounted for 22 per cent of the continents population and 40 per cent of its GDP, while sub-Saharan Africa accounted for 78 per cent of the population and 60 per cent of the GDP. West Africa, with a share in total population of 29 per cent, accounted for

17 per cent of the GDP; East Africa, accounted for 31 per cent of the population and 8 per cent of the GDP; Southern Africa accounted for 15 per cent of the population and 29 per cent of GDP; and Central Africa for 4 per cent of the regions' population and 5 per cent of the GDP.[12] The big five economies of the continent, South Africa, Egypt, Algeria, Nigeria and Morocco, together accounted for 37 per cent of the population and 59 per cent of the GDP. At the other extreme of these countries were 33 Least Developed Countries (LDCs), with 45 per cent of the continent's population and 17 per cent of the GDP.[13] With a per capita income of US$315 (excluding South Africa) at the turn of the century, sub-Saharan Africa was indeed the poorest region. Average output per capita in constant prices was lower in 2000 than it was in 1970, and in some countries it had fallen by more than 50 per cent.[14] In real terms, fiscal resources per capita were smaller for many countries than in the late 1960. The continent's share of world trade plummeted, accounting for less than 2 per cent of world trade. The majority of African countries remained largely primary exporters, just as they were at independence, in contrast with other regions that had diversified their exports. The dominance of agricultural products as the major source of foreign exchange rendered the continent's export earning capacity highly sensitive to commodity price fluctuations. These considerations account for the marginal role that Africa played in world trade and investment. Notwithstanding the excessive dependence on exports of primary goods, African countries failed to boost their competitive edge in this very field. For instance, over the 1970–1994 period, the region's market shares in cocoa beans fell from 80 per cent to 67 per cent; in coffee, from 26 per cent to 15 per cent; in cotton, from 30 per cent to 16 per cent; in timber, from 13 per cent to 7 per cent; and in iron ore, from 12 per cent to 2 per cent.[15] The loss of Africa's markets in cocoa beans, coffee and timber was largely to Asian countries; in iron ore to Latin America; in cotton to Eastern European countries. Although the loss in market share has been contained in the second half of the 1990s, the share lost over the decades could not be regained.[16]

The continent was also both aid-dependent and heavily indebted. Net transfers from foreign assistance averaged 9 per cent of GDP for a typical poor African country – equivalent to 50 per cent of public spending. Indeed, aid helped to bridge the resource gap and hastened the development process in a number of countries, but the bulk of aid shifted from project assistance and structural adjustment loans to humanitarian assistance and peace-building. Competition for aid also intensified, partly because transitional economies in Easter Europe were also competing for aid. In the late 1980s, it was envisaged that aid to Africa would grow in real terms, but net transfers per capita fell sharply from US$32 in 1980 to US$19 in 1998.[17] It fell to US$18.8 billion in 2000 before increasing to US$19.4 (1998 level) in 2001.[18] Donor fatigue accounted for the reduced ODA flows in real terms. But the continent's lower strategic importance to the West also explains the falling development assistance, as testified by the big gap between the level of the international community's response to Sierra Leone and Kosovo crises.[19]

Heavy reliance on foreign financing did not only deepen aid dependence, it also created heavy debt burden. By the close of the century, foreign debt represented a burden of more than 80 per cent of the GDP in net present value terms, and debt service ratio grew to 31 per cent of exports.[20] Up to the late 1970s, the debt burden of African countries was manageable. Debt stock was only US$31 billion by the end of 1970s, accounting for 79 per cent of exports and 20.5 of GDP, and debt servicing was only 7 per cent of export earnings. By the end of the 1980s, the stock of external debt had risen substantially to US$250.6 billion, with a debt to export ratio standing at 264.2 per cent and debt servicing accounting for 29 per cent of export earnings. During the 1990s, total outstanding debt further increased to US$316 billion, representing about 223 per cent of the export earnings and 61 per cent of the GDP, well above the average of 175 and 36 per cent, respectively, for all the developing countries.[21]

The implications of the debt overhang are many. First, debt service requirements burden the budget of government, divert investment resources away from key social and economic sectors, erode the confidence of the private sector and weaken the prospects for sustainable growth and for reducing poverty.

It was the adverse effects of the debt overhang on the overall development prospects of Africa that led to several international initiatives on the debt crises. These include the Baker Plan (1985), The Toronto Terms (October 1986), the Brandy Plan (1989), the London Terms (December 1991), the Naples Terms (1995), the Loyns Terms (1996) and the HIIPC Initiative (September 1996).[22]

Heavy indebtedness was also partly to be blamed for the low level of private capital flows into the continent. Indeed, Africa's share of foreign direct investment, the most important source of external finance for developing countries , dropped from 25 per cent in the early 1970s to just 5 per cent of the GDP in 2000, although these general figures mask a number of interesting trends.[23] Besides the heavy debt burden, other causes of the declining levels of FDI include, first, the risk of policy reversal; second, the high cost of doing business in Africa; third, weaknesses in legal, judicial and financing systems as well as low labour productivity; and fourth, inefficient and unresponsive physical and technological infrastructure, which are essential to long-term competitiveness of the economy.[24] Although nominally FDI inflows to Africa increased from US$11 billion in 2002 to US$14 Billion in 2003, the continent's share in global FDI inflows remained at 2 per cent, and concentrated in the natural resources sectors, even though the African Growth and Opportunities Act (AGOA) of the United States Government boosted investment in the garment sectors in countries like Botswana, Kenya, Lesotho and Mauritius.[25] Africa was also the only major region to see savings per capita decline after 1970. Averaging about 13 per cent of the GDP in the 1990s, the savings rate of a typical African country was the lowest in the world, with domestic savings estimated at 3 per cent for the continent.[26] On aggregate, investment to GDP ratio remained low at the turn of the century (2001) and below the 25 per cent level needed to speed up growth. For the continent as a whole, the investment and savings ratio averaged around 20 per cent in 2001. Only 14 countries had investment ratios above 25 per cent. The largest category of 20 countries had an investment–saving ratio between 10 per cent and 20 per cent; and only eight countries had an investment–saving ratio of 25 per cent; 25 countries had a ratio of less than 10 per cent of the GDP, indicating a huge shortfall in the resources needed to catalyse development.[27] Heavy indebtedness may not be wholly responsible for this; it had however a major role in the decline.

DETERIORATING SOCIAL CONDITIONS

Decades of political flux and general economic difficulties translated into one thing for the common African: poverty. Africans accounted for one out of every two poor persons in the world. Within the continent four out of every 10 African lived in conditions of absolute poverty. According to the United Nations, 80 per cent of the countries with low human development were in Africa.[28] However, the depth and the incidence of poverty varied between and within the sub-regions. In North Africa, only 22 per cent of the population lived under the poverty line before the turn of the century; in sub-Saharan Africa, the proportion of people living under the poverty line was about 51 per cent.[29] Africa was also the only region in the world where both the absolute number and the proportion of poor people were expected to increase on account of the devastating impact of HIV/AIDS pandemic. At the turn of the century, Africa accounted for 70 per cent of the world HIV/AIDS cases. The impact on life expectancy was devastating. The WHO estimated that in 2001 there were 2.3 million AIDS death in sub-Saharan Africa, where the adult prevalence rate had reached 8.4 per cent, and aids orphans made up 11 per cent of the population of the countries most affected.[30] Compounding these problems were malaria and other diseases. At the turn of the twentieth century, Africa saw 223 deaths a year from Malaria per 100,000 inhabitants, a rate that was higher than that of other developing regions. But while the decline had continued elsewhere, the death rate in Africa had soared to 165 per 100,000. Tuberculosis, malnutrition, chronic diarrhoea, acute respiratory infections, goitre and anaemia were all health challenges facing the continent. Despite some gains, more than 200 million lacked access to health services and more than 250 million lacked access to safe drinking water, and with 2 million children dying before their first birth day, child mortality on the continent remained the highest. Illiteracy was also high, with more than 140 million youth remaining illiterate, and less than one-quarter of poor rural females attended primary school.[31] UNESCO estimated that only 10 per cent of high school graduates proceeded to institutions of higher learning.[32] Budgetary constraints, deteriorating and antiquated health care systems, civil conflicts, large-scale human migration, and increasing resistance of diseases to insecticides and drugs were largely blamed for the poor health conditions. But subsequent assessments added the environment and geography to the causes of Africa's health challenges. Sachs, for example, contended that if it "were that the poor were just like the rich but with less money, the global situation would be vastly easier than it is. As it happens, the poor live in a different ecological zones, face different health conditions and must overcome agronomic limitations that are very different from those of rich countries. These differences, indeed, are often a fundamental cause of persisting poverty."[33]

For the African government, the grim scenario presented considerable challenges that needed to be addressed. On the political front, Africa needed peace and security. Civil and political strives raised investment risks in the continent and were therefore a disincentive for foreign investors. They also destroyed physical and human capital, reduced savings, diverted resources from domestic investment, disrupted economic transactions and distorted government expenditure for public services to military expenditure. The combined impact was a reduced growth, which in turn led to increased poverty. A UNECA study demonstrated that this vicious circle of poverty and conflict fed on itself in a downward spiral.[34] According to the FAO, conflict in sub-Saharan Africa resulted in the losses of almost $52 billion in agricultural output between 1970 and 1997, a figure equivalent to 75 per cent of all official development assistance received by the conflict-affected countries.[35] Thus, the immediate mandate of the African Union in this area was to build and consolidate peace and stability, and this could be done only if member states could build institutions that help resolve conflicts: law, a judiciary, free elections, social insurance, social partnerships, representative political institutions, independent trade unions and institutionalized representation of minority groups. Mechanisms such as these guarantee the rights of people and limit gains from social conflict, reward cooperation among social groups and penalize socially uncooperative behaviour.[36]

On the economic front, the continent's challenges were no less daunting. The World Bank estimated that Africa's economies needed to grow at a sustained rate of at least 7–8 per cent annually to lift a significant number of Africans out of poverty and attain the Millennium Development Goals of eradicating poverty by 2015.[37]

Key conditions for such growth were increased resources for investment. But given the low income levels in many African countries, domestic resources were hardly sufficient with the ratio of domestic investment to GDP, declining from 25 per cent in the mid-1970s to about 19 per cent in the 1990s in several countries. In the low income countries, the ratio had remained at around 16 per cent. The inadequacy of such investment to trigger adequate growth made reviving investment and increasing its productivity a major priority in the quest for economic growth on the continent.

African governments also had to address two other issues simultaneously: they must be able to allocate resources efficiently in order to address supply-side constraints and obtain greater market access for their produce. Supply-side constraints in particular had been blamed for the continent's poor performance in international trade. Since independence, the continent's market share fell sharply, even in traditional primary goods, and African economies failed to diversify in any scale.

The continent therefore needed to sustain the fresh momentum of diversification in some cases and initiate it in others.[38] It was felt that the growing African urban population will be able to sustain such diversification, as urban growth and agglomeration create opportunities for new types of economic activity, by lowering transaction costs, concentrating consumer power and skilled labour, and facilitating dense producer network. However, on account of the small size of African economies, diversification drives could hardly be successful if based solely on domestic market. The experience of other developing countries suggests that greater investment triggers higher and sustained growth, increased voluntary savings, and further investments. But without broad and growing markets, investment could not be attracted to Africa.[39] This consideration accounts for the imperatives of regional integration, which could have spillover effects in areas such as telecommunications, power, transportation, water and sanitation, which are vital for economic growth.[40] But the vast distances and low population density compounded Africa's problems in this area by making service provision costly. At the turn of the century, Africa required an estimated US$18 billion in infrastructure investment, although substantial benefits could be reaped from more effective operations and maintenance of existing facilities, and from rapidly equipping itself with adequate information and communications technology infrastructure.[41] Indeed, poor infrastructure was one of the main causes of Africa's low competitiveness. High transportation costs throughout the continent were a burden on competitiveness and growth. For example, in 2001, shipping a car from Japan to Abidjan would cost on average US$1500 (including insurance); shipping that same car from Addis Ababa to Abidjan costs US$5000.[42] This made transport costs higher trade barriers than tariffs in Africa.[43] Indeed, the volume of trade is very sensitive to transport costs, and transport costs are sensitive to the quality of infrastructure measured by variables such as the density of the road networks, the paved road network and the rail network, or the number of telephones per person. Inadequate infrastructure also impeded the integration of domestic markets, which was equally damaging to broadly based growth and poverty reduction. The lack of all-weather rural roads, for example, condemned rural areas to isolation, subsistence production and high risk.

Despite the attraction and the potential gains to be made from regional integration, progress towards a harmonized and integrated sub-regional market remained slow. Although regional economic communities such as the Union Economique et Monétaire Ouest-Africaine (UEMOA) and CEMAC and the Southern African Customs Union had developed into customs unions, others were at varying stages of progress in establishing even free-trade areas.[44]

While African countries needed to deepen national and regional integration, they also had to have greater access to the markets of the OECD, not only for their primary produce but also for their manufactured items. For greater access to OECD market, the World Bank recommended that Africa would have to press the OECD to

- pursue agricultural reforms and reduce tariffs, non-tariff barriers and export subsidies;
- reduce and eliminate tariff escalation, which had seriously hampered vertical and horizontal integration of African Agricultural exports systems;
- include agricultural and agro-industrial commodities in future preferential trade agreements;
- streamline phytosanitary and sanitary requirements and refrain from their abuse as market barriers;
- provide technical assistance to public and private sectors in Africa to improve their capacity to apply WTO regulations and phytosanitary requirements and to strengthen their negotiating skills. African countries must know their rights and must be able to defend themselves against unfair attacks as most African countries could not afford to take action on unfair trade practices in the WTO because it was simply too costly.
- encourage foreign direct investment in agriculture and related activities to promote technology and knowledge transfers and make the sector more competitive.

These requirements account for the importance the continent has attached to the Doha Development Agenda (DDA), which offered promises of greater market access for developing countries' agricultural produce through substantial reductions in tariffs, tariff peaks and tariff escalation, as well as reductions in domestic support and export subsidies by industrialized countries. DDA also aimed at reducing subsidies to cotton growers in the industrialized countries, with a commitment to phasing such subsidies out by a specified time and providing financial compensation to developing countries during the transitional period. On non-agricultural products, the DDA sought to improve market access for manufactured goods through reductions in tariff, tariff peaks and tariff escalation. With regard to public health, the DDA called for the renegotiation and a different interpretation of the agreement on Trade-Related Intellectual Property Rights (TRIPS) so as to ensure that African countries would have the right to protect public health and promote access to medicines for all.[45]

On the social front, Africa needed to break the poverty circle in which the common African was trapped. Because 70 per cent of Africans lived in rural areas, poverty for Africa was therefore predominantly rural, and the root causes of it lay in the agriculture sector. Agricultural revolution was therefore needed to boost general development on the continent.[46] History has shown that trade and industry have almost always developed in the wake of accelerated agricultural growth.[47]

Thus, investment in the agricultural sector was found to be a key to the continent's development and had to be combined with greater market access and elimination of price distorting measures such as OECD farm subsidies. It must also run alongside rising productivity and job-creating growth in the industry.[48] The UNDP identified a number of policy clusters as being preconditions for such job-creating growth. These include investing in people, helping small farmers, promoting industrial development policies, mainstreaming gender and good governance, and sound environmental and urban management.[49]

Investing in people meant investment in human development – nutrition, health (including reproductive health), education, water and sanitation – to foster a productive labour force that could participate actively in the economy.[50] Education in particular was found to constitute the key to creating a highly productive workforce. It is indeed difficult to expect investment in high productive sectors if there is no workforce available to staff such investment. Similarly, a workforce cannot adopt new technologies that would make them more productive if they lack the requisite skills. With globalization having shifted competitiveness of regions from their resources base to skill base, investing in education would produce skilled and educated labour force that can easily raise returns on investment.[51] Investing in people also meant investing in health and specifically addressing the crises of HIV/AIDS. In countries with adult prevalence rates of 10 per cent, economic growth was reduced by one-third; rates of 20 per cent reduced productivity and growth by more than half. And in some areas, for every 1 per cent decrease in life expectancy, the growth rate of GDP fell by 0.7 per cent and the rate of investment by 1.2 per cent.[52] Thus, HIV/AIDS, TB and malaria were not only health problems, they were also part of a broader development crises. They undermined countries' productive capacities, perpetuated poverty, exacerbated social problems, overwhelmed health services and threatened national security. The impact was also felt at the macroeconomic level. HIV/AIDS reduced GDP growth in many African countries by 0.5–0.7 per cent a year on average.[53] In countries with a high burden of TB, the economic loss was estimated at between 4 and 7 per cent of the GDP annually. And Africa's GDP would be as much as US$100 billion higher had malaria been eliminated 30 years ago.[54]

There was a need to increase the productivity of small farmers and help them break away from subsistence farming and chronic hunger by introducing improved technologies, including better seeds, tillage and crop rotation systems, pest and soil management, improved rural infrastructure, such as irrigation systems, storage and transport facilities and roads, and a secure land tenure system. Policies were also required to encourage investment in infrastructure such as power, roads, ports and telecommunication to attract investment in non-traditional areas.[55]

National authorities had to promote special industrial development policies by eliminating excessive regulation, state monopolies and lack of openness to trade. This would attract productivity-enhancing investment and thereby promote productivity and growth.[56] Governments must also mainstream gender, the protection of human rights and the empowerment of poor people through democratic governance. And governments needed to place environmental and urban management at the centre of their policies in order to reduce the vulnerability of the poor and the ecosystem.[57] In sum, the UNDP study concluded that African countries could break the poverty trap by reaching the minimum thresholds in health, education, infrastructure and governance. They only needed to enhance their agricultural productivity and industrial development through appropriate policies that were based on social equity, respect for human rights and the environment. However, increased donor funding, better political governance and good resource management were deemed critical for these efforts to generate the required sustainable growth, which, in turn, would enable the poor countries in the long run to take charge of the financing of their basic public service and infrastructure.

CONCLUSION

The forgoing overview shows the social and economic difficulties Africa faced on the eve of the twenty-first century. These difficulties challenged Africa and Africans in many respects and were to determine the type of preferences Africans pursued collectively. Among these preferences were the need to wrest the continent and its people from the grips of poverty and underdevelopment, by enhancing peace and human security, stimulating job-creating growth across the continent through proper investment, and addressing a host of social ailments such as the prevalence of HIV/AIDs, TB and other infectious diseases, lack of access to education, health care and adequate nutrition. The following chapters look at how the African Union responded to these challenges by examining AU's mandate and activities as well as the effects of those activities on the welfare of the African states either individually or collectively.

NOTES

1. See *NEPAD Basic Document* available at *www.nepad.org/nepad/knowledge/doc/.../nepad-framework-document*
2. "The Heart of the Matter," and "Hopeless Africa" *The Economist*, 11 May 2000, p. 17 and pp. 23–25.
3. See, John Lonsdale, "Globalization, Ethnicity and Democracy: A View from the 'Hopeless Continent'," in A.G. Hopkins, editor, *Globalization in World History* (London: Pimlico 2002), pp. 194–219.
4. See African Development Bank, *Annual Development Effectiveness Review 2012*, p. 19.
5. These statistics are based on an assessment of the internal situation of the 53 member states, on the basis of documents that are publicly available, including the annual reports of the African Union Commission, and reports of the General Secretariat of the of the OAU. Intra-state conflict here covers anything from the presence of a small armed group in a province of a state, to large-scale wars between the central government and single or more armed groups. See also Jeffrey Herbest, Economic Incentives, Natural Resources and Conflicts in Africa, *Journal of African Economies*, Vol.9, 3 (2000) pp. 270–288, and pp. 292–294.
6. UNHCR Figures as at June 2006.
7. The World Bank, *Can Africa Claim the 21st Century* (Washington DC), p. 59.
8. Jeffrey Herbest, Economic Incentives, Natural Resources and Conflicts in Africa, *Journal of African Economies,* Vol. 9, 3 (2000) pp. 270–88, *see also* Betty Bigombe, Paul Collier and Nicholas Sambanis, "Policies for Building Post Conflict Peace," *Journal of African Economies*, Vol. 9 No.3 (2000) 323–347. The World Bank, *Can Africa Claim the 21stCentury* (Washington DC), p. 59.
9. For a case study, see Ibrahim Abdullah, "Bush Path to Distruction: the Origine and Chareter of the Revolutionary United Front/ Sierra Leone," *Journal of Modern African Studies*, 36, 2 (1998) pp. 203–235, especially page 211.
10. World Bank, *Can Africa Claim the 21st Century* (Washington DC), p. 60.
11. Economic Commission for Africa, *Transforming Africa's Economies* (Addis Ababa: UNECA, 2001), p. 20.
12. United Nations Economic Commission for Africa (UNECA), *Economic Report on Africa 1999: The Challenges of Poverty Reduction and Sustainability* (Addis Ababa, ECA, 1999), p. 4.

13. Ibid.

14. World Bank, *Can Africa Claim the 21*st *Century*, p. 8.

15. African Development Bank and OECD: *African Economic Outlook 2002/2003* (Paris: OECD Development Centre, 2003), p. 24.

16. Ibid.

17. World Bank, *Can Africa Claim the 21*st *Century*, p. 236.

18. UNECA, *Economic Report on Africa, 2004*, p. 33.

19. UNECA, *The ECA and Africa: Accelerating a Continents Development* (Addis Ababa, ECA, 1999), p. 74.

20. World Bank, *Can Africa Claim the 21st Century*. p. 9, and UNECA, *Economic Report on Africa 1999: The Challenges of Poverty Reduction and Sustainability* (Addis Ababa, ECA, 1999), 12.

21. Omar Kabbaj, *The Challenges of Africa's Development* (New York, OUP, 2003), p.100; for the origins of the African debt crises, see N.N. Susungi, "The Origins of the Debt Crises and its Aftermath in Africa," in Douglas Rimmer (editor), *Action in Africa* (London: The Royal African Society), 1993, pp.107–114.

22. For more on these initiatives, see Kabbaj*, The Challenges of Africa's Development*, pp. 101–104.

23. For more on this see, African Development Bank: *International Investment in Africa: Trends and Opportunities,* Private Sector Department Working Paper Series No.1 (Abidjan: ADB, 2001). pp. 9–12; and UNECA, *Economic Report on Africa, 2002: Tracking Performance and Progress*, (Addis Ababa 2002), pp. 2 and 28–29.

24. UNECA *The ECA and Africa*, p.18; For more on the obstacles to FDI inflow, see UNECA, *Economic Report on Africa 2004,* p. 29, particularly table 1.2.

25. UNECA, *Economic Report on Africa 2004*, p. 29.

26. Kirk Hamilton and Michael Clemens, "Genuine Savings Rate in Developing Countries," *The World bank Economic Review* 13 (May), cited in The World Bank, *Can Africa Claim the 21st Century*, p. 9.

27. UNECA, *Economic Report on Africa 2004*, p. 40

28. These are countries with high population growth rates, low income, low literacy rate, and low life expectancy.

29. UNECA, *Economic Report on Africa 1999: the Challenges of Poverty Reduction and Sustainability* (Addis Ababa 1999), p. xi.

30. The World Bank, *Intensifying Action against HIV/AIDS in Africa: Responding to a Development Crises* (Washington DC: World Bank, 1999), pp. 16. and also African Development Bank and OECD: *African Economic Outlook 2002/2003*, p. 39

31. The World Bank, *Can Africa Claim the 21st Century*, p. 10; see also UNDPI, *Africa Recovery*, Vol. 17, 3 (Oct. 2003) pp. 10–11.

32. UNESCO, *World Science Report* (Paris, 1998), cited in UNECA, *Transforming Africa's Economies* (Addis Ababa: UNECA, 2001), p. 31.

33. Jeffrey Sachs, "Helping the Poorest of the Poor," *The Economist,* 14 August 1999; OAU, "Inventory of African Conflicts since the Establishment of the Organization of African Unity in 1963" (Addis Ababa, 1998).

34. UNECA, *Transforming Africa's Economies*, p. 26

35. Estimated losses in agricultural output due to conflicts for all developing countries average $4.3 billion per year. See ILO et al., *Issue Paper*, Presented at

the African Union Extra-Ordinary Summit of Heads of State and Government on Employment and Poverty Alleviation in Africa, Ougadougou, 8–9 September 2004, p. 9.

36. Ibid., p. 26; see also Leonce Ndikumana, "Towards a Solution to Violence in Burundi: A Case for Political and Economic Liberalization," *Journal of Modern African Studies.*

37. It has been recognized that while economic growth is necessary for increased public spending on human development, it is hardly sufficient. Some governments neglect such investments or discriminate in their provisions among population groups. This weakens the potential benefits that overall economic growth can provide. See UNDP, *Human Development Report 2003*, p. 67, and several subsequent issues.

38. Ibid., p. 210

39. Ibid.

40. UNDP, *Human Development Report 2003*, p. 23

41. World Bank, *Can Africa Claim the 21st Century*, p. 132.

42. UNECA, *Assessing Regional Integration in Africa*, ECA Policy Research Report (Addis Ababa: ECA 2004), p. 2.

43. Azita Amjadi and Alexander J. Yeats, "Have Transport Costs Contributed to the Relative Decline of African Exports?" Policy Research Working Paper 1559 (Washington DC: World Bank, 1995).

44. UNECA, *Assessing Regional Integration in Africa* ECA Policy Research Report (Addis Ababa, ECA 2004), pp. 1–2.

45. See also UNECA, *Economic Report on Africa 2004* (Addis Ababa: ECA 2004), p. 33.

46. This assertion is in accordance with the theory propounded by Johnson and Mellor some forty years ago in B.F. Johnson and J.W. Mellor, "The Role of the Agriculture in Economic Development," *American Economic Review* 51 (1961), pp. 566–593. Cited in Niek Koning, *Should Africa Protect its Farmers to Revitalize its Economy*, Gatekeepers Series No, 105 (London: International Institute for Environment and Development, 2002), p. 7.

47. C.L. Degrado, J. Hopkins and V. Kelly, *Agricultural Growth Linkages in Sub-Saharan Africa* IFPRI Research Report No. 105 (Washington, D.C. IFPRI 1999), cited in Koning, *Should Africa Protect its Farmers*, p. 7.

48. This definition has been adopted from John Taylor, "Rising Productivity, Improving Standards of Living and Promoting Job-creating Economic Growth in Africa" Paper presented at the 2nd US-Sub Sharan African Trade and Economic Cooperation Forum (2nd AGOA Ministerial Forum), Port Louis, Mauritius 16 January 2003, p. 1.

49. UNDP, *Human Development Report 2003*, p. 18–19

50. In this context, productivity is defined as the quantity of goods and services that a worker produces per unit of time with the skills and tools available. UNDP, *Human Development Report 2003*, p. 18.

51. See D O'Connor and M.R. Lunati, *Economic Opening and Demand for Skills in Developing Countries: Review of Theory and Evidence,* Technical Paper No. 149 (Paris: OECD Development Centre, 1999) cited in Richard K. Johanson, *Implications*

of Globalization and Economic Restructuring for Skills Development in Sub-Saharan Africa, Working Paper No. 29 (Geneva: ILO, 2004), p. 2 and p. 5.

52. Taylor, "Rising Productivity," p. 2.

53. African Union, UNECA, UNAIDS, WHO, *Scoring African Leadership for Better Health* (Addis Ababa, 2004), p. xi.

54. Ibid.

55. UNDP, *Human Development Report 2003*, pp. 18–19.

56. Ibid.; and Taylor, "Rising Productivity," p. 2.

57. Ibid., p. 19.

Chapter 3

The Genesis and Evolution of the African Union

A Study in Intergovernmental Processes

This chapter pitches my argument at two levels: one general and the other more specific. At the general level it will be shown that contrary to functionalists view that integration is best left to technicians and sector specialists functioning outside government circles, the establishment of the African Union involved extensive intergovernmental processes that included negotiation and bargaining at both national and intergovernmental levels. Although several platforms were created for the private sector and non-state actors at the continental level, the African Union remained largely an intergovernmental institution. Governments determined AU's priorities and accounted for all the resources that the Union raised from within the continent.[1] More specifically, the chapter will show that contrary to the general belief, the AU was not the brainchild of the former Libyan Leader Colonel Moamar Gadhafi.[2]

Indeed, the name of the Libyan leader's birth place, Sirte, was associated with the African Union on more than one occasion. It was in Sirte in September 1999 that the heads of state and government of the OAU adopted a declaration calling for the transformation of the OAU into the African Union; it was in Sirte in March 2001 that the heads of state and government of the OAU formally proclaimed the entry into force of the Constitutive Act of the African Union; and it was in Sirte in February 2004 that the heads of state and government formally adopted the Common African Defence and Security Policy.

While the role of the Libyan Leader in the creation of the African Union cannot be ignored, empirical evidence shows that the Libyan Leader did not dictate the text of the Constitutive Act of the African Union. On the contrary, the African Union was more of a product of an intergovernmental process that was led by a multitude of actors. Key among the actors were President Thabo Mbeki of South Africa and President Olusegun Obasanjo of Nigeria.

But even if the African Union constituted an appropriate foreign policy instrument for these leaders, as argued elsewhere,[3] the organization represented for the entire membership an aggregate of the interests and a rational means of advancing collective utility.

Indeed, the end of the Cold War unleashed a wind of change across the world. In Africa, not only did the demise of the Cold War ushered in pluralism and multiparty politics, it also brought to the surface an idealistic undercurrent in the form of a renewed interest in African institutions and a general call for African solutions to African problems. One concrete expression of this new trend was the Abuja Treaty that sought to accelerate the continent's economic integration through a six-stage process over a period of 34 years.[4] The new thinking was further demonstrated by the collective resolve to reappraise existing frameworks and structures. It was such reappraisal of the OAU that revealed that the organization could not meet future demands without serious reforms and reorganization.[5] This exigency of reforming the continental organization was well in line with the individual interest of African leaders who had been awoken by the demise of the Cold War to the limitations of their individual efforts to address the various challenges facing them. Two leaders, Thabo Mbeki of South Africa and Olusegun Obasanjo of Nigeria, spearheaded the reforms.

From the very beginning of its rule, the government of the African National Congress (ANC) made the promotion of democracy on the African continent a foreign policy priority. This objective was conceived during the reign of Nelson Mandela, but was pursued more vigorously by Mandela's successor, Thabo Mbeki. The strategy of Mbeki's Government was to emphasize the need to reconstruct the African identity in order to first conclude the work of the earlier pan-African movement and, second, to reinvent the African state to play its rightful role on the world stage.[6] It was within this context that President Mbeki developed his concept of the African Renaissance as a holistic vision that aims at promoting peace, prosperity, democracy, sustainable development, progressive leadership and good governance.[7]

The need to reform the OAU in order to make it more responsive to the challenges of the time found resonance with Mbeki's African Renaissance, and the president became not only one of the advocates for the reform of the OAU, he also led it. According to him, a reformed OAU would be stronger, so that in its work will "focus on the strategic objective of the realization of the African Renaissance."[8]

In his drive to reform the OAU, President Mbeki found a partner in President Olusegu Obasanjo, whose own reform plans consist in resuscitating his Conference on Security, Stability, Development and Cooperation in Africa (CSSDCA), which was abandoned in the wake of his imprisonment. The CSSDCA proposed benchmarks for judging the behaviour of African leaders in four key areas: security, stability, development and cooperation.[9] The idea is for African leaders to develop a common African agenda based on unified objectives and purpose to confront Africa's security, stability and development challenges. Since the OAU did not have the institutional mechanism necessary for the common African agenda, it became necessary for Obasanjo to subscribe to the call for the restructuring of the continental organization.[10]

It was against this background that presidents Obasanjo and Mbeki went to Algiers in July 1999, seeking not only to get in motion a series of reforms but also relaunch President Obasanjo's CSSDCA and to promote President Mbeki's concept of African Renaissance. Thus, Mbeki was credited for convincing his colleagues to orientate the OAU towards the promotion of stronger and democratic institutions by outlawing coup d'état on the continent.[11] This is the background that is lost on those critics that saw the African Union as being little more than the brainchild of one person: the Libyan leader Gadhafi

Yet the role of the Libyan leader in the creation of the African Union cannot be ignored. At Algiers, support for reforming the OAU was so overwhelming that a decision was taken to convene an extraordinary session to discuss the reform agenda.[12] And the Assembly unanimously accepted the offer of the Libyan leader to host the extraordinary summit in Sirte.

Observers of Libyan politics maintain that the leader of the Libyan Revolution was prompted to offer to host the summit on various considerations. First, Colonel Gadhafi sensed that the two most powerful African leaders were teaming up to reform the OAU for the advancement of their own interest.[13] Second, hosting the summit offered the Libyan leader the opportunity to solidify his return to the geopolitics of black Africa and to demonstrate his renewed commitment to the pan-Africanism project.[14]

In addition to accepting to convene an extraordinary summit, the Algiers summit was important in many ways. In the declaration[15] they adopted at the end of the session, the leaders made commitments in various areas: on security and economic matters, they called for the establishment of appropriate mechanisms for the eradication of corruption as well as the trafficking in drugs and arms. On human rights, they reiterated their commitment to the promotion and protection of human rights and fundamental freedoms. On globalization, they called for democratic and an all-inclusive globalization that will foster development on the basis of human solidarity and prosperity of all people. They also called for a democratic global governance. On terrorism, they called for international cooperation in drawing up an international legal instrument for combating terrorism under the auspices of the United Nations. They even went further to ask for an international conference on terrorism. And finally on international economic relations, they called for equity and for a partnership that will promote the development and unity of the continent. In addition to the declaration, the leaders took several decisions, including the decision to convene an extraordinary session to examine the continent's challenges in detail.[16]

The 4th Extraordinary Session of the Assembly of the OAU was convened in Sirte, Libya, on 8 and 9 September 1999. It had only one item on its agenda: *strengthening of Africa's capacity to deal with the challenges of the new millennium.* As per the established practice, The Assembly's session was preceded by a preparatory ministerial session in Tripoli from 6 to 7 September 1999, which examined two items: (a) Draft Charter of the Federation of the United States of Africa, proposed by Libya, and (b) The Draft Sirte Declaration.

Instead of the more ambitious plan to have a Federation of the United States of Africa as proposed by Colonel Ghadafi, and which was an item on the agenda for the preparatory ministerial session in Tripoli, the outcome of the Sirte I summit was a Declaration that called for the following:

1. to establish an African Union in conformity with the ultimate objectives of the Charter of the OAU and the provisions of the Treaty establishing the African Economic Community;
2. to accelerate the process of implementing the Treaty establishing the African Economic Community, in particular by
   - shortening the implementation periods of the Abuja Treaty;
   - ensuring the speedy establishment of all the institutions provided for by the Abuja Treaty, such as the African Central Bank, the African Monetary Union, the African Court of Justice and the Pan African Parliament;
   - strengthening and consolidating the regional economic communities as the pillars for achieving the objectives of the African Economic Community and realizing the envisaged Union.

The 4th Extraordinary Session of the OAU Assembly represented a watershed for Africa in many ways. First, it witnessed the highest turnout of heads of state and government in several years.[17] Second, it gave African leaders a unique opportunity to reflect collectively on their predicament and to chart a new course of action. And, third, it heralded the demise of the OAU and the advent of a new continental structure to replace the OAU, which, the leaders unanimously agreed, could not respond to the challenges of the twenty-first century. However, Sirte I also shows clearly that African leaders did not want a radical break with the past. Thus, while the African Union represented a leap into the future it was not a total divorce from the past, as much of the declaration centred on the need to operationalize the provisions of the Abuja Treaty and shorten the various timeframes which the treaty provides.

In addition to providing a shorter timeframe for the implementation of various provisions of the treaty, the Sirte Declaration also provided the following timeline:

- the adoption of the Constitutive Act of the proposed union at the 36th Ordinary Session of the Assembly, scheduled to take place in Togo in June 2000;
- completion of the ratification process by December 2000;
- formal launching of the African Union on 1 January 2001 during an extraordinary session scheduled to take place in Sirte on 1 January 2001;
- the establishment of the Pan African Parliament before 2000;
- convening of an African Ministerial Conference on the CSSDCA.

The implementation of the provisions of the declaration became the preoccupation of the OAU Secretariat and the member states. Shortly after the Sirte summit, the Secretary General of the OAU, Salim Ahmed Salim, appointed a panel of experts to produce a draft Constitutive Act for the African Union. The draft text, first discussed by African Experts in Addis Ababa on 17–21 April 2000, proposed three options:

1. an African Union based on the fusion of the existing OAU and the AEC;
2. a Union based on a revised OAU charter, which is to coexist with the AEC;
3. a set of continental organizations, where the OAU will constitute the framework, and the African Union and the AEC will constitute the pillars.

The first expert meeting failed to reach a consensus on the *nature* of the proposed union, although they managed to examine the draft texts of the Constitutive Act. The expert meeting on the Constitutive Act continued in Tripoli, Libya, on 27–29 May, 2000 before the First Ministerial Conference on the Implementation of the Sirte Declaration was opened on 31 May. The difficulties during the conference centred on the nature of the proposed Union and there were clear indications that the Ministers would not have reached consensus either. However, the unexpected arrival at the opening ceremony of the ministerial session of the presidents of Mali, Ghana, Liberia, Sudan and Senegal, alongside the Libyan leader Gadhafi. Thus, what was planned to be a ministerial conference turned into a mini summit. In his address to the ministerial gathering, the Libyan leader emphasized the urgency with which the question of the African Union ought to be treated. He reminded the ministers that the African leaders had unanimously taken the decision to set up the African Union, and that Libya's draft Charter of the United States of Africa provided a response to the questions relating to the nature, the shape, the principles and the objectives of the union. Other speakers reiterated the need to implement quickly the desire of the leaders, which consisted in putting in place a structure other than the OAU that would best respond to the challenges of the twenty-first century.[18] The ministers on their turn also underscored the need to go beyond the OAU and to find a solution to the impasse that bedevilled the meeting of experts and senior government officials. No doubt, the presence of the heads of state placed considerable pressure on the ministers and forced them to find a solution to the impasse.

It was on this basis that an ad hoc committee of 15 members was set up under the chairmanship of Modibo Sidibe, Minister of Foreign Affairs of Mali, who was chairman of the Council of Ministers, to examine and submit a report on the draft Constitutive Act and on the Draft Protocol on the Pan African Parliament. In its turn, the ad hoc committee set up a three-member sub-committee composed of Mali, Libya and the Secretary General of the OAU. It was this subcommittee which finally came up with the draft Constitutive Act, which was adopted by the larger ad hoc committee before being adopted by the Council of Ministers as a whole. The draft text contained a preamble and 30 articles. The council mandated the Secretary General to put the agreed text in a proper legal language, and to communicate the text to the member states for their views and comments. It was agreed that the draft text would be adopted during the 36th Session of the Assembly, scheduled to take place in Lomé, Togo in July 2001.

Getting the text through the summit in Togo proved to be more difficult than most people had anticipated. The preparatory ministerial meeting in particular started off badly. A number of delegations proposed that the adoption of the draft Constitutive Act be postponed to a later date in order to allow a bigger section of their national constituencies to discuss it and thereby participate in the historic process of setting up the African Union. Proponents of postponement argued that the draft text was not submitted to them in time to allow for wider consultation on it. They also stressed the need for a gradual approach and the need to strengthen the existing regional economic communities in the first instance.

In the opposite camp were the other group of states that insisted that the Sirte Declaration was a political act that was unanimously subscribed to by all the heads of states, that the ministers were bound to implement the terms of the declaration in accordance with the timeline that the assembly had agreed upon, and that the first ministerial meeting on the implementation of the Sirte I declaration did a good job.

A solution to this impasse was found when an ad hoc 15-member ministerial committee was set up to examine in detail the text submitted by the Secretary General.[19] The recommendations of the ad hoc committee enabled the Council of Ministers to approve the draft Constitutive Act.[20] However, the consensus at the level of the Council of Ministers did not save the Assembly from having a lengthy debate on the Constitutive Act. However, at the end of the debate, they took a decision[21] to, among other things:

1. adopt the Constitutive Act of the African Union;
2. urge member states to sign and ratify the Act as soon as possible in order to ensure the rapid implementation of the instrument.

Twenty-five countries signed the Act during the course of the summit, and several others followed suit thereafter. The required number of ratifications was obtained within a year, and the Act entered into force on 26 May 2001, upon Nigeria's deposit of the 36th instrument of ratification on 25 April 2001.

The entry into force of the Constitutive Act of African Union was one of the items on the agenda of the 5th Extraordinary Session of the Assembly, which took place in Sirte on 1 and 2 March 2001.[22] The debate of the heads of state and government revolved around two issues: (a) whether to declare at that session the entry into force of the African Union before the required number of ratifications was obtained; or (b) to wait until the required number of ratifications were obtained before the union could be solemnly proclaimed.

Speakers in favour of the immediate proclamation of the establishment of the African Union and the entry into force of the Constitutive Act included leaders of Libya, Sudan, Togo and Senegal. Those calling for a delay until the required number of ratifications are obtained included President Obasanjo of Nigeria, Museveni of Uganda, and the leaders of Tanzania, Namibia, Ghana, Lesotho, Zambia, Mali, South Africa and Gabon.

It was the proposal of the Egyptian delegation that was to save the day. In his intervention, Amr Moussa, the Minister of Foreign Affairs of Egypt, proposed a draft decision that provided as follows:

1. that the 5th Extraordinary Session of the Assembly of the OAU hereby declares the creation of the African Union;
2. that the Constitutive Act of the African Union will enter into force 30 days after the deposit of the instrument of ratification by two-thirds of the OAU member states;
3. that the 37th Session of the OAU will take the necessary decisions concerning the entry into force of the Constitutive Act as well as the setting up of the organs.

On the basis of the Egyptian proposal, a drafting committee was set up to draft the decision, which was adopted by the Assembly on 2 March 2001. Accordingly, the 5th Extraordinary Session of the Assembly decided:

1. to declare solemnly the creation of the African Union by the collectivity of the member state;
2. that the legal disposition of the declaration will be completed when the 36th instrument of ratification of the Constitutive Act is deposited;
3. that the Constitutive Act of the Union will enter into force 30 days after the deposit of the instrument of ratification of two-thirds of the member states of the OAU, as stipulated in Article 28 of the Act;
4. that the 37th ordinary session of the Assembly will take necessary decisions relating to the transformation of the OAU into the African Union, in accordance with Article 33 of the Constitutive Act, and to draw up draft protocols relating to the organs and institutions.

By all means, the decision represents a compromise between those who wanted a fast approach and those who preferred a gradual movement. This cleavage was classic to African continental politics. It characterized African affairs during the period before and immediately after independence, and was to recur within a few years of the inception of the African Union.[23]

THE TRANSITIONAL PERIOD

When the 37th Ordinary Session of the Assembly of the OAU was convened in Lusaka, the process of transforming the OAU to the AU had already begun. The highlight of the Lusaka Summit was therefore the selection of the principal change agent – the Chief Executive Officer – who would drive the whole transformation process to its logical conclusion. For that position, three candidates vied to replace Salim Ahmed Salim as the Secretary General of the OAU: Amara Essy, former foreign minister of Cote d'Ivoire; Lasana Kouyaté, former Executive Secretary of the Economic Community of West African States (ECOWAS) and Theo Ben Guirarb, former cabinet minister of Namibia. Lasana Kouyaté dropped out at the third round and Amara Essy won the two-thirds majority at the eighth round.[24]

In Lusaka, the Assembly also decided to mandate the Secretary General to undertake consultations with member states on the various organs of the Union.[25] Such consultations were expected to produce draft rules of procedure of the organs, in particular the Assembly, the Executive Council, the Commission and the Permanent Representatives Committee. The Secretary General was also mandated to revisit and reorient the programmes of the General Secretariat in order to enable it to undertake the additional responsibilities and programmes arising from the implementation of the Constitutive Act and the operationalization of the African Union during the transitional period.[26] Most significantly, he was asked to review the programme budget and to reallocate the budgetary appropriations contained therein in a manner that would enable the Secretariat to carry out a number of transitional activities. And while the Assembly called on member states and development partners to make extra-budgetary contributions, it authorized the Secretary General to undertake studies on alternative sources for funding the activities and programmes of the African Union.[27]

The Assembly's decision on the operationalization of the African Union covered ten other areas, including the popularization of the African Union in member states, the structure and competences of the Economic and Social Council,[28] the Mechanism for Conflict Prevention, Management and Resolution, [29] Regional Economic Communities (RECs), Specialized Technical Committees; the devolution of assets and liabilities as well as symbols of the African Union.[30] Most importantly, the decision provides that the transitional period would be one year and that the African Union would be formally launched during the following session of the Assembly, scheduled to take place in Durban, South Africa, in July 2002.

The Secretary General's report on the activities undertaken to implement the Lusaka Decision during the one-year transitional period was examined at the special session of the Council of Ministers in Durban on 1–2 July 2002.[31] Accordingly, the implementation of the Lusaka Decision begun immediately upon the assumption of office of the new Secretary General. The process was characterized by consultations with member states, the UN, the civil society and other international partners. Internal consultations were held within the secretariat through brainstorming sessions, and a Transition Planning Support Team was established within the Secretariat with the financial support of the UNDP.

These processes facilitated the establishment of the organs by producing the draft rules of procedure of the Assembly, the Executive Council, and the PRC. With regard to the Commission, the Secretariat secured funding from the International Labour Organization (ILO) for a study that would help identify the organizational chart of the Commission (organigram) and the job profile and job description of the proposed posts. The terms of reference of the study also included an audit review of the institutional and organizational setup of the current OAU Secretariat and the future Commission, human resource development plan, especially the formulation of training programmes and retrenchment packages, and the development of new and competitive staff management tools.

As part of its popularization efforts, the Secretariat established a website of the OAU/AU and reached out to media representatives, universities, civil society organizations and extended collaboration with bodies such as the ECA, which organized a symposium on the African Union in the margins of the 3rd African Development Forum (ADF) in Addis Ababa in 2002.

Consultations were also held on the ECOSOC mainly through the OAU-Civil Society Conference in Addis Ababa in June 2001 and with the Regional Economic Communities. Also envisaged were a number of activities aimed at setting up and fully operationalizing the OAU specialized agencies and specialized technical committees. More significantly, the Secretariat began to work on how to strengthen the mechanism for conflict prevention, management and resolution. The consultations on the mechanism resulted in the recommendation to elaborate a protocol that would create a legally binding peace and security council as one of the principal organs of the African Union.[32] On the alternative source of funding, the Secretariat commissioned a study on the way forward, but work on this area remained inconclusive. The activities during the transitional period also covered gender mainstreaming. A working group on gender was established within the Secretariat and a workshop was organized on gender mainstreaming in the African Union. Nothing much was done on the court of justice and the financial institutions.

The report of the Secretary General recommended that the rules of procedure of the Assembly, the Executive Council and the PRC be adopted during the Durban session and that work on the other organs as well as the structure and the financial implications of the Commission be allowed to continue and reported on within a year. Work on other areas such as the alternative sources of funding was also to continue. The most important recommendation related to the interim arrangements. The report recommended that in accordance with the provisions of the Constitutive Act,[33] the OAU Secretariat General should be designated the interim commission of the Union and the Secretary General the interim chairperson of the Union.

With little difficulty, the council examined and recommended the adoption of the draft rules of procedure of the Assembly, the Executive Council and the PRC, as well as the draft statutes of the commission. It also considered the Secretariat's report on the Draft Protocol relating to the establishment of the Peace and Security Council of the African Union, and unanimously took a decision on the establishment of the PSC and agreed to make the body more effective than the Central Organ by giving it appropriate authority to enable the AU to fulfil its mandate in the area of peace and security.

It was the question of the interim period that dominated the debate during the extraordinary session, and this revolved essentially around two positions. The first is that since the transitional period ended on 9 July 2002, according to the provisions of the Constitutive Act,[34] the OAU Secretariat would have to be automatically transformed into the interim commission of the AU pending the establishment of the commission. The second position was only slightly different in that it negates the automaticity of the Secretariat becoming the interim secretariat. Proponents of this position insisted that the one-year mandate the Assembly had given to the Secretary General to implement the Lusaka Decision lasted till the end of the transitional period, and that the council would therefore have to propose new arrangements and modalities for managing the interim period. On the length of the interim period, two divergent views emerged. One was that the interim period should be a year with a clearly marked calendar and programme of activities to complete the pending work. Proponents of this view suggested that the Secretary General be designated the interim chairperson, and the assistant Secretaries General as interim commissioners, so that they could complete the priority tasks assigned to the Secretariat General. Others suggested that the chairperson and the deputy chairperson of the commission be elected within six months and be entrusted with the task of completing the priority tasks within the remaining six months, so that by the time the next ordinary session of the Assembly was convened, all the key organs of the Union would be in place.

Another group suggested that the interim period should be six months and that the Secretary General should be appointed as interim chairperson of the commission for six months, so that he could complete arrangements for the election of the chairperson, deputy chairperson and commissioners, so that they could be elected at the next ordinary session of the Assembly.

After a lengthy deliberation, the Council of Ministers decided to recommend to the Assembly an interim period of one year, to retain the incumbent Secretary General as the interim chairperson of the commission, the assistant Secretaries General as interim commissioners, and the Secretariat General as the interim commission. This was endorsed by the Assembly.[35]

No sooner was the AU established than the process of a structural change begun. Within a year of its inception, a number of amendments to the Constitutive Act were proposed and adopted, suggesting the dissatisfaction with the most fundamental document of the Union.[36] But the proposal that threatened AU's already shaky foundation was that of establishing the Union Government that would lead to the United States of Africa. Although the proposal constituted a threat to the African Union, it triggered a series of consultations that further demonstrated the centrality of intergovernmental processes in the formation and evolution of the African Union.

TOWARDS THE UNITED STATES OF AFRICA

Indeed, the idea of a United States of Africa has been an old one. Since Marcus Garvey mentioned it in his poem "Hail United States of Africa"[37] in 1924, the idea continued to live on in the minds of pan-Africanists over the decades. It was mooted intermittently during later days of the OAU and the early days of the AU. But by the mid-2000s, Ghadafi's infatuation with the idea turned the idea of a United States of Africa into a vexing item on the agenda of several AU meetings. Thus, from 17 to 18 November 2006 the Executive Council of the African Union met in Addis Ababa at its 9th Extraordinary Session to consider the proposal of a Union Government that would lead to the United States of Africa in 2015.[38] Two views emerged during the debate. One group of states[39] led by Libya supported the proposal to create the Union Government by 2007 and to proclaim the United States of Africa by 2015. The majority of member states, however, opposed this proposal on the grounds that the African Union was young and fragile and that the Union should be allowed to mature before a process of fundamental change could be considered. This group also maintained that the proponents of the transformation had failed to make a convincing case for their cause because the tasks assigned to the proposed Union Government constituted the mandate of the existing African Union. But the debate on the Union Government did not end there. The 8th Ordinary Session of the Assembly, which took place in Accra in July 2007, was entirely devoted to "the Grand Debate on the Union Government." The outcome of the "Grand Debate" was a reaffirmation of the cleavage between the "maximalists," those calling for Union Government now, and their opponents the "Gradualists."[40] At the end of the Accra Summit, the leaders adopted a declaration that was sufficiently vague to satisfy both camps. In essence, the declaration restated the leaders commitment to the acceleration of the economic and political integration of the continent, including the formation of a Union Government for Africa and the subsequent creation of the United States of Africa. The leaders also outlined the steps to be taken to attain the Union Government. These included:

1. the rationalization of regional economic communities and harmonization of their activities which lead to the creation of an African common market through the stages set out in the Treaty establishing the African Economic Community (Abuja Treaty), with a reviewed and shorter timeframe to be agreed upon in order to accelerate the economic and, where possible, political integration;
2. auditing the commission as well as the other organs of the African Union;
3. the establishment of a ministerial committee to:

    a. identify the contents of the Union Government concept and its relations with national governments;
    b. identify the domains of competence and the impact of the establishment of the Union Government on the sovereignty of member states;
    c. define the relationship between the Union Government and the Regional Economic Communities (RECs);
    d. elaborate the roadmap together with timeframes for establishing the Union Government; and

e. identify additional sources of financing for the activities of the Union.

For most observers, the Accra meeting and the measures recommended brought some respite to the incessant wrangling that characterized the deliberation of the African Union on the Union Government or the United States of Africa. The audit exercise was undertaken, but the recommendations that the audit report made remained largely unimplemented by 2012. Libya's assumption of the rotating chairmanship of the Union in 2009 did not only rekindle the Union Government debate, it also gave it a new contour. Already during Tanzania's chairmanship in 2008, the African Union Authority was proposed as a compromise between the gradualist and maximalist positions. At the time, this was acceptable to both camps, and a decision was taken to transform the African Union Commission into African Union Authority.[41] But it was not clear how this was to be achieved. When Ghaddafi took over the chairmanship of the Union, he pressed for two things: change of the AU symbols and a decision on the implementation modalities of the African Union Authority. He succeeded on both scores. The flag was replaced with the current green flag of the Union that he had himself proposed. He also succeeded in getting the Assembly to adopt a decision during its 9th Ordinary Session in Sirte in 2009[42] that instructed the African Union Commission to:

1. prepare the legal instruments for amendments to the Constitutive Act, the rules of procedure of the Assembly, the Executive Council, the Peace and Security Council, the Permanent Representatives Committee (PRC) and the Statutes of the Commission.
2. to convene a meeting of experts and the permanent representatives on the structure of the new AU Authority, taking into account the mandate given to the Authority; and the financial applications of the transformation of the commission into the AU Authority.

The commission did indeed convene an expert meeting on the legal instruments of the Union as well as on the structure of the proposed authority. But those meetings were not conclusive. Therefore, when the Assembly met in July 2010, it took note of the interim report of the commission on the experts' meeting and instructed that follow-up meetings of government experts, the Permanent Representatives' Committee (PRC) and ministers of justice be convened to consider and approve the draft legal instruments.[43] By January 2011, government experts had revised most of the legal texts of the Union, but again the Assembly could not take any concrete action on the subject. Instead, it requested the commission to convene further meetings of government experts and ministers of justice to finalize work on the legal instruments.[44]

The Assembly took another full year before it considered the Union Government again.[45] When the subject was finally considered in January

2013, the leaders took a decision that largely strengthened the hands of the gradualists. Instead of putting in place the African Union Authority, the leaders agreed to strengthen the commission and all other organs as well as the relations between AU organs and the Regional Economic Communities. With respect to the African Union Authority, the leaders decided

> to consider, at the appropriate time, all related issues, on the basis of all the relevant reports, recommendations and declarations, as well as decisions of the Assembly, the different Committees of Heads of State and Government, the Executive Council, and the Ministerial Committees that have considered the issue, as well as the recommendations of the High-Level Panel on the Audit of the Union.[46]

The decision effectively removed the transformation of the African Union Commission into African Union Authority from the list of AU priorities. Attention was refocused instead on strengthening the African Union Commission.

A number of factors have contributed to the development. Among the factors were the end of term of Alpha Omar Konaré as Chairperson of the Commission, the death of Ghadaffi of Libya and the departure of President Wade of Senegal. These events considerably weakened, if not killed, the spirit of maximalists. However, a major contributing factor was the election of Dr Nkosazana Dlamini-Zuma as Chairperson of the Commission of the African Union. As South Africa's Foreign Minister and member of the Executive Council of the African Union for several years, Dr Zuma was one of the leading supporters of the African Union agenda and programmes. However, she was never unequivocal about her support for a more realistic and pragmatic approach to African unity. Therefore, her arrival at the helm of the African Union strengthened the position of the gradualist and arguably paved the way to Decision 454 of 2013 that suspended sine die the processes of transforming the Commission into the African Union Authority. Priority was given instead to the development of the African Union Strategic Plan 2014–2017 and, most importantly, to the 50-year plan and vision entitled *Agenda 2063*.[47]

CONCLUSION

By many counts the Durban Summit represented a watershed in African integration. First, it marked the formal end to the transitional period from the OAU to the new African Union. Second, Durban offered the most fitting burial ground for an organization that spent its entire existence fighting for the liberation of South Africa and other African territories. And third, as a locomotive of African development, South Africa was also a fitting ground to launch the new African Union, whose mandate was more of lifting the entire continent from poverty and underdevelopment through peace building, good governance and economic reconstruction.

In accordance with the mandate of the interim commission, the interim period was devoted to the completion of the priority tasks such as the preparations for the election of the chairperson, the deputy chairperson and the commissioners, as well as the establishment of the structure of the new commission. Thus, the election of the chairperson, the deputy chairperson and the commissioners in Maputo in July 2003 brought to an end the interim period and ushered in a new era in African continental politics.[48] The election of the commissioners and the processes that preceded it shows clearly that the African Union was the outcome of intergovernmental processes as Liberal intergovernmentalists posit. Similarly, the processes that the proposal for the United States of Africa triggered offer additional confirmation that the AU was an intergovernmental institution that operates on the basis of consensus rather than coercion. This consideration underlines the poverty of the claim that the Union was a pet project of the former Libyan leader, Ghadafi.

NOTES

1. As we shall see (chapter 11), AU member states funded the operational budget of the African Union organs, but accounted for about 10 per cent of the programme budget of the Union.

2. See *The Europa Year Book 2002*, p. 278; Keith Gottschalk and Siegmar Schmidt, "The African Union and the New Partnership for Africa's Development: Strong Institutions for Weaker States," available at www.weltpolitik.net/attachment/international politik und gesellschaft 2004.

3. For more on how the African Union served the Foreign Policy objectives of these leaders, see, Thomas Kwasi Tieku, "Explaining the Clash and Accommodation of Interests of Major Actors in the Creation of the African Union," *African Affairs,* 103 (2004), pp. 246–247.

4. See page 71 for more on the Abuja Treaty.

5. Corinne A.A. Parker and Donald Rukare, "The New African Union and its Constitutive Act," *American Journal of International Law*, 92, 2 (20020, pp. 365–378, cited in Tieku, "The Creation of the African Union," p. 252.

6. G.Evans, "South Africa's Foreign Policy After Mandela: Mbeki and his Concept of an African Renaissance", The Round Table, 88, 352 (1999), cited in Tieku, "Explaining the Clash and Accommodation of Interests", p. 255.

7. Department of Foreign Affairs of the Republic of South Africa, Foreign Policy of South Africa, available at http://www.dfa.gov.za/department/ cited in Tieku.

8. Thabo Mbeki, speech delivered on the occasion of the launch of the African Renaissance Institute, Pretoria, 11 October 1999.

9. For more on the CSSDCA, see Olusegun Obasanjo and Felix G.N. Mosha (eds.), *Africa: rise to Challenge, Conference Report of the Kampala Forum* (Abeokuta, Nigeria: Africa Leadership Forum, 1992).

10. For the role of Nigeria, see J.K. Shinkaye, "Nigeria's role in shaping the African Union," in Nigerian Ministry of Cooperation and Integration in Africa, *African Union and the Challenges of Cooperation and Integration,* Proceedings of the National Seminar 15-15 May 2001 (Abuja: Spectrum Books Ltd. 2002), pp.11–29.

11. For more on the OAU's position on the anti-constitutional change of governments, see p. 146.

12. Declaration No. AHG/Decl.XXXV).

13. Tieku, "The Creation of the African Union," p. 260.

14. Asteris Huliara, "Qadhafi's Comeback: Libya and Sub-Saharan Africa in the 1990s," *African Affairs* 100, 398 (2001), p.17.

15. Algiers Declaration AHG/Decl.1-2 (XXXV) of 14 July 1999.

16. Decision AHG/Dec 140 (XXXV).

17. In total 43 heads of state and government attended the summit, and the remaining 10 countries were represented by their foreign ministers and other senior cabinet officials.

18. See Al Mamoun Baba Lamine Keita *Union Africaine,* (2002).

19. The ministerial committee was composed of Mali (Chair), Libya, Lesotho, Ghana, Uganda, Republic of Congo, SADR, Nigerial, Tchad, Guinea Equatorial, Gabon, Mozambique, South Africa, Algeria, Gambia, Mauritius, Togo, Tanzania, Tunisia, Sudan and Ethiopia.

20. Decision No. CM/Dec 519 (LXXII).

21. Decision No. AHG/Dec 143 (XXXVI).

22. The other items on the agenda of the assembly were the Pan African Parliament, Africa's external debt, the CSSDCA and the Lockerbie affair.

23. See chapter 12, pp. 47–50.

24. The votes were as follows: 1st round: Essy 18 votes, Theo 18 votes, Kuyateh 12; 2nd round: Essy 22, Theo 17, and Kuyateh 9: 3rd round: Essy 24, Theo 16, Kuyateh 9. From the fourth to the seventh round, Essy and Theo scored 30 and 18, respectively. Theo withdrew after the 7th round and Essy obtained 42 out of 48, 2 voted against, 3 abstained and 1 was invalid.

25. Decision No. AHG.Dec/160 (XXXVII).

26. Ibid.

27. Ibid.

28. For more on the instructions in these areas, see Decision No. AHG.Dec/160 (XXXVII.

29. Report of the Secretary General on the Implementation of the Lusaka Decision on the African Union (AHG/Dec.160 (XXXVII) Document SP/CM/AU/2.

30. Ibid p. 13

31. Article 33 (4)

32. Articles 33 (1) and 33 (4)

33. Decision As/AU/Dec.1(I)

34. See Protocol to the Amendments to the Constitutive Act of the African Union 2003, available at www.au.int/.../PROTOCOL_AMENDMENTS_CONSTITUTIVE_ACT_OF_ THE_AFRICAN_UNION.pdf

35. Available at http://www.poemhunter.com/poem/hail-united-states-of-africa/

36. In January 2005, a committee of seven heads of state was set up to study the Libyan proposal for a Union Government that entails transforming the existing Commission of the African Union into the government of the continent. The committee was composed of the heads of state from Uganda (Chair), Senegal, Botswana, Chad, Ethiopia and Niger. At the group's first meeting in Kampala on 13 June 2005, only the heads of state of Senegal and Uganda were present; all the other heads of state were represented. The committee's second meeting took place in the margins of the summit in Sirte, in July 2005. The main thrust of their proposal is the creation of a continental government, where the chairperson of the Commission of the African Union would be the prime minister of Africa and commissioners would become ministers. This proposal constituted the most controversial item on the agenda of the Assembly in Sirte in July 2005. While a number of countries saw the merit of a continental government, others saw it as being premature at best. The division over the issue prompted the Assembly to meet in a tightly closed session, at which only the heads of state and heads of delegation were allowed to take part. Those consultations led to a decision to establish another committee of heads of state and government to consider all the positions on the issue that came out during the debate. The committee was chaired by President Obasanjo of Nigeria, and comprised the heads of state of Algeria, Kenya, Senegal, Gabon, Lesotho and Uganda. During its 7th Ordinary Session, held in Banjul in July 2006, the Assembly received the report of the committee and mandated the Executive Council to convene an extraordinary meeting to consider the report and submit its recommendation to the Assembly during the January Session.

37. Comprising Libya, Mali, Senegal and to some extent Nigeria.

38. For more on this, see Thimoty Murithi, editor, *Towards A Union Government for Africa: Challenges and Opportunities,* ISS Monograph Series No. 140 2008.

39. Decision No. Assembly/AU/Dec 233 (XVII) 2008.

40. Decision No. Assembly/AU/Dec 263 (XIII) 2009.

41. Decision No. Assembly/AU/Dec 298 (XV) 2010.

42. Decision No. Assembly/AU/Dec 341 (XVI) 2011, Decision No. Assembly/AU/Dec 372 (XVII) 2011, Decision No. Assembly/AU/Dec 415 (XVIII) 2012

43. The Assembly did not consider the item during its sessions in July 2011, January 2012 and July 2012.

44. Decision No. Assembly/AU/Dec 454 (XX) 2013.

45. Agenda 2063 Framework Document was submitted to the Council of Ministers in January 2014. The document outlined a vision for Africa in 2063 and a plan to attain that vision. This is a vision of an Africa that is prosperous and enjoys inclusive growth and sustainable development; integrated and unified; enjoys good governance, respect for human rights, rule of law and justice for all; is peaceful and secure; is a citadel of culture, values and ethics; places its people, especially youth and women, at the centre of its development; and is an influential global player and a strong partner. Enablers and drivers identified for the attainment of the vision include conducive

policy and legal environment, strong human and institutional capacity, as well as responsible and efficient private sector and media. Social and economic inequalities, inability to manage diversity, terrorism and organized crime, religious extremism and ethnicism, corruption, nepotism and natural disasters constitute major risks that the framework document has identified. In my view, apart from the new timeframe of the vision, Agenda 2063 is a return to the past. The seven axes of the vision have been fully articulated in various blueprints from the Lagos Plan of Action to the Abuja Treaty and NEPAD. In recent years, they were articulated almost word for word by the Commission for African that the former British Prime Minister Tony Blair set up in 2004. The mandate of the Blair African Commission was to generate new ideas and actions for a strong and prosperous Africa, to help African institutions deliver implementation of existing international commitment towards Africa, to understand and help fulfil African aspirations. In its final report, the commission formulated the following recommendations:

i. Africa should strengthen good governance by promoting accountability and transparency, fighting corruption and strengthening information systems. To do this, the leaders should embark on capacity building because lack of capacity lies at the heart of bad governance.
ii. Africa should make peace a priority by building the continent's capacity to prevent, manage and resolve conflict. They should also be able to embark upon post-conflict reconstruction.
iii. Africa should pay closer attention to social development, through education, health, including the promotion of sanitation and provision of clean water, prevention and treatment of HIV/AIDS and the establishment of social protection schemes.
iv. African Government should promote economic growth strategies that will allow poor people to participate in that growth. In other words, the strategy of economic growth should mainstream equitable income distribution through effective job creation.
v. to increase the continent's economic growth, African countries should be able to trade more with the outside world. This would require greater market access as well as the removal of supply-side constraints.
vi. both increased growth and increased trade require investment. For this reason, the commission recommended the overhaul of development aid in terms of quality and quantity. This should be coupled with effective debt relief that would free resources for investment in the growth sectors as well as in the social sector.
vii. for the recommendations to be effectively implemented, African multilateral institutions (AU, IDB, ECA, NEPAD, etc.) must be strengthened, and global multilateral institutions such as the IMF, the World Bank and the WTO overhauled, in order to give African, countries greater voice in the decision-making and strategic leadership.

46. The chairperson, and the deputy chairperson of the Commission as well as six of the eight commissioners were elected in Maputo. Alpha Oumar Konare of Mali became the first substantive chairperson of the commission; Patrick Mazimhaka (Rwanda) was elected deputy chairperson, Ambassador Said Djinnit (Algeria) Commissioner for Peace and Security, Julia Dolly Joiner (The Gambia) Commissioner for Peace and Security, Dr Bernard Zoba (Republic of Congo), Commissioner for Infrastructure and Energy; Bience P. Gawanas (Namibia) Commissioner for Social Affairs, Elizabeth Tankeu (Cameroon) Commissioner for Trade and Industry, Rosebud Kurwijila (Tanzania), Commissioner for Rural Economy and Agriculture. A Tunisian was elected Commissioner for Human Resources Science and Technology, but later declined the post. She was replaced by Dr Nadia Mohammed Essayed (Libya) Commissioner for Human resources, Science and technology. The election of Dr Nadia and Dr Maxwell Mkawezalamba (Malawi) as Commissioner for Economic Affairs completed the college of commissioners. They were all elected for a four-year term. See pp.189–190 for the election of subsequent commissions.

Chapter 4

Decolonization and After

The OAU and Africa's Challenges

This chapter is the first substantive analysis of the preferences of African leaders. It shows how decolonization and stability represented the most pressing preference of African leaders from the 1960s up to the independence of South Africa in 1991. The chapter outlines the manner in which the OAU managed its mandate in these areas, and concludes that the OAU succeeded in its decolonization struggle because the organization was properly mandated and equipped to attain that objective. It shows that to some extent the organization also succeeded in reducing interstate conflicts, but was less successful in managing civil wars and in addressing socio-economic problems of its members because it had limited autonomy in these areas. The chapter argues that the OAU's failure in addressing civil wars and socio-economic problems must be seen in the context of agent–principal relationship and cannot be isolated from the collective responsibility of OAU member states.

By many counts, the founding conference of the Organization was in itself a brilliant feat of diplomacy. Convened in Addis Ababa in May 1963, the conference represented a climax of a string of pan-African gatherings that begun from the London conference in 1900 to the Monrovia and Lagos gatherings in May 1961 and January 1962, respectively.[1] With all but two of the leaders of the 32 independent African countries in attendance, the Addis Ababa conference also epitomized the spirit of compromise that finally prevailed between the different camps.[2] Despite their differences, African leaders' collective experience of colonialism, apartheid and white-minority rule made decolonization of the continent a key preference that the leaders assigned to themselves and their newly created organization.

In addition to the emancipation of the continent, the OAU's mandate included the promotion of unity and solidarity among African states, improvement of the standards of living of the African people, as well as the defence of sovereignty and territorial integrity of African state. These objectives were anchored on several principles, including the sovereign equality of member states, non-interference in internal affairs of each other, respect for the sovereignty and territorial integrity of each state and non-alignment in the East–West power politics.

The OAU's record in these areas resembles a roller coaster, with peaks representing successes and valleys representing failures. The following sections outline the organization's balance sheet and highlight its achievements and failures. The merit of this exercise is to allow me to contextualize the activities of the African Union whose task was more of dealing with matters arising from the OAU's legacy than with completely new issues.

DECOLONIZATION, SELF-DETERMINATION AND HUMAN RIGHTS

When the OAU was being transformed into the African Union in 2001, 53 African states took part in the process. The increase in the number of member states is attributable to a single historical factor: decolonization of the continent. The role of Africans in this process has long been a subject of debate in the dense historiography of decolonization and among students of the OAU. The temptation to take part in this debate is irresistible, but the risks of being side-tracked are equally overwhelming. It suffices therefore to note that 30 years from the inception of the OAU, membership of the continental body increased from 32 to 53 states.[3] This was no mean feat, and the organization deserves credit for the achievement even if only because decolonization constituted one of the organization's raison d'être. As one commentator observed, it was the common stand on colonialism and racial oppression that brought the representatives of 31 African states to a summit conference of heads of state and government of independent African states in Addis Ababa during the period 23–26 May 1963, where they signed the Charter of the Organization of African Unity. Some of the assembled leaders expressed reservation about the charter and the character of the organization. However, no objection was strong enough to justify abstention. To do so would have been to risk being named as a dissident in Africa's united stand against colonialism and apartheid.[4]

Opposition to such views abound because they were seen as a narrow interpretation of the founding fathers' intentions which went beyond decolonization and the fight against apartheid and racialism. Accordingly, such a limited purpose would have meant that the raison d'être of the OAU would dissipate with the independence of Namibia and the achievement of black majority rule in South Africa.[5]

This debate, in my view, adds little value to the present enterprise, and need not therefore delay me any further. It is, however, my contention that decolonization was a fundamental objective of OAU founders, and one which the organization pursued most successfully. Action in this area was a combination of diplomatic offensive against colonialism and white minority rule and direct financial and military assistance to liberation groups on the continent.

The organizations records show that decolonization was high on the agenda of the founding conference and one of the key resolutions adopted was that on the total liberation of the African continent.[6] The debate on the issue was long and heated, but eventually led to a consensus that required all independent African countries to make monetary contribution to the independence struggle. And where the nature of the independence struggle required it, African states were to give weapons and military training to liberation fighters; and states sharing borders with the colonial territories were to facilitate transit and the movement of men and material to and from the front. African countries also had to mount diplomatic campaign against colonial authorities and white-minority regimes.[7]

To implement this consensus, a committee of nine was set up to receive and distribute assistance as well as coordinate the diplomatic offensive.[8] The body was initially called the *Committee of Nine*, before it was renamed *the Coordinating Committee for the Liberation of Africa*, the *Liberation Committee* in short. An Executive Secretariat, headed by a Tanzanian diplomat, was established in Dar es Salaam to service the committee, and a special fund was established to finance the various activities.[9]

The committee had three standing sub-committees on general policy, defence and finance. The committee on general policy looked at politics of the liberation struggle, information and public relations. The committee on defence dealt with defence and military training and on finance with financial matters. The Executive Secretariat was organized along similar divisions.[10]

At its inaugural session in June 1963, the Liberation Committee identified 16 colonial territories, which it decided to help achieve independence.[11] These territories were in three categories: the first category was composed of countries that were in the process of gaining independence, and included Northern Rhodesia (Zambia), Bechuanaland (Botswana), Basutoland (Lesotho) and Swaziland. In these countries, the OAU's support went mainly to political parties and was intended to help them organize themselves to contest elections. Apart from Zambia, where United National Independence Party (UNIP) won elections and became the first ruling party of Zambia, the political parties supported in other British colonies in Southern Africa failed to win pre-independence elections.

The second category consisted of territories in which colonial governments and white-minority regimes were determined to perpetuate their rule over the African populations and were using force to achieve this. These included Angola, Mozambique, Guinea Bissau, Zimbabwe, Namibia and South Africa. The objective of the OAU in these countries was to assist the liberation movements with money, weapons and training.[12]

In between the two categories were the colonial territories in which the colonial governments appeared undecided about independence. These were Djibouti, Comoros and Mauritius.[13] The OAU strategy in these territories was to bring pressure to bear on the colonial authorities to concede independence.

The first success story of the OAU in the decolonization struggle was the independence of Zambia, where the party that the Liberation Committee supported won pre-independence elections. The OAU's role in the liberation of the other High Commission Territories is less clear because parties other than those which the organization supported actually won the elections in Botswana, Lesotho and Swaziland. However, with the independence of these territories, the OAU was left with territories in the second category. The main landmark of the Liberation Committee's activities in these territories was the Accra Declaration of 1973. The Declaration, adopted as a result of the intensification of liberation struggle, called for greater assistance to be given to territories under Portuguese and white-minority rule. It also called on African states to help the frontline states to resist aggression by the colonial and racist regimes, launch a concerted international campaign in support of the liberation struggle to isolate the racist and the colonial regimes in Africa, and to get the United Nations to provide assistance to liberation movements.

On the diplomatic front, two special UN Security Council meetings were convened in 1963 alone to examine Africa's demand that Portugal and South Africa be expelled from the United Nations. Although outside support against Portugal was limited, considerable support was garnered against Apartheid. Consequently, the UN Security Council passed a resolution proscribing arms to South Africa, and in December the same year, the council adopted another resolution, which enlarged the scope of international embargos against South Africa. A UN Expert Group on South Africa also recommended the imposition of a worldwide economic sanction against South Africa. Although that recommendation, as well as the Security Council resolutions banning arms sales, was generally ignored, African countries' pressure on the international community went unabated. As a result, African states succeeded in removing South Africa from the United Nations Economic Commission for Africa, and from the Commission for technical Cooperation in Africa. South Africa was also forced to withdraw from UNESCO, ILO, WHO, FAO, as well as from the international Olympic Games. And an OAU decision also closed African airports and seaport to South African aircrafts and vessels.

Similarly, the Liberation Committee sent out goodwill missions to the USSR, China, and other socialist countries, Scandinavia and the Arab countries. In accordance with the Accra Declaration, the bulk of the assistance generated through the goodwill missions went to the territories under Portuguese rule that were soon to win their wars of independence.[14] In fact, records show that only two of the goodwill missions had been undertaken before the Portuguese colonies began to gain independence. Thus, the 25th Ordinary Session of the Liberation Committee in Dar es Salaam had to review the Accra Declaration and to adapt it to the new development. The resulting strategy was contained in a document entitled the Dar es Salaam Declaration, and shifted emphasis to Southern Africa: Zimbabwe, Namibia and South Africa. For this region, the Liberation Committee adopted a double-barrelled approach to the liberation struggle. This consisted in giving priority to peaceful negotiation for the achievement of independence, and in resorting to armed struggle, should negotiations fail. The Dar es Salaam Declaration was adopted by the Council of Ministers in an extraordinary session on Southern Africa, held in Dar es Salaam in April 1975. At that session, the council appealed to member states to settle their arrears of contributions to the special fund and to offer additional assistance to the liberation movements. In response to this call, a number of member states launched fundraising campaigns for popular subscription, which, together with the generous donations from countries outside Africa, enabled the Liberation Committee to allocate and deliver much larger sums of money to the liberation movements than it had ever dreamt of doing in the past.

The assistance enabled the Patriotic Front of Zimbabwe to step up its military pressure on Smith's regime and thereby forced Smith to the Conference table in Geneva and subsequently in Lancaster House in London where Smith finally accepted defeat and agreed to a new constitution that paved the way for the emergence of independent Zimbabwe under an African majority government. Similarly, OAU assistance enabled SWAPO to increase its pressure on Vorster's government of South Africa both in the military and in the diplomatic fields to the extent that the South African government for the first time showed its readiness to negotiate seriously with the UN for Namibia's independence. A by-product of this pressure was the emergence of the contact group of five Western countries, namely the United States, Britain, France, the Federal Republic of Germany and Canada in the negotiations for Namibia's independence. Equally important was the role the organization played in the liberation of South Africa. The African National Congress fought hard to obtain OAU's exclusive backing. As recent studies indicate, the diplomatic support that the OAU gave to the ANC proved to be pivotal during the negotiations that ushered in black majority rule in South Africa.[15]

The organization's role in the decolonization of the continent and its standing in the eye of the liberation movements were best captured in the statement that Samora Machel of Mozambique gave during the 24th Ordinary Session of the Liberation Committee. According to Machel:

> OAU's Liberation Committee was a "blood bank," that succeeded in popularizing the cause of liberation throughout the continent. ...The Liberation Committee has been a precious instrument for international mobilisation in favour of our cause, both at the UN and with the specialised agencies and before international public opinion. The Liberation Committee was, above all, an essential instrument for channeling to us the resources of African solidarity. It is true that these resources did not always correspond to the needs of the struggle or to the possibilities of Africa. However, this is a situation for which the Committee cannot be held responsible.

It is clear from the above analysis that the tendency in the literature to downplay the OAU's role in the decolonization process cannot be supported by empirical evidence. In the liberation struggle, the OAU was a player in a team of players, and its role was as significant as that of other actors. The OAU's efforts prompted the United Nations General Assembly to recognize the legitimacy of the liberation struggle by African nationalists. As a result, the General Assembly in its resolution 2555 called upon all specialized agencies of the UN to give material assistance to the liberation movements.[16] Similar efforts by OAU member states prompted the Security Council to hold a special session on African territories in 1972. Several peace and goodwill missions were sent overseas to lobby for both moral and material support.[17] Indeed, the support given to the freedom fighters was immense, and the OAU was instrumental in mobilizing that support.[18]

Critics of the organization also paid scant attention to the circumstances under which the continental body operated. In addition to pressure from different member states, the organization was also subjected to pressure from the different interests that existed within independence movements themselves.[19] But the most debilitation constraints was the state of its finances. Initially, the Special Fund was about 700,000 pound sterling. By 1973, it had only risen to some 1.4 million pounds or 3.3 million US dollars. It remained stagnant at that level well into the 1980s and decreased to some 3.1 million dollars for the financial year 1987–1988. Even when the number of groups requiring support decreased, the funds were not sufficient to cater for the remaining liberation movements. Arrears owed by member states rose from US$2 million in 1970 to US$12 million in 1978. They remained at that height up to the late 1980s. There is no doubt the committee's shortcomings cannot be overlooked, but they must be seen against both the material and other difficulties the body also faced.

THE OAU AND CONFLICT RESOLUTION IN AFRICA

Parallel to the decolonization struggle were efforts to resolve conflicts that greeted independence in many African countries. In all 80 successful military coups, 108 failed attempts and 139 reported plots were recorded on the continent between 1956 and 2001.[20] Added to these were about 30 violent conflicts, which ranged from full-scale wars involving extra-continental powers (Algeria, Angola, Mozambique and Ethiopia)[21] to armed liberation struggles (Rhodesia, Namibia, South Africa), cross-border attacks (Somalia into Ethiopia in 1977 and Tanzania into Uganda) and genocide (Rwanda); the rest were civil wars.[22] About 10 million people lost their lives and as five times as many were wounded. More than 20 million became refugees or were internally displaced in their own countries.[23]

The OAU attempted to deal with African conflicts first by adopting during its session in Cairo in 1964 resolution AHG/Res.16 (1), which called member states to respect the borders "existing on their achievement of national independence."[24] Indeed, the continent's numerous problems offered sufficient justification for the continent's leaders wish not to be involved in endless boundary disputes, despite the fact that the frontiers were drawn by colonial powers to suit themselves, with the result that some of the newly independent states had difficulty in holding themselves together. Although the organization's approach did not appeal to various ethnic groups that have been carved up in sensitive ways, it is remarkable that the first secessionist movements have had little success.

The organization also set up the Commission on Mediation, Conciliation and Arbitration to deal with interstate conflict in Africa. The Commission was, however, still-born. Its mandate was limited to interstate conflicts and few such conflicts were referred to it. Moreover, it lacked the necessary financial resources, as member states failed to pay their contribution to its budget.[25] Attempts to revive it in the mid-1970s failed largely because member states showed little interest. African Governments instead referred their disputes to ad hoc dispute settlement committees, composed of heads of state or ministers. The first such body was constituted as early as 1963 to mediate in the Algerian Moroccan dispute. Similar committees were created to grapple with the Somalia-Ethiopia dispute, Rwanda-Burundi dispute, the dispute between Angolan warring factions, the Congo crises and in the Nigerian Civil war. Despite its precariousness, the OAU ad hoc arrangements managed to contain disputes between member states. And considering the potential for border conflict, there were relatively few. Most of the dispute, as those between Nigeria and Cameroon, Tanzania and Malawi, Upper Volta and Mali, were either settled without force or kept simmering at a non-violent level through OAU diplomacy.[26] Even where border conflicts escalated to armed hostilities (as between

Algeria and Morocco over their Saharan frontiers or between Ethiopia and Somalia over Ogaden), OAU mediation brought about quick cease fire.[27]

It was civil wars that tested the organization's conflict resolution capacity the most. According to the United Nations, in 1996 alone, 14 of Africa's 53 states were involved in armed conflicts resulting in the death or displacement of some eight million people.[28] Throughout its existence, the OAU espoused a principle of non-interference in the internal affairs of member states. This led to a policy that automatically gave support to a member government.[29] The result was that the organization was incapable of acting as a mediator in the internal conflicts of member states, and where it did, as in Chad, the dearth of resources and uncertain legal and institutional framework placed the organization's efforts in jeopardy.

It was largely these constraints that prompted the Assembly to adopt at its 29th Session in Cairo in 1993 the *Declaration on the Establishment, within the OAU, of a Mechanism for Conflict Resolution, Management and Resolution*.[30] The objective, as stated in the declaration, was to bring a new institutional dynamism to the process of dealing with conflicts on the continent by anticipating, preventing and resolving crises.[31] Both civilian and military observation missions to conflict zones were provided for. The overall direction and coordination of the activities of the mechanism were entrusted to a 19-member Central Organ, composed of members of the Bureau of the Assembly, who were elected annually, as well as the outgoing and the incoming chairpersons of the Assembly. The Central Organ operates at the levels of the Assembly, the Council of Ministers and the Permanent Representatives' Committee. A special fund was created and benefited from appropriations from the OAU regular budget and donations from member states and members of the international community. By March 2002, the resources of the fund stood at US$42 million. By many counts, the adoption of the mechanism breathed fresh life into the area of conflict resolution. In the 1990s alone the OAU has been involved in peace-making and peace-building activities in several African countries and regions. Military observer missions were deployed in Rwanda (1991–1993), Burundi (1993–1996), the Comoros (1998–2002), the Democratic Republic of the Congo (from 1999) and Eritrea and Ethiopia (from 2000).

Parallel to the mechanism was the Conference on Security, Stability, Development and Cooperation in Africa (CSSDCA). Originally the brainchild of Olusegun Obasanjo, then chairman of the African Leadership Forum, the CSSDCA was endorsed by the Assembly of heads of state and government in Sirte in 1999 In 2000, the Assembly adopted the Solemn Declaration on the CSSDCA, making it a programme of the OAU and attaching it to the Secretariat with a budget of US$500,000, although the officials in charge did not take up their position before December 2001. In addition to the regular budget, the CSSDCA benefited from a US$1 million contribution from

South Africa and Nigeria. The CSSDCA process provides a framework for the coordination, harmonization and promotion of policies aimed at preventing, containing and eliminating internal and interstate conflicts in Africa, as well as accelerating regional integration and development on the continent. In particular, it sought to reinforce Africa's capacity for conflict prevention, management and resolution by strengthening and supporting the mechanism for conflict prevention, management and resolution.[32] The first ministerial session on the CSSDCA took place in Abuja, Nigeria, in May 2000.[33] In addition to these, a number of initiatives were taken to address Africa's political and social crises. These include the Bamako Convention on the Ban of the Import into Africa and the Control of Trans-boundary Movement and Management of Hazardous Wastes within Africa; The Bamako Declaration on an African Common Position on the illicit Proliferation, Circulation and Trafficking of Small Arms and Light Weapons; The Kempton Park Plan of Action on Land Mine-Free Africa 1997; Declaration and Plan of Action on Drug and Illicit Trafficking Control in Africa, 1996; Convention for the Elimination of Mercenarism in Africa, 1977; and the African Nuclear Weapons Free-Zone Pelindaba Treaty, 1998.

CONCLUSION

The conclusion that can be draw from the above assessment of the history of the OAU is that the organization's " inactivity" was more of a myth than reality. From its inception, the organization sought to achieve three objectives for the continent: independence, peace and development. To achieve these objectives, African leaders adopted within the framework of the OAU 24 treaties on areas as diverse as peace and security, agriculture, health, education, industrial relations, trade and economic development. Of these, 14 treaties were already in force by 2001. The organization might have experienced failures in several areas, but as Chazan, Mortimer, Ravenhill and Rothchild observe, it

> remained a focal point for collective initiatives and for conflict management. The attempt to construct solidarity at the continental level is not a sentimental illusion but rather a reasoned response to Africa's dependent position in the global economic system. African leaders are conscious of the utility of cooperation at the same time that they found cooperation difficult to achieve in practice.[34]

There is no dearth of tributes such as this in the literature, although they remain largely scattered. But the most fitting remark for the tombstone of the OAU is provided by Colin Legum, who summed up the organization's 30-year history thus:

> It has contributed largely to the defeat of the Smith regime in Rhodesia and to the abdication of Portugal's centuries-old rule in Africa by its support for the liberation movements and through international pressures. It also contributed to the international campaign to isolate the Apartheid regime. However, it failed in one of its major aims – to create five economic regions within the region as a nucleus of a continent-wide economic system to overcome Africa's balkanized economies. It succeeded in preventing any serious border conflicts and limiting the effects of the few that occurred. But it failed to intervene in serious internal conflicts affecting it member states because of its charter's prohibition of such intervention. However, in 1990, this prohibition was changed and an elaborate machinery established for the prevention of conflicts and conciliation in disputes.[35]

There is hardly a better statement that sums up the OAU's history, and with which this chapter should be concluded.

NOTES

1. For more on these meetings, see Vincent B. Thompson, *Africa and Unity: The Evolution of Pan Africanism* (London, Harlow 1969); W.S. Thompson, *Ghana's Foreign Policy: Diplomacy, Ideology and the New State, 1957–1966* (Princeton, Princeton University Press, 1969) especially chapter 1 and 2; Colin Legum, *Pan Africanism: A Short Political Guide*, Revised Edition (New York: Praeger 1965).

2. In attendance were the leaders of Algeria, United Arab Republic (Egypt), Tunisia, Sudan, Libya, Somalia, Mauritania, Ethiopia, Cameroun, Senegal, Congo Brazzaville, Congo-Leopoldville, Uganda, Niger, Tanganyika, Chad, Gabon, Burundi, Dahoumey, Nigeria, Rwanda, Sierra Leone, Cote d'Ivoire, Haute Volta (Burkina Faso), Guinea, Mali, Madagascar, and the Central African Republic. Morocco and Togo were absent. For more in the ideological divisions, see V.B. Thompson, *African and Unity*; and W.S. Thompson, *Ghana's Foreign Policy.*

3. A starting point in this regard is Prosser Gifford and WM Roger-Louis, editors, *Decolonization and African Independence: The Transfer of Power, 1960–1980* (Connecticut: Yale University Press 1988). pp. 527–635, in particular, offer a guide to the specialized studies.

4. Zdenek Cervenka, "Major Policy Shift in the Organization of African Unity," in K. Ingram (ed.) *Foreign Relations of African States* (London: Butterworth 1974), quoted in Olatunde J.C.B. Ojo, D.K. Orwa and C.M.B. Utete, *African International Relations* (London and Lagos: Longman 1985), p. 84; Doudou Thiam, The *Foreign policy of African States* (New York 1965), cited in Olatunde J.C.B. Ojo, D.K. Orwa and C.M.B. Utete, *African International Relations;*

5. Olatunde J.C.B. Ojo, D.K. Orwa and C.M.B. Utete, *African International Relations,* p. 84.

6. Resolution No. CIAS/Plen.2/Rev.2 (10 sections A and B).

7. C.O.C. Amate, *Inside the OAU: Pan Africanism in Practice* (London: Macmillan 1986), p. 212.

8. The committee was composed of Algeria, Egypt, Ethiopia, Guinea, Nigeria, Senegal, Tanzania, Uganda and Zaire.

9. For more on the Special Funds and contributions of member states, as well as the beneficiaries of the Special Fund, see Amate, *Inside the OAU,* pp. 213–14.

10. Ibid.

11. These were Angola and Cabinada, Mozambique, Guinea Bissau, Cape Verde, Northern Rhodesia, South West Africa, South Africa, Swaziland, Basutoland, Bechuanaland, Comoros Islands, Rio de Oro (Sahara), Fernando Po, Spanish Guinea, Djibouti and La Reunion.

12. Amate , *Inside the OAU*, p. 286

13. For more on this, see, Xavier Yacono, *Histoire de la colonization Francaise*, 6e edition (Paris 1993), Xavier Yacono, *Les Etapes de la decolonisation Francaise* (Paris, Presse Universitaire de France 1971).

14. For more on this see, Amate, *Inside the OAU*, p. 299

15. For more on this see, R. Pfister, "Gateway to International Victory: The Diplomacy of the African National Congress in Africa, 1960–1994", *The Journal of Modern African Studies*, Vol. 41, No. 1 (2003) , pp. 51–73.

16. OAU, *The Organization of African Unity: A Short History* (Addis Ababa, OAU Secretariat, 1977).

17. Ibid.

18. For more on this see. Leonard T. Kapanga, "The OAU's Support for the Liberation of Southern Africa" in Yassin El Ayouty, editor, *The Organization of African Unity After Ten Years: Comparative Perspectives* (New York: Praeger Publishers, 1975), pp. 135–151.

19. For more on these internal struggles, see Colin Legum et al, *Africa in the 1980s: A Continent in Crises* (New York: McGraw Hill Book Co. 1979), pp. 29–32.

20. See Patrick J. McGowan, "African Military Coups D'Etata, 1956–2001: Frequency, Trends and Distribution," *Journal of Modern African Studies,* Vol. 41, 3 (2003), pp. 339–370.

21. Colin Legum, *Africa since Independence* (Bloomington and Indianapolis: Indiana University Press, 1999), pp. 31–32.

22. These include the Nigerian Civil War, 1967–1970; Shaba Crises in Zaire, 1977 and 1978;Chadian Civil War 1979–1982; Chadian Civil War 1983-1984; Chadian Civil War, 1986; Sudanese Civil War 1982–2002; Somali Civil War; 1991; Rwandan Civil War 1992–1993; Burundian Civil War 1993–2005; Civil Strive in Congo Brazzaville 1993; Angolan Civil War 1993; Liberian Civil War 1989; See K. Van Walreven, *Dreams of Power: the Role of the Organization of African Unity in the Politics of Africa, 1963–1993*, Research Series 13/1999 (Lieden: African Studies Centre 1999), p. 295.

23. Colin Legum, *Africa since Independence*, p. 32; see also Ibrahim Elbadawi and Nicholas Sambanis, "Why are There so Many Civil Wars in Africa? Understanding and Preventing Violent Conflict," *Journal of African Economies*, vol. 9, 3 (2000), pp. 244–269.

24. Resolution AGH/Res.16 (1).

25. See report of the Secretary General to the 5th Ordinary Session of the Assembly of Heads of State and Government. Cited in OAU Secretariat, *Resolving Conflicts in Africa: Implementation Option* (Addis Ababa, nd)

26. For more on this, see Colin Legum, "The Role of the Organization of African Unity in Dealing with Violent Conflicts," in Colin Legum et.al. *Africa in the 1980s: A Continent in Crises* (New York: McGraw-Hill Book Company, 1979). pp. 38–43.

27. Ibid.

28. UN Secretary General, "The Causes of Conflict and Promotion of Durable Peace and Sustainable Development in Africa," Report to the UN Security Council 1998.

29. The only exception was the Angolan Civil War, which broke out at a time when there were no recognized government. The OAU's approach to the crises was to give equal recognition to the three warring factions before the external intervention of the Soviets and the Cubans on the side of the MPLA and the intervention of South Africa and some Western countries on the side of UNITA and the FNLA prompted two-thirds of OAU member states to limit their support to the MPLA.

30. The decision to set up such an instrument was taken in Dakar in 1992. The Cairo Declaration was the concrete expression of the Decision.

31. Paragraphs 12 and 15 of the declaration.

32. See also African Union, *Concept Paper on the Establishment of a Common African Defence and Security Policy* (Addis Ababa: Commission of the African Union, 2003), pp. 20–21.

33. Preparations for the CSSDCA begun in 1990, with a brainstorming session in Addis Ababa in November 1990, steering committee meeting in February 1991 in Addis Ababa, International Roundtable meeting in Cologne, in March 1991. African NGO consultative meeting on CSSDCA in Lagos in April 1991. The Kampala Forum on CSSDCA in May 1991. For further background, see Olusegum Obasanjo and Felix G.N. Mosha (editors), *Africa: Rise to Challenge – Towards a CSSDCA* (Lagos: Africa Leadership Forum 1993). See also Francis M. Deng and I William Zartman, *A Strategic Vision for Africa: The Kampala Movement* (Washington DC: Brookings Institution 2002).

34. Naomi Chazan, Robert Mortimer, John Raven Hill, and Donald Rothchild, *Politics and Society in Contemporary Africa* (Boulder: Lynne Reinner, 1992), pp. 323–324, cited in Stephan Wright, "The Changing Context of African Foreign Policies," in idem, editor, *African Foreign Policies* (Boulder, Westview), 1999. p. 18.

35. Colin Legum, *Africa since Independence*, pp. 47–48.

Chapter 5

From the Lagos Plan of Action to NEPAD

The Development Blueprints of a Continent

Many problems faced by our countries today can be solved by the Union, because if our economies are linked, we will be obliged to sit down and discuss issues instead of going to war [1]

The persistent economic crises that Africa became associated with during much of the post-independence period accounts for the generalized perception that African leaders paid scant attention to the socio-economic development of their countries. Indeed, conditions on the continent at the turn of the twenty-first century were sufficiently dire to lend credence to such a view. Africa not only accounted for the bulk of the world's intra-state conflicts; the continent also started the twenty-first century as the poorest, the most indebted and the most marginalized region. This chapter extends my analysis of the preferences of African leaders and shows that despite the bleak balance sheet at the turn of the century, socio-economic development constituted one of the key preferences of African states and remained a cornerstone of their collective efforts at regional and continental level. For the continental leaders, the most appropriate response to the developmental challenges consists in integration and coordinated development planning. This accounts for the attention given to regional integration and continental development blueprints such as the Abuja Treaty and NEPAD.

PRELUDE TO THE ABUJA TREATY

One of the organizations created under Article 10 of the OAU Charter was the Economic and Social Commission.[2] The importance that member states attached to this organization can be gleaned in the mandate they assigned to it. In addition to being assigned with the responsibility of studying the problems relating to Africa's economic and social development, the commission was expected to promote intra-African trade by encouraging the creation of African free-trade areas and by establishing a common commodity fund to stabilize African commodity prices. It was also expected to create an African clearing house and an African monetary zone, as well as coordinate and harmonize development plans across the continent.[3]

The commission was credited for pushing African leaders to adopt a number of statements and declarations on Africa's economic conditions. These include the Assembly's resolutions and declarations taken in Algiers in September 1968, in Addis Ababa in August 1970 and May 1973, all of which underlined the importance of economic integration of the continent to the realization of the objectives of the OAU. Other instruments include a declaration that the Confernce of Minsters adopted in Kinshasa in December 1976 on the establishment of an African Economic Community as an objective to be attained in successive stages; the Monrovia Declaration of Commitment on Guidelines and Measures for National and Collective Self Reliance in Economic and Social Development for the Establishment of the New International Order. These processes paved the way for the adoption in April 1980 of the Lagos Plan of Action for the Economic Development of Africa 1980–2000.

Drafted by a team of African experts led by Professor Adebayo Adedeji,[4] The Lagos Plan of Action sought to foster economic growth in African countries by increasing agriculture and food production, promoting industrialization and boosting the energy sector, as well as ensuring environmental protection. The plan provided for the establishment of an Africa Economic Community (AEC) by the year 2000[5] to promote the economic, social and cultural integration of Africa. It called on the OAU to work to strengthen existing regional economic communities and establish similar economic groupings in regions where they did not exist. The continental body was also to strengthen sectoral integration at the continental level, particularly in the fields of agriculture, food, transport and communications, industry and energy. In addition, it was called upon to promote, coordinate and harmonize policies, plans and practices of existing and future economic groupings for the gradual establishment of an African Common Market. In the mind of its proponents, the Lagos Plan of Action would strengthen sectoral integration and subsequently lead to the creation of an African Economic Community.[6]

A review of the progress on the Lagos Plan of Action shows that the OAU's member states largely failed to implement the Lagos Plan of Action, despite several efforts to address some of the obstacles member states faced. Even though regional economic communities were established, African economies remained far apart, with intra-regional trade hovering under 8 per cent in the mid-1980s. The failure was blamed on several factors including colonial economic structures that African countries inherited, the collapse of commodity prices, high cost of international lending, acute dependency of African economies on foreign resources, lack of skilled manpower, and extraneous factors such as drought, desertification and the subversive activities of Apartheid regime in Southern Africa. It was also revealed that African countries lacked the political will to do what was required to establish the African Common market. In particular, they failed to harmonize customs tariffs, trading standards and procedures as well as to adopt uniform investment codes and implement the various conventions on customs.[7]

Thus, despite the fact that several initiatives were adopted, including the African Priority Programme for Economic Recovery 1986–1990 and the United Nations Programme of Action for African Economic Recovery and Development 1986–1990, both of which sought to push Africa's economic recovery, the OAU failed to make any noticeable headway in fostering socio-economic development on the continent.[8]

THE ABUJA TREATY

The failure to implement the Lagos Plan of Action was not to discourage African leaders, but to prompt them to adopt the Treaty of the African Economic Community at the 27th Session of the Assembly in Abuja in June 1991. The Abuja Treaty, like the Lagos Plan of Action, sought to

1. promote economic, social and cultural development and the integration of African economies;
2. establish, on a continental scale, a framework for the development, mobilization and utilization of the human and material resources of Africa;
3. promote cooperation in all fields of human endeavour;
4. coordinate and harmonize policies among existing and future economic communities in order to foster the gradual establishment of the community.

For the attainment of these objectives, a number of measures were to be put into place, including the reinforcement of existing regional economic communities, the establishment of other communities where they did not exist, and the promotion of closer cooperation among them; the liberalization and promotion of inter-African trade and the adoption of a common trade policy vis-à-vis third states as well as the establishment and maintenance of a common external tariff; the harmonization and promotion of Community activities in the fields of agriculture, industry, transport and communications, energy, natural resources, trade and finance, human resources, education, culture, science and technology. The community was to be established gradually in six stages of variable duration over a period not exceeding 34 years.

The first stage envisaged the reinforcement of existing regional economic community within five years from the date of entry into force of the treaty and the establishment of economic communities in regions where they did not exist. The second stage, spanning a period of eight years, envisaged trade promotion through the gradual removal of tariff and non-tariff barriers to regional and intra-community trade and for the gradual harmonization of customs duties in relation to third states, as well as strengthening of sectoral linkages at the regional and continental levels. The third stage involved the creation of free-trade areas within ten years. In the fourth stage, member states were to establish, within two years of the establishment of the FTAs, customs union at the continental level. This was to be followed in the fifth stage by the establishment of the African Common Market to be consolidated in the sixth stage, which was also to see the full implementation of the provisions relating to the free movements of people, goods, capital and services, as well as the integration of the economic, political, social and cultural sectors, and the establishment of the pan-African economic and monetary union. The final stage was also to see the establishment of the Pan African Parliament.

By many counts, the Abuja Treaty represented a renewal of commitment by African leaders to the goals of economic and social development they set for themselves in the Lagos Plan of Action. It entered into force in May 1994, following ratification by two thirds of OAU member states. The fact that it entered into force barely three years after adoption suggests the considerable enthusiasm with which the treaty was received.

However, like the Lagos Plan of Action, the implementation of the Abuja Treaty did not take off in many areas. Regionalism thrived somewhat on the continent, but this was limited to building institutions. Progress in other areas remained stalled. Intra-African trade, for example, remained at 8 per cent[9] and the limited FDI inflows came mainly from outside the continent.[10] All other economic and social indicators pointed towards the wrong direction. Average economic growth throughout the 1990s was around 3 per cent. Half of the continent's population continued to live on less than US$1 per day; the mortality rate of children under 5 years of age was 140 per 1000; and life expectancy at birth was only 54 years.[11] Only 58 per cent of the population had access to safe drinking water. The rate of illiteracy for people over 15 years of age was 41 per cent. There were only 18 mainline telephones per 1000 people in Africa, compared with 146 for the world and 567 for high-income countries.[12]

Notwithstanding these challenges, the Abuja Treaty remained relevant and its provisions were integrated into the Constitutive Act of the African Union. As a result, the main objectives of the African Union became the achievement of unity and solidarity of the countries and the people of Africa,[13] the acceleration of the political and socio-economic integration of the continent,[14] coordination and harmonizing of the policies between the existing and future regional economic communities for the gradual attainment of the objectives of the union.[15] The Abuja Treaty also underpinned the RECs as the treaty offered a detailed guidelines for the economic, political and institutional mechanisms for attaining the goals of the African unity as defined in broad terms by the Charter of OAU and the Constitutive Act of the African Union.[16]

Attempts to to forge unity did not begin with the Abuja Treaty; they could be traced as far as back to the period preceding and immediately following the independence of many African countries.[17] Earlier examples include the Ghana–Upper Volta Trade Agreement, the African Common Market linking Algeria, United Arab Republic (Egypt), Ghana, Guinea, Mali and Morocco; the Equatorial Customs Union, the precursor to the Customs Union of Central African States (1962), joined Cameroon, Central African Republic, Chad Congo, and Gabon; the East African Community (1967) comprising Kenya, Tanzania and Uganda. While most of the earlier groupings ended up being dissolved, Africa still remained dotted with a multitude of regional groupings.

As table 5.1 shows, by the time the African Union was established in 2002, Africa had 14 regional integration groupings, with two or more in each region. In West Africa, Union Economique et Monétaire Ouest-Africaine (UEMOA) and the Mano River Union coexist with the Economic Community of West African States (ECOWAS). In Central Africa, the Economic Community of Central African States ran side by side with the Central African Economic and Monetary Community and the Economic Community of the Great Lakes Region. Eastern and Southern Africa shared six regional Economic Communities: the Common Market for Eastern and Southern Africa (COMESA), the East African Community (EAC), the Intergovernmental Authority on Development (IGAD), the Indian Ocean Commission (IOC), the Southern African Development Community (SADC) and the Southern African Customs Union (SACU). North Africa had only the Arab Maghreb Union (UMA) before the advent of the CEN-SAD, although CEN-SAD straddled across various Economic Communities and sub-regions.[18] In assessing regional economic communities, the United Nations Economic Commission for Africa (UNECA) identified six general and specific factors that account for the proliferation of regional economic blocs.

First, regional integration provides low barriers to trade among member-countries. And because advocates of free trade argue that free trade improves welfare by enabling citizens to procure goods and services from the cheapest source, there are welfare gains in regional integration arrangements. For individual members, however, the effect of regional integration depends on whether it is *trade creating* or *trade diverting*.[19]

Table 5.1 Africa's Regional Groupings

Community	*Members*	*Specified Objectives*
Arab Maghreb Union (UMA)	Algeria, Libya, Mauritania, Morocco, Tunisia	Full economic union
Central African Economic and Monetary Community (CEMAC)	Cameroon, Central African Republic, Chad, Republic of Congo, Equatorial Guinea, Gabon	Full economic union
Common Market for Eastern and Southern Africa (COMESA)	Angola, Burundi, Comoros, Democratic Republic of Congo, Djibouti, Egypt, Eritrea, Ethiopia, Kenya, Madagascar, Malawi, Mauritius, Namibia, Rwanda, Seychelles, Sudan, Swaziland, Uganda, Zambia, Zimbabwe	Common market
Community of Sahel Saharan States (CEN-SAD)	Benin, Burkina Faso, Central African Republic, Chad, Djibouti, Egypt Eritrea Gambia, Libya, Mali, Morocco, Niger, Nigeria, Senegal, Somalia, Sudan, Togo, Tunisia	Free-trade area and integration in some sectors
East African Community (EAC)	Kenya, Tanzania, Uganda	Full economic union
Economic Community of Central African States	Angola, Burundi, Cameroon, Central African Republic, Chad, Democratic Republic of Congo, Republic of Congo, Equatorial Guinea, Gabon, Sao Tome and Principe, Rwanda	Full economic union
Economic Community of Great Lakes Countries	Burundi, democratic Republic of Congo, Rwanda	Full economic union
Economic Community of West African States	Benin, Burkina Faso, Cape Verde, Cote D'Ivoire, Gambia, Ghana, Guinea, Guinea Bissau, Liberia, Mali, Niger, Nigeria, Senegal, Sierra Leone, Togo	Full economic union
Indian Ocean Commission (IOC)	Comoros, Madagascar, Mauritius, Réunion, Seychelles	Sustainable development through cooperation on diplomacy, environment and trade
InterGovernmental Authority on Development (IGAD)	Djibouti, Eritrea, Ethiopia, Kenya, Somalia, Sudan and Uganda	Full economic union
Mano River Union	Guinea, Liberia, Sierra Leone	Multi-sectoral integration
Southern African Customs Union	Botswana, Lesotho, Namibia, South Africa, Swaziland	Customs union
Southern African Development Community (SADC)	Angola, Botswana, DRC, Lesotho, Malawi, Mauritius, Mozambique, Namibia, Seychelles, South Africa, Swaziland, Tanzania, Zambia, Zimbabwe	Full economic union
West African Economic and Monetary Union	Benin, Burkina Faso, Cote d'Ivoire, Guinea Bissau, Mali, Niger, Senegal, Togo	Full economic union

Source: Economic Commission for Africa

Second, regional integration increases the scale and competition for small countries with little or no endowments by combining markets, thereby enabling firms to expand and compete. While the evidence both in favour of and against this position is substantial, there is consensus that regional integration offers developing countries substantial benefits, even though these benefits can be obtained otherwise, such as through unilateral trade liberalization.

Third, regional arrangements are credited for encouraging investment by reducing distortions, enlarging markets and enhancing the credibility of economic and political reforms. This, in turn, can raise the return on investment, make larger investments more feasible and reduce economic and political uncertainty. And customs union can encourage foreign investors to engage in tariff jumping, that is, investing in one country in order to trade freely with all members of the community. It also promotes knowledge and technology transfers and spillovers in member states.

Fourth, regional integration enhances members bargaining power, particularly in international trade negotiation, provided all members negotiate as a bloc.[20] It also enhances cooperation of member states to promote regional public goods such as shared rivers, roads, rail links and electric grids, and combat regional ills such as pollution and transport bottlenecks.[21]

Fifth, one of the attractions and one that has yet to be fully acknowledged is the impact of regional integration on peace and security of the region. Studies have indicated that regional integration reduces the risk of conflict in two ways. First, by increasing interdependence among member states, regional integration makes conflict less likely and more costly. Second, regular political contact among members can build trust and facilitate cooperation in various areas, including security. However, it should be recognized that although regional economic integration may lead to regional political integration, thereby reducing risk of internal conflict, it can also create tensions among members, particularly if economic benefits are not shared equitably.[22]

The sixth consideration is that although the direct link between regional integration, growth has yet to be fully established, there is growing evidence on the link between trade on the other hand and growth on the one hand and between regional integration and increasing trade. Thus, by increasing a country's total volume of trade, regional integration indirectly increases growth.[23]

These factors made regional integration specifically attractive to African countries, whose internal conditions were characterized by bad policies, poor infrastructure, low income, ineffective institutions, unhealthy political environment and lack of capital. The asphyxiating debt burden and low investments also compounded the internal difficulties and made the continent the poorest and the most distressed.[24] These realities prompted the World Bank to conclude that Africa could relaunch development only if it acted to improve governance, resolve conflicts, invest in people, increase competitiveness, diversify economies, reduce aid dependence and strengthen partnerships.[25]

If the advantages of regional integration attracted African countries to regional arrangements, the proliferation of these institutions constituted major challenges too. Not only did blocs have overlapping memberships, they also pursued identical mandates and objectives. The multiplicity of these groupings also tends to dissipate efforts towards the common goals of the African Union, as it risked producing counterproductive competition among communities and institutions.[26]

The overlap also added to the burden of member states. Countries belonging to two or more regional economic communities not only faced multiple financial obligations, they also had to cope with different meetings, policy decisions, instruments, procedures and schedules. For example, customs officials, despite being ill-equipped, had to deal with different tariff reduction rates, rules of origin, trade documentation and statistical nomenclatures. The range of requirements risked multiplying customs procedures and paper work and defeating the trade liberalization goals of facilitating and simplifying trade.[27]

Furthermore, it was member states that were required to implement at the national level the various protocols, decisions and agreements relating to economic integration. For this, they required national mechanisms to plan, organize, coordinate and follow-up on their individual commitments. While a number of countries had established such mechanisms, including ministries responsible for integration issues, others did not do so. And even where they existed, such mechanisms were often too loosely defined or insufficiently equipped with human, material and financial resources to make the necessary impact at the national level. The result was that most governments failed to translate their commitment at the regional level into substantive policy at the national level. National governments were also unwilling to subordinate immediate national political interests to long-term regional economic goals.[28] In addition to the problems associated with the multiplicity of the groupings, the various communities were plagued by problems of inadequate financial resources. Although recurrent budgets were based on contributions assessed to member states, actual payments of contributions had declined in such a way that the majority of the communities found themselves in serious financial difficulties,[29] as many governments did not have a specific budget for activities and programmes on the topic.[30] As a result, most RECs depended on external funding for their activities during much of the period under consideration. Thus, the financial difficulties that the RECs faced, together with the lack of capacity in member states to implement community policies and decision, presented the African Union with several challenges.

Key among these was the challenge of rationalizing the RECs by identifying and retaining communities that were critical to the African integration process. As the ECA concluded, multiple, uncoordinated and poorly financed Regional Economic Communities could hardly be sufficiently solid to constitute the building blocks of the African Union.[31] The commission also had to find means to strengthen the capacity of member states in internalizing the integration imperatives.[32]

A number of measures were taken to respond to this requirement. First, during its summit in Banjul, Gambia in July 2006, the Assembly took a decision to reduce the number of groupings recognized as regional economic community from fourteen to eight and not recognize any new group as being a regional economic community.[33]

The second measure consisted in the AU Commission strengthening its relationship with the RECs. For a long time, the relationship between the commission and the RECs was characterized by mistrust.[34] As a result, there were duplications, lack of cooperation, lack of experience sharing and lack of information exchange between the commission in Addis Ababa and the communities.[35] The commission even complained about RECS denying the commission's representatives access to Communities closed-door meetings.[36] In order to address this particular problem, AU Commission and the RECs concluded a protocol on their working relations in 2007.[37] A key element of the protocol was the joint undertaking of all sides to coordinate their policies, measures, programmes and activities with a view to avoiding duplication. (Article 4). To operationalize this protocol, the AU and RECs took a number of measures, including the adoption in January 2008 of a Memorandum of Understanding (MoU) on Cooperation in the Area of Peace and Security. The MoU provides for the establishment of liaison offices to facilitate coordination and cooperation between the parties. With the exception of the Community of Sahel–Saharan States (CEN-SAD) and the Arab Maghreb Union (AMU), all the RECs had sent their Liaison Officers to Addis Ababa by 2012. On its part, the commission also attached liaison offices to the RECs.[38]

In the same vein, the commission and the RECs jointly drew up a Minimum Integration Programme (MIP), comprised a set of activities, projects and programmes to be implemented by the REC's in order to accelerate the regional and continental integration processes.[39] Areas covered within the framework of the MIP and MIP action plan included trade, infrastructure development, free movement of people, as well as peace and security. A related activity that the commission embarked upon was the assessment of the role, capacity and ability of the RECs to deliver on a standardized integration programme. The exercise was meant to facilitate a more effective management of the continental integration process, and to help the Regional Economic Communities develop coherent sectoral policies. From October 2009, the legal advisors of the commission and the RECs, too, met regularly to exchange views on best practices and the roles of the legal advisors in promoting synergies and effective cooperation between the different organizations.

Clearly, the African Union and the RECs moved over time away from a relationship that was characterized by mutual suspicion and lack of cooperation to an arrangement that fostered cooperation and coordination of policies and practices of the various communities. Despite the progress registered, a number of challenges remained. For example, the MIP action plan faced a number of problems, including the lack of funding. As a result no major progress was made with respect to the implementation of MIP for many years. Other challenges included AUC's weak capacity to coordinate the activities of the RECs. Even though, the level of coordination between the AUC and the RECs registered some progress especially in the operationalization of some components of the peace and security architecture, such as the ASF and Continental Early Warning System (CEWS), coordination was weak with respect to other components of APSA such as the Panel of the Wise, the Peace and Security Council and the Peace Fund. Furthermore, while the RECs recognized and accepted the principle of subsidiarity in their relations with the AUC, there was less clarity on its application. Some RECs were of the view that the AUC should not view itself as an implementing agency; it should rather play a coordinating role.[40]

SOCIO-ECONOMIC DEVELOPMENT

By many counts, the Abuja Treaty represented the first most comprehensive programme on regional integration in Africa. It incorporated the essence of all the previous integration and development plans, and was premised on the conviction that Africa could only develop through regional integration and eventual union. Integration was seen to be the only arrangement by which Africans could enlarge their markets, improve their infrastructure, enhance human development and productivity, and bring an end to violent conflicts through dialogue and regular contact that would constitute the hallmark of the integration process. However, the slow implementation of the provisions and terms of the Treaty and the failure of all the regions to meet the various milestones underlined the formidable nature of the realities on the ground. African economies remained too delinked to achieve any of the targets of the Abuja Treaty within the specified timeframe. The volume of intra-regional trade stagnated at around 12 per cent of the continent's total trade. While a number of factors account for this, the fundamental causes of the limited achievement lay in the absence of complementarities among African economies.[41] Most countries continued to be dependent on the production and export of a few primary products. And because of their small industrial base, African countries were also heavily dependent on the importation of manufactured capital goods and other consumer goods from non-African sources. Little wonder therefore that African integration efforts neither generated sizeable intra-regional trade nor promoted rapid economic growth during the period under consideration.

These failures prompted renewed and deeper reflection into Africa's economic future and led to the conclusion that Africa's renewal would require a radical intervention, spearheaded by African leaders themselves, to develop a new vision that would address the excruciating level of poverty, underdevelopment and the continued marginalization of the continent. These considerations account for the initiative that became known as the New Partnership for Africa's Development (NEPAD).[42]

For its proponents, NEPAD represented the most comprehensive and holistic indigenous development blueprint for Africa. It complimented the Abuja Treaty by charting a development path that would lead the economies of the continent to eventual union. Indeed, the Abuja Treaty was strong on end, but weak on means. This is where the strength of NEPAD lay according to the proponents of the framework.

In essence, NEPAD's objectives included the eradication of poverty, attainment of sustainable development on the continent, halting the marginalization of the continent in the globalization process, enhancement of its integration into the global economy and the empowerment of women. These objectives were to be pursued on the basis of several principles, which constituted the conditions for sustainable development. These include

1. good governance as a basic requirement for peace, security and sustainable political and socio-economic development;
2. African ownership and leadership and participation by all sectors;
3. self-reliance;
4. partnership between and among African peoples;
5. acceleration of regional and continental integration;
6. forging of a new international partnership; and
7. ensuring that all partnerships are geared towards the achievement of the Millennium Development goals.

The NEPAD strategic framework document spells out a programme of action that the proponents of the initiative saw as the right prescription for the revival of Africa. The programme of action covered several sectors.

In the infrastructure sector, the NEPAD Heads of State Implementation Committee approved 20 priority short-term action plan projects. These included studies, quick win projects in energy, transport, water and sanitation, information and communication technologies, as well as capacity building. The total cost of these short-term projects alone was put at US$8.12 billion, with half of the cost of the investment projects expected to come from the private sector.

In the area of health, a strategy was drawn up consisting of seven main components: strengthening commitment, enabling stewardship and harnessing multi-sectoral efforts, launching sustainable health systems and building evidence-based practice, scaling up disease control, reducing health risks associated with pregnancy and childbirth, empowering people to improve their health, and mobilizing sufficient sustainable workers for the health sector.

In education, NEPAD identified eight priority areas: meeting the Millennium Development Goals on basic education,[43] improving the quality of education, achieving gender equality in education, developing effective feeding and nutrition programmes in schools, as well as capacity building in the public sector, improvement of mathematics and science education, assisting the educational system in the post-conflict states, and promoting HIV/AIDS education.

Over 250 projects were included in the NEPAD Environment Action Plan, which was adopted in Maputo in July 2003.[44] A similar action plan was drawn up on tourism, focusing on eight priority areas: creation of enabling regulatory environment, strengthening institutional capacity, promotion of tourism marketing, promotion of research and development, promoting investment in tourism infrastructure and products, reinforcement of human resources and quality assurance, establishment and adoption of a code of conducts and ethics for tourism, and mobilization of financial resources.

The centrepiece of NEPAD's agenda on agriculture was the Comprehensive Africa Agriculture Development Programme (CAADP). A key aspect of CAADP was the goal of allocating at least 10 per cent of national budgetary resources to agriculture within five years as agreed in the Maputo Declaration on Agriculture and Food Security in Africa, adopted in Maputo in 2003. CAADP also sought to strengthen agriculture research and development. Similar programmes have been drawn up on science and technology as well as on Africa's industrialization.

With respect to funding, NEPAD placed strong emphasis on the need to mobilize domestic savings and investments, improve management of public revenue and expenditure, improve Africa's share in international trade, attract foreign direct investment and increase capital inflow through ODA and debt reduction.

Through the various measures, NEPAD sought to create a peaceful and conflict-free Africa, firmly placed on the path of effective poverty eradication, where democracy, good governance and respect for human rights would be entrenched in the body politics and that would have heightened level of regional integration, and would possess effective capacity for policy development, coordination and negotiation in the international arena, and that would be in genuine partnership with developed countries.

Indeed, few people can quarrel with the objectives enunciated in the NEPAD Programme. First, it was a visionary approach to the construction of a prosperous and stable future for the continent based on principles universally accepted as essential for political and economic development. According to NEPAD proponents, past attempts at continent-wide action plans for development failed because they ignored the key principles on which NEPAD was based: good governance and public financial accountability.[45]

Second, NEPAD was seen as a home-grown initiative that represented the determination of African leaders to assume the ownership of the development process in their countries and to establish new forms of partnership with the international community.[46] Such ownership was a critical prerequisite for development initiatives to succeed. The Africa Peer Review Mechanism (APRM) was considered one of the most important ingredients of the ownership process.[47]

Third, NEPAD was based on sober assessment of the development challenges the African continent faced as well as the new realities that were being created by the rapidly globalizing world economy.[48] While stressing the importance of ownership and self-reliance, NEPAD recognized the importance of external assistance to Africa's development. For this reason, it proposed a new partnership between African countries and the international donor community based on shared principles and binding commitments to obligations and objectives.

By and large, NEPAD was well received by all the major development partners including the G8, the European Union, the UN and the Brettonwoods Institutions. They all agreed on the unique problem and the need for special arrangements in a range of development areas. They applauded the African governments for taking ownership and responsibility for their development process. The G8 in particular called NEPAD a bold and clear-sighted vision, and pledged to provide greater support – from aid and debt relief to trade and investment. A set of pledges were made in the Africa Action Plan (AAP), which the G8 adopted in Kanananskis in 2003 and which they saw as a solid foundation for future cooperation. Under the AAP, each G8 country pledged to establish "enhanced partnership with African Countries whose performance reflects the NEPAD commitment."[49] The G8 also welcomed the APRM, which it considered an innovative and potentially decisive element in NEPAD.

With regard to sectoral programmes, some progress was reported during the initial period. The energy sector, for example, benefited from funding from the African Development Bank (ADB); and the Government of Canada provided funding for CAADP's agriculture research and development programme. The United Nations provided support in the form of assistance from its own resources and mobilization of international support. Direct UN support came in the form of technical assistance for institutional development, capacity building, project development, resource mobilization and advocacy.[50] To enhance international support, the Secretary General set up a 13-member advisory panel to review and assess the adequacy of international support for NEPAD, conduct dialogue with the donor community in order to raise support and make recommendations on actions that the international community should take to expedite the implementation of NEPAD programmes.

Despite these initial advances, the implementation of the NEPAD programme remained slow to such an extent that early enthusiasts such as the former president of Senegal Abdoulaye Wade could not mask their disenchantment. Indeed, various assessments show that the considerable moral support that the initiative received did not translate into effective material support. The NEPAD programme estimated that for Africa to achieve 7 per cent annual economic growth, which was needed to reduce by half the number of people living in poverty by the year 2015, the continent would need to fill an annual resources gap of about 64 billion.[51] Although NEPAD supporters maintained that Africa could meet much of the funding requirement through increased export earnings, and foreign investment and by reversing the trend of capital flight, they conceded that Africa would hope to receive 10–12 billion more a year as aid[52] to achieve the established targets of expenditure because most African countries faced severe fiscal constraints. Progress in the infrastructure sector in particular was impeded by the problem of long project-approval cycles in partner institutions, limited grant resources for project preparation and severe technical capacity constraints at the national and regional levels.

In agriculture, despite noticeable progress in the implementation of CAADP, several problems persisted. Countries were not only unable to meet the target of allocating 10 per cent of national budgetary resources to agriculture, they also failed to allocate adequate resources to agriculture extension services or build a critical mass of technical experts. As the Secretary General of the UN indicated, all these problems were compounded by the declining share of aid devoted to agriculture in the developing countries in general and Africa in particular.[53]

With regard to the health sector, there were the twin problems of shortage of staff due the massive flight of health professionals to overseas, and the increasing instance of health care personnel falling victim to the HIV/AIDS pandemic. And in a number of countries, the educational sector was not only underfunded, it also experienced severe loss of professionals for more or less the same reason as the health sector.

With respect to support from the UN, the Secretary General identified challenges and constraints that the UN faced in providing adequate support to NEPAD. First, increased financial commitment by the United Nations system for NEPAD was dependent on the United Nations and the agencies receiving additional financial resources for these programmes. Second, while the organizations of the United Nations system were required to initiate an increasing amount of joint programming and new initiatives, the lack of additional financial resources limited the scope and prospects of joint activities.[54] In addition to the problem of increasing the level of support, there was the difficulty of achieving policy coherence. As the Report of the Secretary General shows, the lack of complementarities in debt, aid and trade policies towards Africa made policy coherence as much of a challenge as increasing the volume of aid. For much of the past 20 years ODA to Africa was offset by debt service. Furthermore, the sharp decline of Africa's market share during the 30 years before the turn of the century amounted to an estimated income loss of US$70 billion per year, almost five times the average annual amount of ODA to Africa.[55]

These difficulties were captured by Ibrahim Assane Mayaki, the Chief Executive Officer of NEPAD Planning and Coordination Agency in a statement marking the tenth anniversary of the framework. According to Mayaki, "Africa's own limited resources … and the difficulties and unpredictability of external support have inevitably affected the pace at which NEPAD's ambitious programmes have been implemented."[56] Mayaki's admission was echoed by Erastus Mwencha, deputy chairperson of the African Union Commission, who in his address to the same gathering admitted the vexing problem of funding that NEPAD programmes faced.[57] Thus, the two executives brought to the fore the biggest weakness of NEPAD: making the implementation of major strategies such as PIDA, CAADP and CARMMA contingent upon the goodwill of the development partners.[58]

But while the disenchantment with NEPAD grew, even among its original proponents such as President Abdoulaye Wade of Senegal, NEPAD was not to be put aside. The revival strategy of the African leaders took the form of an Assembly decision taken in 2010 to transform what was NEPAD Secretariat based in Midrand, South Africa, into NEPAD Planning and Coordinating Agency, and integrating it into the structure and the processes of the African Union.

The transformation of the NEPAD Secretariat into NEPAD Coordinating Agency and attaching it to the AU Commission might have addressed the problem of duplication and rivalry that existed between the then NEPAD Secretariat and the African Union Commission; however, it did little to enhance NEPAD efficiency and effectiveness with respect to service delivery and implementation of development programmes. For much of the ten-year period, service delivery and implementation of development programmes remained AU's weaknesses. Save for peace and security, and to some extent governance, there was hardly any best practices that NEPAD could have learnt from the AU Commission, especially with respect to service delivery and implementation of development programme.

Besides talks of focusing on harnessing internal capacity development and mobilizing more domestic resources, the new arrangement did not come up with any proposal to address the resource constraints that plagued NEPAD during the ten years. The irony was compounded by the AU's own reliance on development partners for the bulk of AU programmes.

CONCLUSION

The above overview shows that despite its bleak development results at the turn of the twenty-first century, the African continent was preoccupied with socio-economic development since independence. The number of development frameworks put in place, including the Lagos Plan of Action, the Abuja Treaty and NEPAD, all sought to foster progress and socio-economic development on the continent. Notwithstanding the promise these frameworks held, Africa failed to implement them for various reasons. The lack of political will, lack of capacity at the national level as well as the absence for the most part of the complementarity among African economies were among the factors that aborted the implementation of the Abuja Treaty on time. With respect to the NEPAD initiative, it has been shown that the frameworks greatest weakness was the inability to raise domestic resources, therefore making the implementation of major strategies dependent on the goodwill of the development partners.

In spite of these difficulties, Africa had come a long way. For close to ten years, the average growth rate of the continent was over 5 per cent. Although the impact of growth on poverty in the continent remained a major subject of debate, the economic performance certainly occasioned a change of perception of the African continent from what *The Economist* described as "a hopeless continent" to "Africa rising."[59]

NOTES

1. Amara Essy, in an interview with the *New African* , June 2002
2. The other two were the Educational, Scientific, Cultural and Health Commission, and the Defence Commission.

3. See Olatunde J.C.B. Ojo et al., *African International Relations*, p. 91.

4. Former Executive Secretary of the United Nations Economic Commission for Africa.

5. See OAU, *Lagos Plan of Action for the Economic Development of Africa, 1980–2000* (Addis Ababa, 1988); Gino J. Naldi, *The Organization of African Unity,* pp. 169–170.

6. Ibid., p. 169.

7. Ibid.

8. It should be noted however that the regional economic communities such as ECOWAS, and COMESA have made considerable headway and inspired similar bodies in other parts of the continent. The result is that by the first-half of the 1990s, almost all African countries belong to one or more regional groups.

9. Omar Kabaj, *African Development.* Supplement of the African Development Bank Report (Oxford: OUP, 2003) p. 72.

10. For more on this, see United Nations Conference on Trade and Development, *Foreign Direct Investment in Africa: Performance and Potential* (UNCTAD, 1999).

11. The World Bank*, Can Africa Claim the 21st Century* (Washington: World Bank, 2000), pp. 86–87.

12. See UNDP *Human Development Report 2003* (New York, OUP, 2003), pp.51–60.

13. Constitutive Act, Article 3 (a)

14. Ibid, Article 3 (c)

15. Ibid. Article 3 (l)

16. UNECA*. Assessing Integration in Africa*, ECA Policy Research Report (Addis Ababa: ECA 2004), p.27.

17. This section of the study draws liberally on the report of the UNECA on the progress of integration on the continent. UNECA*, Assessing Integration in Africa*, ECA Policy Research Report (Addis Ababa: ECA 2004). Analysts would go as far back as the beginning of the 20th Century and would site as examples the Southern African Customs Union, which begun in 1910, and the Rhodesian Customs Union, which was formed in 1949 between South Africa and Rhodesia. Because I am dealing with Africa's post-independence international relations, I have chosen to deal with efforts by independent African countries only.

18. UNECA*, Assessing Regional Integration*, p. 39

19. It is beyond the scope of this study to elaborate on these technical terms in detail. What is provided here is just a rudimentary definition to enable readers unfamiliar with the terms to be able to grasp the basic points. Thus *trade creation* refers to instances where expensive domestic goods and services from extra-regional sources are replaced with cheaper products from regional sources. *Trade diversion* refers to the reverse situation where expensive regional products replace cheaper non-regional non-community products.

20. World Bank, *Trade Blocs* (Washington DC: World Bank, 2000) pp. 17–19.

21. Ibid.

22. ECA, *Assessing Regional Integration in Africa*, p. 15.

23. Ibid., p. 16; World Bank, *Trade Blocks*, p. 16.

24. P. Collier and J Gunning, "Explaining African Economic Performance", *Journal of Economic Literature* 37 (1) 1999, pp. 64–111.

25. World Bank, *Can Africa Claim the 21*st *Century?* pp.48–64, 103–120, 235–255.

26. Ibid., p. 41.

27. Ibid.

28. Ibid., pp. 50–51.

29. For more on the financial difficulties facing the regional groupings, see UNECA, *Assessing Regional Integration,* pp. 44–45.

30. African Development Bank et al. *African Economic Outlook 2013*, p. 14.

31. UNECA, *Assessing Regional Integration,* p. 64.

32. Commission of the African Union *Strategic Plan of the Commission of the African Union Vol.1: Vision and Mission of the African Union,* (May 2004), p. 31.

33. Decision Assembly/AU/Dec.112(VII) 2006.

34. Commission of the African Union, *Solidarity Budget for the Financial Year 2005, Part X, Department of Economic Affairs* (2004), p.13.

35. Ibid.

36. Discussion with Commission Official, Addis Ababa, 2004.

37. African Union, *Protocol on Relations between the African Union Commission and the Regional Economic Communities (RECs).*

38. Commission of the African Union *Strategic Plan of the Commission of the African Union Vol.1: Vision and Mission of the African Union,* (May 2004), p. 31.

39. Commission of the African Union, *Strategic Plan of the Commission of the African Union Vol. 2: 2004–2007 Strategic Framework of the Commission of the African Union*, (May 2004), pp. 29–30.

40. For more on this, see chapter 7, pp. 126.

41. Kabbaj, *The Challenge of African Development*, p. 73. See also World Bank, "Recent Trade Performance of Sub-Saharan African Countries: Causes for Hope or More of the Same?" available in *http://www.worldbank.org/afr/findings/english/find176.htm* p.1–3.

42. NEPAD is an amalgamation of the Millennium Partnership for the African Recovery Programme, which was spearheaded by President Thabo Mbeki of South Africa, Abdoulaziz Bouteflika of Algeria, Olusegum Obasanjo of Nigeria and Hosni Mubarak of Egypt, and the OMEGA Plan of President Abdoulaye Wade of Senegal. To some extent, too, NEPAD draws on the ECA report entitled the *Compact for African Development.*

43. The eight MDG were to: eradicate poverty and hunger; achieve universal primary education; promote gender equality and empowerment of women; reduce child mortality by two-thirds; improve maternal health; combat HIV/AIDS, malaria and other diseases; ensure environmental sustainability; develop global partnership for development.

44. See, United Nations Environment Programme (UNEP), *Development of an Action Plan for the Environment Initiative of NEPAD* (UNEP 2003) and www.environment-directory.org/nepad/content

45. Kabbaj, *The Challenges of Africa's Development* p. 3

46. Ibid., p. 89

47. For a short overview of the APRM, see pp.151–152.

48. Kabbaj, *The Challenges of Africa's Development*, p. 89.

49. United Nations, "Funding for NEPAD: Africa Still Waiting for Genuine Partnership" available at http://www.un.org/en/africarenewal/sgreport/repdfs/partners.pdf.

50. Secretary General of the United Nation, New Partnership for Africa's Development: Report on Progress in Implementation and International Support" June 2004, Doc. E/AC.50/2004/6 and Doc. A/59/150/, pp. 17–22.

51. The New Partnership for Africa's development, paragraph 144.

52. United Nations, "Funding for NEPAD" p. 5

53. Secretary General of the United Nations, *The New Partnership for Africa's Development*

54. Ibid. p. 22.

55. World Bank, "Africa Region Trade Progress Note", available at www.worldbank.org/afr/trade/wb-assistance_2003-03 pdf; cited in Secretary General of the United Nation, The New Partnership for Africa's Development, p. 17.

56. Cited in Baffour Ankomah, "NEPAD, 10 Years on", *The New African* London 8 May 2012.

57. Ibid.

58. The admission of this weakness was much to the enchantment of NEPAD critics such as President Yahya Jammeh of the Gambia, who used to refer to NEPAD as the "knee-pad" that Africa would need to remain on its knees in order to get financial support from the Western development partners.

59. *The Economist*, 13 May 2000, Cited also by Abdoulie Janneh, Executive Secretary of the United Nations Economic Commission for Africa, in Bafour Ankomah, NEPAD 10 Years on, *The New African*.

Chapter 6

Breaking the Poverty Trap

The Human Development Agenda of the African Union

This chapter extends the examination of AU's preferences by focusing on social questions, especially the Union's mandate and challenges it faced in the area of health, education, gender and population. It shows that by and large, the African Union had little to its credit in these areas other than a few legal instruments. In my view, AU's ineffectiveness in the area of human development was due to its limited autonomy, just as limited autonomy reduced the Union's effectiveness in various other areas.

Academics and development professionals have been grappling with the notion of human development for some time. At the heart of the exercise are the different perceptions of poverty. A widely held view is that the poor are those living on or less than US$1.25 per day. While this income measure tells us who is poor, it does not tell us how they are poor. An attempt to fill this gap has been made by Oxford Poverty and Human Development Initiative (OPHI) of the University of Oxford. What OPHI offers is a multidimensional poverty index (MPI) that measures poverty on the basis of health, education and living standards.[1] The present chapter approaches the question of human development from OPHI perspective and offers an assessment of Africa collective efforts to address the problems of health, education, gender, population and migration. Although these issues do not exhaust the multidimensional nature of poverty, they constitute representational samples of the human development challenges Africa faced.

HEALTH

Africa's health challenges were sufficiently serious to threaten the development gains the continent had made.[2] Between 1960 and 1990, life expectancy at birth rose from 40 to 50 years, adult mortality decreased both for males and females, and the under five mortality rate decreased tremendously from 254 to 155 per 1000 live births. By the end of the twentieth century, these positive trends were reversed, with life expectancy falling to about 47 and adult mortality rising.[3] These reversals were blamed on the emergence of deadly diseases such as HIV/AIDS and the resurgence of malaria and tuberculosis in more virulent forms and epidemic proportions. The World Health Organization (WHO) estimated that Africa had the highest number of People Living with HIV/AIDS (PLWHA), and accounted for most deaths from HIV/AIDS, TB and malaria. More than 75 per cent of global AIDS death, 22 per cent of TB deaths and 90 per cent of all malaria-related deaths occurred in sub-Saharan Africa.[4] Together with poor socio-economic conditions and weakening health systems, these diseases were largely responsible for the deterioration of African health situation in the 1990s, and their combined socio-economic impacts threatened the continent's development prospects by reducing national savings and investments, undermining countries productive capacity, overwhelming provision of health services and challenging national security.

The impacts of these diseases at the micro-economic level can be gauged by their effect on growth. It was estimated that the HIV/AIDS reduced GDP growth in Africa by between 0.5 per cent and 2.6 per cent a year on average, and that the early elimination of malaria would have added US$100 billion to Africa's GDP over the past 30 years.[5] And in countries with a high burden of TB, the loss of productivity due to the disease was estimated at 4–7 per cent of GDP.[6]

HIV/AIDS also changed the demographic profile of several countries in Africa, consequently increasing the dependency ratio drastically. In various communities, young adults had to support a growing number of orphans and elderly people. Often children were withdrawn from school to care for family members who were ill and to regain lost income. As more adults died, more children become orphans. Families faced income losses and high costs for health care and funerals.[7] Malaria too reduced work performance by impairing physical ability, causing significant loss of work life, productive time, income and savings. Because it frequently occurred concurrently with HIV/AIDS, tuberculosis also affected the most productive age group of the population and accounts for 3–4 months per year of lost work time, as well as the loss of earnings of at least of 20–30 per cent of TB affected household income.[8] The consequence of the epidemic on the productive capacity of the continent was obvious. Employers of all types face high rates of turnover, absenteeism and illness, and high cost of training, insurance and employee benefits.

Ill health and death from these diseases caused a decline in crop output, reductions in input, decreases in area planted, changes in cropping patterns and loss of agricultural knowledge. At the core of the impact on agriculture was the loss of potential able-bodied adult labour force as well as reduction in labour quality, time diverted from agricultural activities towards caring for the sick and attending funerals, and reduced funds to hire seasonal casual labour.

The private sector also suffered from the impacts of these epidemics. In addition to low productivity, absenteeism and general shortage of labour, the private sector faced problems associated with poor work place environment brought about by the stigmatization of people living with HIV/AIDS.

Even before the emergence of HIV/AIDS and the worsening of TB and malaria, public health sectors in most African countries already had difficulty providing basic services to the population, due to inadequate resource input and inefficient use of available resources. Thus, the onslaught of the diseases on top of this had imposed additional pressure by further overstretching the health system.

The alarming impact of these epidemics on education could be seen in their potential to erode the returns on investment in African education at all levels.[9] And the ability of African countries to respond to these health challenges continued to be undermined by the impact of the diseases.

The gravity of these problems prompted responses at three levels. At the local level, African countries sought to improve access to new drugs and treatments. At the international level, the UN Secretary General established a Commission on AIDS and Governance in order to equip policy makers with the tools required to address the profound structural impact that HIV/AIDS was having on the continent's capacity to meet its development challenges.

At the continental level, African leaders responded by adopting a number of continental instruments. These include the Declaration on Health as a Foundation for Socio-Economic Development (1987), Dakar Declaration on the AIDS Epidemic in Africa (1992), Tunis Declaration on HIV/AIDS and the Child in Africa (1994), the Addis Ababa Declaration and the African Plan of Action Concerning the Situation of Women in Africa in the Context of Family Health (1996), and the Harare Declaration on Malaria Prevention and Control in the Context of African Economic Recovery and Development.

But among all these, the most ambitious and far-reaching instruments were the Abuja Declaration on the Roll Back Malaria in Africa (2000) the Amsterdam Declaration to Stop Tuberculosis (2000), the Addis Ababa Consensus and Plan of Action (2000) and the Abuja Declaration on HIV/AIDS, Tuberculosis, and Other Related Infectious Diseases (2001).

The Abuja Declaration and Plan of Action on Roll Back Malaria in African was adopted during the Special Summit on Roll Back malaria (RBM) in Africa in Abuja in April 2000. In it, the heads of state and government pledged to improve access to prevention and care, through the reduction and waiving of taxes and tariffs on mosquito nets and materials, insecticides, anti-malaria drugs and other malaria-related commodities. The declaration endorsed the Roll Back Malaria goals of halving the prevalence of malaria in the world by 2010 and designating 25 April each year as Africa's Malaria Day. It also facilitated the Roll Back malaria partnership that was subsequently initiated and which provided an opportunity for mobilizing resources to support malaria control activities in member states.

The Amsterdam Declaration to Stop Tuberculosis enunciated the commitment of the 20 countries that account for 80 per cent of the world's tuberculosis burden to accelerate action against TB. The Amsterdam meeting, that adopted the Amsterdam Declaration, also resulted in the establishment of the global fund for TB through partnership led by the World Bank.

The Addis Ababa Consensus and Plan of Action, adopted at the African Development Forum 2000, underscored the importance of leadership in overcoming the HIV/AIDS epidemic in Africa. It urged member states to take concrete actions by establishing national aids commissions and strategic plans to tackle HIV/AIDS, backed up by appropriate legislation and modalities for involving people living with HIV/AIDS and other stakeholders in the decision-making process and mechanisms for regular monitoring of progress. The leadership exigency was advanced further by the Abuja Declaration and Framework of Action on HIV/AIDS, TB and other related infectious diseases (ORID), which was adopted during the OAU Summit in Abuja in 2001. Within the Abuja Framework, the African leaders expressed their commitment to provide leadership in the fight against poverty, HIV/AIDS, TB, malaria and other infectious diseases, which constitute impediments to better political, social and economic development of the continent.[10]

The Abuja Summit also declared AIDS as a "state of emergency in Africa," and called for the inclusion of the fight against HIV/AIDS, TB and other infectious diseases in the agenda to reduce poverty and foster sustainable development. One of the key components of the Abuja Declaration was the commitment by the heads of state and government to increase domestic spending on health to 15 per cent of the annual national budget and raise additional external resources from the international community.

Thus, in the area of health, there is no dearth of initiatives and frameworks. Together they constitute the mandate of the African Union. The challenge, however, was to translate these commitments into concrete measures for prevention and care. More specifically, the African Union was required to implement the commitments of the leaders to forge partnerships and networks especially at the regional and international levels.

The importance of regional networks in particular stems from the fact that cross-border movements are extensive in many African regions, and they tend to carry diseases across borders. In this regard, the African Union was required to coordinate African governments' efforts to raise international assistance in order to respond to the epidemics. The organization was also required to put in place mechanism to monitor progress and measure the impact of the responses of national governments. In this context the African Union had to devise ways to grapple with the linkages between foreign policy and funding for international campaigns against deadly diseases as demonstrated by Western donors attempt to exclude Zimbabwe from the Global Fund for the fight against HIV/AIDS.

African Union's achievements in the health sector were modest by many counts. The Union adopted the African health strategy 2007–2015 and declared 2011–2020 Africa's decade of traditional medicine. The commission also regularly monitored and reported on the implementation of the Abuja call for accelerated action towards universal access to HIV/AIDS, TB and malaria services and other infectious diseases in Africa. The Campaign on Accelerated Reduction of maternal, infant and child mortality in Africa (CARMMA) was launched in July 2009 and the problem was chosen as the theme of Summit in Kampala in 2010. And as part of the implementation of the leaders' commitment to forge partnerships at regional and international levels, the African Union Commission created a network of experts to harmonize e-health and telemedicine programmes. The fact that apart from these activities little else could be shown on the ground is indicative of the challenges that the African Union continued to face in the health sector.

EDUCATION

Goal 2 of the United Nations Millennium Development Goals aimed at attaining universal primary education by 2015, by ensuring that all children were able to complete primary education. For African countries this objective was particularly important in that it constituted one of the key elements of human development, on which the continent's future development wholly rested. Indeed, human capital development lies at the heart of social and economic change in the advanced and emerging economies. Therefore, for Africa to move ahead, priority must be given to basic education, which equips recipient with essential literacy and numeracy skills needed for high yield on investment and for enhanced labour productivity.[11]

However, like in many areas, Africa's performance in the area of education was far from satisfactory. Between 1980 and 1993, for example, primary school enrolments dropped from 80 per cent to 72 per cent.[12] What is more, less than a quarter of secondary school age children were enrolled in secondary school. And many adults had little or no education. Income, region and gender continued to determine whether the children would be enrolled. Overall, primary enrolments were low but were more acute among the poor rural females In the 1990s, for example, only 24 per cent of this group was enrolled in 16 African countries.[13] Secondary enrolment was also low representing about 7 per cent of the poorest rural group in the majority of African countries and a negligible 3 per cent in the poorest countries.[14]

The implication of this poor performance of the educational sector is that a large per cent of the African population was excluded from acquiring the capabilities they needed to contribute to the growth of the modern economy. Low female enrolment in particular slowed down the demographic transition, reducing the prospect of African countries moving towards a virtuous circle of growth, demographic transition and savings.[15]

The poor performance of the 1980s and the early 1990s persisted into the late 1990s. While net primary enrolment increased by 3 per cent by the end of the 1990s, less than 60 per cent of the children were enrolled.[16] Moreover, enrolment did not mean completion. Globally, just over half of the children who started school finished it. In sub-Saharan Africa, only one in three completed.[17]

Competition for places in underfunded secondary schoolswas also a problem, as places tended to be skewed towards males and the well-off in urban areas. Enrolment in higher education was even lower, representing less than 10 per cent and in several cases less than 1 per cent.[18]

Poor performance in the educational sector of developing countries in general and Africa in particular is due to three main factors. They are limited resources, inequity and inefficiency. In contrast to rich countries, developing countries in general and Africa in particular spent less per student as a proportion of GNP at all levels of education. And when spending is low, rich people often capture a much larger share of it, and so poor people do not benefit as much. Inefficient spending went for teachers' salaries, leaving little for learning materials. In addition, low-quality teaching meant that students did not learn as much as they could have.[19]

To reverse this trend African leaders through the AU and the OAU, before it took several steps, including sectoral consultations that led to the establishment of the Association of African Universities; the centre for the Study of Language and History through Oral Tradition in Niamey, Niger; and the Scientific, Technical and Research Commission in Lagos, Nigeria. In 1996, African leaders declared the period 1997–2006 as the *Decade of Education in*

Africa and mandated the OAU to prepare a plan of action for the implementation of the declaration. The plan of action was adopted by the first conference of African Ministers of Education in Harare, in March 1999, and subsequently endorsed by the Assembly of heads of state and government during its 35th session in Algiers, in July 1999. The plan of action focused on equity and access, quality, relevance and effectiveness of education, complementary learning modalities, and capacity building.

However, as is the case with several African initiatives, the first decade of education in Africa did not yield expected results. An evaluation report revealed that most of the goals set in the plan of action were not achieved for various reasons. First it was revealed that the first decade was not accompanied by a plan of action in a timely manner. The plan of action was adopted only two years after the declaration. Second, the communication component of the plan was weak as the publicity given to the initiative remained grossly inadequate. Consequently, there was little evidence of ownership by the stakeholders, and little support came from the continent's development partners who had their own parallel and disconnected programmes.[20] At the national level, member states designed their education programmes and negotiated donor support individually, without any specific link to the goals agreed upon at the continental level within the framework of the initiative.

Thus, the challenges Africa faced in the area of education remained formidable. An ECA study summed up these challenges.[21] Accordingly, African countries needed to invest in people by taking the following measures:

1. Scale-up investment in education that is skills-intensivewhich effectively deploys human resources in the provision of social services.
2. Ensure that primary school enrolment increases, accompanied by rising completion rates, by implementing global school feeding programmes, removing fee system and educating parents on the benefits of education.
3. Promote gender parity in education systems not only at the primary level but also at secondary and tertiary levels, especially investing in boarding and transportation facilities for girls.
4. Ensure that curricula include reproductive health education and similar information.
5. Match vocational training and education to public and private sector employment needs.

It was perhaps in recognition of these persistent challenges that the ministers of education of the African Union recommended to the Assembly that there be a second decade for education in Africa, running from 2006 to 2015. This second decade was accordingly proclaimed in 2006 and, unlike the first decade, was immediately supported by a plan of action that included appropriate monitoring and evaluation mechanisms, incorporated bench marks and performance indicators. The guiding principles designed to ensure the success of the second decade included gathering political support for the initiative at the national level and enhancing mutual assistance among member states.[22] Expected outcomes comprised a functioning Educational Management Information Systems (EMIS); increased access to education by the population, enhanced quality, efficiency and relevance of education to development; and gender equality in primary and secondary education and in sciences. For this purpose, an African Education Development Fund was envisaged to fill the gaping funding gap.

In order to avoid the type of failure experienced during the first decade, a monitoring and evaluation mechanism was put in place. Under this framework, member states were required to submit to their regional economic communities a detailed plan for the implementation of the plan of action with goals, timeframes and funding plans. The RECs were required to evaluate the individual country's plans and assess their compatibility with the Continental Plan and the feasibility of its funding arrangement. The communities were also required to monitor the implementation of the country's submit reports to the Steering Committee, which would report to Conference of Ministers of Education (COMEDAF).[23]

The African Union also established the Africa Education Observatory as recommended in the plan of action for the second decade of education for Africa. In collaboration with the Association for the Development of Education in Africa (ADEA), the observatory carried out capacity building activities for education planning officials from over 40 member states. Similarly, indicators for monitoring performance were developed and used to produce a biennial analytical report entitled "African Education Outlook." But perhaps the most significant step that the African Union took in the area of education was the establishment of the Pan African University.

The Pan African University was launched in December 2011 in collaboration with the Association of African Universities. A coordinating unit was established as a precursor of the PAU Rectorate, and the statutes and other policy documents of the PAU were adopted in January 2012; and the curriculum for a selected number of postgraduate programmes was finalized. The PAU received support from a number of international agencies and donor countries including Germany, Sweden, India, China, Spain, Japan, the European Union, and the ADEA. Within the framework of the "Africa Project," the European Commission also supported the development of Africa-focused Masters and PhD programmes.

The African Union also undertook to harmonize higher education in Africa, and in collaboration with UNESCO revised the Arusha Convention for the Mutual Recognition of Degrees and Certificates in Africa. This was endorsed by COMEDAF IV. The pilot project to harmonize university curricula across the continent received funding from the European Union.

The AU also established the Mwalimu Nyerere Scholarship programme which received European Union support in the tune of 40 million Euros under the "Intra-ACP Mobility Scheme." The basic scheme sponsored 43 African students to study in African universities, most of them outside their own countries. In the first call in 2011, 28 African universities in three networks were awarded a total of 7 million Euro to cover Masters and PhD scholarships as well as academic staff exchange. The second call was launched in January 2012. And within the framework of the India–Africa partnership, the Indian government offered 300 scholarships in agricultural sciences, tenable in Indian universities. And four countries were selected to host India–Africa institutions of higher education. By 2012, the business plans of the institutions were developed and the MOU for the India-Africa Institute for Education Planning and Administration in Bujumbura was signed. There were plans to have the India–Africa Institute for Foreign Trade in Kampala, India–Africa Institute for ICT in Accra, and India–Africa Institute for Diamonds in Botswana. Three other countries were identified to host scientific research institutes.

In order to respond to the lack of qualified teachers in the continent, especially in the area of science, mathematics and technology, the AU conducted a feasibility study on the establishment of regional teacher development centres (with focus on science and mathematics education), took steps to promote teacher development through open and distant learning, and developed a protocol on the mobility of professionals across borders.

GENDER MAINSTREAMING

That poverty has a female face may appear as one of those clichés that gains ephemeral currency before they die out. But the situation of African women in three critical area of human development shows that women do indeed represent the bulk of poor people on the continent, and do therefore give poverty a predominantly feminine feature.

No doubt some progress was made. The 1990s and 2000s saw significant increases in the gross and net enrolment ratios for both boys and girls, with a good number of countries achieving 100 per cent enrolment for boys and girls. At the secondary level, a few countries reported having achieved parity between boys and girls or reducing gender gaps. Several African countries also reported significant progress in reducing illiteracy levels, particularly among women.

However, despite these improvements, Africa was still by far the region with the lowest number of children in schools. Only 58 per cent of children of school-going age were actually enrolled in school. With the exception of a few countries, educational statistics from across the region showed gender disparities. Female-to-male school enrolment, retention and completion ratios favoured males in a majority of countries. Moreover, the highest illiteracy rates in the world were found among African women. Because of low levels, of education, women constituted a disproportionate large part of the under-employed and working poor. At the tertiary and university levels, the low participation for women continued to be a major source of concern because it undermined national efforts for human capital development, particularly as the gender gaps remained pronounced in science fields, mathematics and computer sciences.[24]

African women also suffered the highest mortality rate in the world. It was estimated that the chances of an African woman dying during child birth or pregnancy was 1:13. More than 250,000 women die each year from complications in pregnancy and child birth, compared to 150 in Europe.[25] About 20 per cent of maternal mortality is attributable to illegal abortions.

In addition to being subjected to harassment and violence , African women rarely had a secure tenure to the land they worked on, despite the fact that they were responsible for 80 per cent of agricultural production and all of the household production in most African regions.[26] One of the implications caused by the insecurity of tenure was the inability of women to generate adequate income by raising credit and making appropriate investment.[27]

The African Union's response to these challenges came in various forms. First, while the charter of the OAU did not provide for gender mainstreaming, the Constitutive Act of the African Union specifically provides that the African Union shall function in accordance with the promotion of gender equality.[28] During its meeting in March 2002, the Council of Ministers urged the secretariat to accord the issue of gender the importance it deserved and to convene a meeting to map out strategies on how to promote gender mainstreaming on the continent. In response to these demands, a working group on gender was established at the Secretariat to spearhead activities meant to advance the gender mainstreaming agenda. Workshops and similar consultative meetings were held to map out the way forward.[29] Another step taken in that direction was the decision to locate the Directorate on Gender in the office of the interim chairperson of the commission.[30]

However, the first most remarkable step in this respect was the adoption in Durban of the decision on gender parity in the Commission of the African Union. According to this decision, the college of ten commissioners would be composed of five female and five male.

The second was the adoption in Addis Ababa by the Assembly of the Solemn Declaration on Gender Equality in Africa (SDGEA). In addition to reaffirming and expanding the scope of commitments made within such a frameworks as the Beijing Platform of Action, the SDGEA made additional and innovative pledges. It included the commitment to accelerate the implementation of gender-specific economic and legal measures aimed at combating the HIV/AIDS and other pandemics; provide women with treatment and social services at the local level; enact and reinforce legislation protecting women's rights, including rights to property and inheritance; end discrimination against women living with HIV/AIDS; protect women against crimes; facilitate the full and effective participation of women in peace processes; work towards the general prohibition of child soldiers and the abuse of girl children as wives and sex slaves; ensure the education of girls and literacy of women; and extend the principle of gender parity adopted with regard to the Commission of Africa Union to all other organs of the Union, including NEPAD and the regional economic communities.[31] The heads of state committed themselves to annually report on the implementation of the SDGEA[32] and obliged the chairperson of the African Union Commission to submit an annual report on the measures taken to implement the principles of gender equality and gender mainstreaming.[33]

By far, the most comprehensive continental instrument on gender mainstreaming was the protocol to the African Charter on Human and People's Rights on the Rights of Women in Africa. Adopted in 2003, the protocol built on a number of instruments, all of which recognize and seek to advance the rights of women.[34] But more than any other instrument, the protocol holds considerable promise with regard to gender equality on the continent. It required state parties to ensure that their national constitution and other legal instruments provided for and took into account gender equality.[35] To ensure that women enjoy rights to life, integrity and security, the protocol enjoined state parties to enact and enforce laws prohibiting all forms of violence against women including unwanted or forced sex.[36] It also required state parties to prohibit all forms of harmful practices that adversely affect the rights of women and which were contrary to international standards.[37] Furthermore, state parties were called upon to enact and enforce legislation on marriage age, marriage register as well as on divorce, and divorce procedure.[38] Several other aspects of human rights were covered, including the right to justice and equal protection before the law, right to participate in political and decision-making processes, right to peace, to education, to food security and housing, and to protection during armed conflicts.[39] Elderly women, women in distress and women with disability were singled out for special treatment.[40]

Perhaps the provisions that best guaranteed effective gender mainstreaming were those on education and right to properties.[41] As seen earlier, female-to-male school enrolment, retention and completion ratios favoured males in a majority of African countries, and the highest illiteracy rates in the world were found among African women. Therefore, what the protocol sought to do was to reverse the trend by requiring state parties to eliminate all forms of discrimination against women and to guarantee equal opportunity and access to education and training, eliminate stereotypes in text books and other education materials, and protect the girl child from abuse. State parties were also to promote education and training for women at all levels, particularly in the field of science and technology, and promote the enrolment and retention of girls in schools.[42]

As widows have no right to the properties of their spouses in many African countries and other developing societies, the protocol sought to address the problem by providing that in the case of separation, divorce or annulment of marriage, men and women shall have the right to an equitable share of the joint property deriving from the marriage.[43] A widow shall have the right to an equitable share in the inheritance of the property of her husband and shall have the right to continue to live in the matrimonial house. And finally, women and men shall have the right to inherit, in equitable shares, their parents' properties.[44]

Other gender-related initiatives include the AU gender policy (adopted in 2009), Assembly declaration of the decade 2010–2020 as the African Women's Decade, and the 10-Year Gender Action Plan and Road Map. There was also the fund for African women. Practical measures taken included the location of gender directory in the office of the chairperson of the commission in accordance with Article 12 (3) of the Statutes of the Commission to ensure that the principle of promoting gender equality was adhered to, as well as facilitate gender mainstreaming within the commission itself and other AU structures. The African Union Commission also report that a number of outreach activities which were undertaken including a workshop on gender response economic policymaking, which sought to reinforce the capacities of the persons in charge of economic policies, budget and development planning, in order to enable them to plan and develop plans and programmes that are sensitive to gender considerations.

Like in many other areas, the African Union leveraged on its convening power to have various frameworks and initiatives adopted at the continental level. Further research will be needed to determine the full impact of these initiatives in the welfare of women at all levels. What is clear for now is that the goal of gender equality remains remote and cannot be achieved by mere continental frameworks and initiatives without any enforcement mechanism. For example, the protocol on the rights of women came across difficulties as soon as it was drafted. Already at the negotiation conference a number of countries expressed their reservation on articles dealing with the family, including the right of the mother to transfer her nationality to her child of a foreign father, inheritance, traditional practices and reproductive right of the women. And a number of countries reserved their right to submit reservations with their individual instruments of ratification. Although at the country level gender-based violence had been outlawed in most African countries, a number of practices, such as female genital mutilation, remain a major challenge across the continent.

MIGRATION AND POPULATION

Poverty in Africa affected not only education, health and women, but it also constituted a push factor that spurred migration both within the continent and to other regions. The United Nations estimated that there were over 16.3 million migrants in Africa in 2002,[45] and close to 13.5 million internally displaced persons.[46] The rising number of migrants and IDPs, and the fact that the trend was growing, made the migration issues major challenges for the African Union and its member states. But the challenge was not only to stem the flow of migration, but also to manage migration properly, as evidence shows that a well-managed migration has the potential to yield significant benefits to origin and destination states. For instance, labour migration, had played an important role in filling labour needs in agriculture, construction and other sectors, thus contributing to economic development of many destination countries in Africa. The benefits of migration, such as remittances, knowledge and skills transfers and returning migration, had also made major contributions to economies of origin countries. Mismanaged or unmanaged migration, however does have serious negative consequences for states and migrants themselves; it destabilizes national and regional security, as well as jeopardize interstate relations.[47] The African Union's response to this need included the adoption of the Abuja Treaty that urged member states to adopt employment policies that would allow the free movement of persons within the African Economic Community.[48] The OAU Labour Commission and the Council of Ministers made several recommendations regarding the legal, economic, political, social and administrative aspects of migration. And during its 74th Ordinary Session in Lusaka, Zambia, in July 2001, the Council of Ministers called for the development of a strategic framework on immigration that would address the challenges posed by migration, and strengthen intra-regional and inter-regional cooperation in the field.[49] The draft policy framework that was subsequently developed sought to encourage member states to mainstream migration issues into their national and regional development agenda. More specifically, it offered to guide member states' policies in the various areas, including labour migration, border management, irregular migration (like migrant smuggling, human trafficking, return and admission), forced displacement, human rights of migrants, internal migration, migration and development, and migration data management.[50] The implementation of the framework took various forms. At the continental level, it prompted the African Union to take two important measures.

The first measure was the decision of the Executive Council at its inaugural session in Durban, South Africa, to mandate the commission of the African Union to work with the African diaspora and to support their involvement in the programmes of the union. The decision led to the creation of Africa Citizens Directorate, CIDO, which sought to foster the participation of diaspora in Africa's development and coordinate their activities. A related undertaking was the process of establishing the Africa Institute for Remittances which began in 2010, with the aim of boosting remittances to the continent by lowering costs, increasing transparency and stimulating healthy competition among service providers.

The second measure was the launching in 2009 of AU-Commit Campaign that aimed at galvanizing activities to combat trafficking in human being in Africa, and outreach to policy makers and law enforcement officials of member countries about the Ouagadougou Action Plan to combat trafficking in human beings, especially women and children.

In the area of population, the speed at which Africa's population grew constituted a source of preoccupation for the African Union. In 1950, Africa had a population of 215 million people. The number had risen to 906 million by 2005 and was hovering around 1 billion in 2012. It is expected to rise to 1.355 billion by 2025 and to 1.994 billion by 2050.[51] This prompted analysts to conclude that Africa's population was part of its problems. Accordingly, if Africa's overall growth, level of poverty and social development remained constant, sub-Saharan African countries would remain stuck in a poverty-demographic trap.[52]

In order to face the challenge of rapidly growing populations, especially that of transitioning from high fertility to low fertility levels, Africa leaders took a number of steps, both on their own and in concert with the international community. The bottom line of all the activities was the consensus that the individual well-being and respect for individual human rights were fundamental to socio-economic development.[53] It was within this context that the African Population Commission was established in 1994 to coordinate the activities of the national population commissions, monitor and evaluate the implementation of decisions, declaration and resolutions that the African leaders had taken on population. The commission's main policy organ was the general assembly, which was composed of the chief executives of the national population bodies (or their representatives). It met biannually, and had a secretariat jointly manned by the African Union and Economic Commission for Africa.[54]

An additional step taken in the area of health in general and population control in particular was the provision in the protocol to the African Charter on Human and People's Rights on the Rights of Women that gives women the right to decide on their reproductive health. Although this provision was resisted from various quarters, its insertion represented a progressive step in many respects. In the same spirit, the African Committee of Experts on the Rights and Welfare of the Child (ACERWC) and the Advisory Council on Ageing (ACA) were set up and the decades 1999–2009 and 2009–2019 were declared African decades of persons with disabilities.

CONCLUSION

In assessing human development in Africa, the reader can be easily carried away by the grim statistics of failures that are juxtaposed alongside successes in a handful of cases. According to those grim figures, almost half of Africa's 800 million population lived in poverty in 2010; one in three people living in Africa were undernourished; half the population had no access to electricity, and water-borne diseases affected an equal number of the population. More women continued to die at childbirth in Africa than in other regions, and malaria continued to kill more than 1 million on the continent. Although these global figures mask impressive advances that some countries made, they do underscore the magnitude of human development challenges Africa faced. Elsewhere, I have demonstrated that on an input-impact continuum much of the activities that the African Union undertook were outputs that had no outcomes at the country level.[55]

No doubt the union developed and adopted frameworks in health, education, gender mainstreaming as well as population control and migration. More significantly, the African Union established the Pan African University and launched the Mwalimu Nyerere scholarshi programme for African students in African universities outside their home countries. The importance of both the PAU and the scholarship programme is indisputable. But apart from these two facilities, there is hardly any other human development area where the impact of the African Union can be measured in concrete terms. For example, under various AU frameworks, African states undertook to increase their health budget and to commit a minimum of 10 per cent of their national budgets to agriculture. In 2010, only three countries allocated more than 15 per cent of government budget to health;[56] an equally low number of countries had passed the Maputo threshold of allocating 10 per cent of national budget to agriculture.[57] Thus, for the most part, AU human development activities were limited to the development and adoption of agreements and charters that took several years to implement on the ground. It was often much easier for African Union officials to report on the legal instruments that had been signed and ratified, or the workshops and conferences that had been convened than to demonstrate the impact that these activities had at the ground level. The organization's ineffectiveness in these areas is a factor of its limited autonomy or lack of enforcement and implementation capacity at the country and regional level. This goes to demonstrate the argument of the Institutionalists that integration involves the creation of institutions, but the effectiveness of the institutions depends on the degree to which they are empowered, which in turn depends on the preferences of the principals.

NOTES

1. These three dimensions are measured on the basis of ten indicators: for health: nutrition, child mortality; education: years of schooling, school attendance; living standards such as cooking fuel, sanitation, water, electricity, floor, assets. See Sanina Alkire and Andy Sumner, *Multidimensional Poverty and the Post-2015 MDGs* February 2013; also available at www.ophi.org.uk.

2. One of the most comprehensive assessment of the impact of Africa's health challenges on the continents development is African Union, UNECA, et al., *Scoring African Leadership for Better Health*, (Addis Ababa: ECA, 2004).

3. Ibid., p. 3.

4. For more on this see, World Health Organization, *World Health Report 2002: Reducing Risks, Promoting Health Life* (Geneva: WHO, 2002) available at (ww.who.int/whr).

5. AU, ECA et al., *Scoring African Leadership* p. 23.

6. Ibid, and UNECA, *Harnessing Technologies for Sustainable Development*, ECA Policy Research Report (Addis Ababa, ECA, p. 146.

7. UNECA, *Harnessing Technologies*, p. 136.

8. AU, UNECA etl all *Scoring African Leadership*, p. 26.

9. Ibid., p. 33.

10. African Union, *Report of the Meeting of (African) Ministers of Finance on the G8 Meeting in Gleneagles, Scotland, Libya*, 29 June 2005, p. 7.

11. Kabaj, *The Challenge of African Development*, p. 16.

12. The World Bank, *Can Africa Claim the 21 Century*, p. 87.

13. Ibid., p.88.

14. Ibid.

15. Ibid., p.89.

16. UNDP, *Human Development Report*, 2003 p. 92

17. Ibid, p. 93. See also, Commission for Africa, *Our Common Interest: Report of the Commission for Africa*, (March 2005), p. 182, UNECA, *Millennium Development Goals for Africa: Progress and Challenges*, pp. 6–7

18. Commission for Africa, *Our Common Interest*, p. 182

19. UNDP *Human Development Report 2003*, p. 93

20. African Union, *The 2nd Decade of Education for Africa 2006–2015: Plan of Action* (Addis Ababa: 2006), p. 1; See African Union, *Decade of Education in Africa*

(1997–2006) An Assessment , Document AU/Educ/2/(1), submitted to the conference of Ministers of Education of the African Union 8–11 April 2005.

21. UNECA *The Millennium Development Goals in Africa: Progress and Challenges* (Addis Ababa, 2005)

22. African Union, *The 2nd Decade of Education for Africa 2006–2015: Plan of Action* (Addis Ababa: 2006), p. 2.

23. African Union, Algiers Declaration of the Ministers of Education of the Member-States of the African Union, Document AU/EDUc/4(1) Rev 1. April 2005.

24. Omar Kabbaj, *The Challenge of African Development*, pp.16–18.

25. Ibid., p.198.

26. UNDP, *Human Development Report 2003,* p. 90.

27. For concrete examples, see Commission for Africa: *Our Common Interest*, p.43 and p. 208.

28. *Constitutive Act of the African Union* Article 4(1).

29. Organization of African Unity, *Introductory Note to the Report of the Secretary General to the 38th Session of the Assembly of Heads of State and Government and the 76th Session of the Council of Ministers*, Durban 4–10 July 2002. p. 105.

30. Ibid., p. 106.

31. African Union, *Solemn Declaration on Gender Equality in Africa*, Addis Ababa, July 2004, Doc. Assembly/AU/Dec.1(III), Rev.1

32. Article 12

33. See Commission of the African Union, *Chairperson's Progress Report on the Implementation of the Solemn Declaration on Gender Equality in Africa,* Document EX.CL/170/(VII), Report Submitted to the 7th Ordinary Session of the Executive Council, Sirte, Libya 28 June – 2 July 2005.

34. These include, as stated in the preamble, the African Charter on Human and People's Rights, Heads of State Resolution on the Recommendation of the African Commission on Human and People's Rights to elaborate a Protocol on the Rights of Women in Africa Doc. AHG/Res.240(XXXI), Universal Declaration of Human Rights, the International Covenant on Civil and Political Rights, the International Covenant on Economic, Social and Cultural Rights, the Convention on the Elimination of Forms of Discrimination Against Women and its Optional Protocol; the African Charter on the Rights and Welfare of the Child; UN Security Council Resolution 1325 (2000) on the Role of Women in the promotion of peace and security..

35. African Union, "Protocol to the African Charter on Human and People's Right's on the Rights of Women in Africa" Doc Min/Wom.rts/Prot II Rev.5 Article 2.

36. Article 4.

37. Article 5.

38. Articles 6 and 7. It should be noted that this particular section attracted a number of reservations of AU member states. Marriage age, marriage register, child's right to mother's nationality, inheritance and health and reproductive rights were some of the areas that attracted reservations.

39. Ibid., articles 8–21.

40. Articles 22, 23, 24.

41. Article 12.

42. Article 12.

43. Article 7 (d)

44. Article 21.

45. United Nations Population Division, International Migration Report 2002, cited African Union, "Draft Migration Policy Framework for Africa," Document EX.CL/176/(VII) June 2005. p. 3. See also The Demographical Impact of Migration: Evidence, Report of the UN Expert Group meeting 3 December 2012, available at www.un.org/migrationtrends2012/

46. Ibid., p. 3

47. For more on this, see African Union, "Draft Migration Policy Framework", pp. 4–7.

48. Article 71 (e) of the Treaty Establishing the African Economic Community.

49. Decision No. CM/Dec614 (LXXIV)

50. See African Union, "Draft Migration Policy Framework."

51. African Union, *The State of the African Population 2006* (Addis Ababa, 2006).

52. African Union, *Review of the Millennium Declaration and Millennium Development Goals (MDGs): An African Common Position* Doc. EX.CL/181 (VII), June 2005.

53. This consensus found expression in a number of international gatherings including the International Conference on Population and Development (ICPD) in Cairo in 1994, The Earth Summit in Rio De Janero in 1991, the Children Summit in New York in 1991, The Fourth World Conference on Women in Beijing in 1995, The Social Summit in Copenhagen in 1995, the Habitat Summit in New York in 2000.

54. African Union, Report of the 5th Ordinary Session of the African Populations Commission (APC) Document EX.CL/ 187 (VII) June 2005.

55. See Omar Alieu Touray, "Final Review Report on the Implementation of the African Union Commission Strategic Plan 2009–2012" (Addis Ababa, AUC 2012) p. 11.

56. Botswana, Rwanda, and Zambia. See WHO, *State of Health Spending in Africa*, January 2013, available at www.afro.who.int/.../8698-state-of-health-financing-in-the-african-region. html.

57. The countries are Burkina Faso, Ethiopia, Malawi and Mali; see Shenggen Fan, Tewodaj Mogues, and Sam Benin "Setting Priorities for Public Spending for Agricultural and Rural Development in Africa" *IPFRI Policy Brief No.12 April 2009;* available at http://www.ifpri.org/sites/default/files/publications/bp012.pdf

Chapter 7

"An Agenda for Peace"[1]

The Theory and Practice of Collective Security in Africa

An argument I advanced at the beginning of this study was that the African Union and the OAU were aggregates of national interests and constituted rational means of advancing national preferences in the face of limited individual capacity. The manner in which the union pursued its political, social and economic preferences has been covered in the preceding chapters. This chapter extends my examination of the AU's preferences by looking at the peace and security agenda of the continent.

A cursory review of African politics during the period under consideration reveals that there is hardly any area that has attracted the African Union's attention more than peace and security. Between 2004 and 2012, the Union's Peace and Security Council (PSC) met 349 times, and the Central Organ, the body that the PSC replaced, had met 96 times at ambassadorial level between 1993 and 2003.[2] The frequency of the consultations illustrates the importance of consensus on peace and security matters. In addition, the bulk of the international financial and other forms of support that the AU received during 2002–2012 went to peace and security.[3] Policy makers alone did not show interest in peace and security issues; the civil society community too showed their preoccupation in various instances. The bulky literature on the subject is also indicative of both the interest of the academic community and of the centrality of security issues in the academic discourse on the African Union.

Such generalized interest in security issues offers sufficient justification for an undertaking like the present study, and also strengthens my argument that peace and security constituted a major objective of the African Union. It will be shown that although collective security was a long-standing preoccupation, it was taken more seriously only in the aftermath of the Cold War. But even then, the collective approach to peace and security brought to the fore a major agency problem: limited autonomy, as epitomized by limited financial capability, and other constraints that the AU faced. The result was that the implementation of the continental peace and security agenda suffered from "ambition–capacity gap": a disjuncture between what the AU wanted to do and what capacity it had to implement.

This chapter is divided into three parts. The first part looks at the legal and institutional frameworks that underpin the union's peace and security agenda. The second part looks at the practical operationalization of the peace and security frameworks on the ground. It shows that despite the multiplicity of arrangements and frameworks, the AU's peace and security agenda can be reduced to two main components: (a) *conflict prevention / preventive diplomacy* and (b) *peacekeeping*. The third part offers an overview of the key factors that affected the implementation of the union's peace agenda.

THE INSTITUTIONAL AND LEGAL FRAMEWORKS OF AFRICA'S PEACE AND SECURITY AGENDA

Collective defence and security has been a long-standing preference of African leaders. Although few of them supported President Nkrumah's proposal for a common defence system with a single military High Command,[4] all African leaders remained preoccupied with collective defence and security. The multitude of bilateral, regional and sub regional defence and security arrangements that dot the political landscape of the continent are a strong testimony of that preoccupation.[5] The raison d'être of the OAU itself was not least based on collective defence and security exigency, as the organization was looked upon to offer a platform on which African leaders , inter alia, could together settle inter-African disputes, promote common defence as well as undertake economic and social programmes.[6] However, the ideological differences of the post-independence leaders allowed neither a supranational organization nor a stronger defence structure, such as the one suggested by Nkrumah. Instead, a loose entity, the Commission on Mediation, Conciliation and Arbitration, was created to serve as the peace and security organ of the organization. Composed of 21 legal professionals, the quasi-legal body was still-born. Its mandate was limited to interstate conflicts and few such conflicts were referred to it. Moreover, it lacked the necessary financial resources, as member states failed to pay their contribution to its budget.[7] Attempts to revive it in the mid-1970s failed largely because member states showed little interest in it. Instead, disputes were referred to ad hoc dispute settlement committees, composed of heads of state or ministers. The first such body was constituted as early as 1963 to mediate in the Algerian–Moroccan dispute. Similar bodies were created to grapple with the Somalia–Ethiopia dispute,

Rwanda–Burundi dispute, the dispute between Angolan warring factions, the Congo crises and the Nigerian civil war. Despite its weaknesses, the OAU ad hoc arrangements managed to contain disputes between member states. Most of the border disputes, as those between Nigeria and Cameroon, Tanzania and Malawi, Burkina Faso and Mali, were either settled without force or kept simmering at a non-violent level through OAU diplomacy.[8] Even where border conflicts escalated to armed hostilities (as between Algeria and Morocco over their Saharan frontiers or between Ethiopia and Somalia over Ogaden), the OAU mediation brought about quick ceasefire.[9]

It was civil wars that tested the organization's conflict resolution capacity most. According to the United Nations, in 1996 alone 14 of Africa's 53 states were involved in internal armed conflicts resulting in the death or displacement of some eight million people.[10] At the heart of the OAU policy on civil wars was the principle of non-interference in the domestic affairs of member states[11]. This principle was criticized for being used as an excuse for inaction. Where the organization got involved in internal affairs of a country, support was automatically given to a member government.[12] As a result, the organization was incapable of acting as a credible disinterested mediator in the internal conflicts of member states. Furthermore, the dearth of resources and uncertain legal and institutional framework impeded the organization's experiment with peacekeeping in places such as Chad and Zaire.

These limitations, and the escalation of violent conflicts across the continent, with their attendant implications for the regions, brought about a reappraisal of security and national sovereignty. By the early 1990s, the principle of non-interference was discarded and the concept of security broadened to include not just state security, but also human security.[13]

It was within this context that the Assembly adopted at its 29th Session in Cairo in 1993 *the Declaration on the Establishment, within the OAU, of a Mechanism for Conflict Resolution, Management and Resolution.*[14] The objective of the Declaration, was to bring a new institutional dynamism to the process of dealing with conflict on the continent, by anticipating, preventing and resolving them.[15] Both civilian and military observation missions to conflict zones were provided for. The overall direction and coordination of the activities of the Mechanism were entrusted to a 19-member Central Organ, composed of members of the Bureau of the Assembly, who were elected annually. The outgoing and the incoming chairpersons of the Assembly were also ex-officio members. The Central Organ operated at the levels of the Assembly, the Council of Ministers and the Permanent Representatives' Committee. A special fund was created and benefited from appropriations from the OAU regular budget and donations from member states and members of the international community. By March 2002, the resources of the Fund stood at US$42 million.[16]

A scourge that brought about a heightened sense of insecurity in Africa was international terrorism. The continent suffered from international terrorism long before the terrorist bombings of the twin towers of the World Trade Centre in New York on 11 September 2001. Algeria and Egypt stood out in this respect, but several sub-Saharan African countries, too, suffered from incidents such as the bombing of UTA flight over Niger in September 1989, the simultaneous bombing of US embassies in Dar es Salaam and Nairobi. It was in response to these threats that African leaders adopted at their 35th Ordinary Session in Algiers in July 1999 the OAU Convention on the prevention and Combating of Terrorism. The convention sought to combat and eliminate terrorism and organized crimes by strengthening cooperation among member states. It came into force in December 2002, following the ratification by 15 countries. An Inter-Governmental High Level meeting on the Prevention and Combating of Terrorism in Africa was convened in Algiers from 11 to 14 September 2002, and adopted a plan of action and recommendation for the implementation of the Convention. An additional protocol was drafted to complement the Algiers Convention. It highlighted modalities for preventing terrorists from using sophisticated technology and communication systems, as well as weapons of mass destruction.

Several other initiatives were taken to address security challenges on the continent. These include the Bamako Convention on the Ban of the Import into Africa and the Control of Trans-boundary Movement and Management of Hazardous Wastes within Africa; The Bamako Declaration on an African Common Position on the Illicit Proliferation, Circulation and Trafficking of Small Arms and Light Weapons; The Kempton Park Plan of Action on Land Mine-Free Africa 1997; Declaration and Plan of Action on Drug Control and Illicit Trafficking in Africa, 1996; Convention for the Elimination of Mercenarism in Africa, 1977; the African Nuclear Weapons Free Zone Treaty (ANWFZT) commonly known as the Pelindaba Treaty, 1998.

Parallel to the OAU initiatives was the Conference on Security, Stability, Development and Cooperation in Africa (CSSDCA), which was spearheaded by President Olusegun Obasanjo, then a civil society leader. In essence, CSSDCA sought to complement the OAU Mechanism in coordinating, harmonizing, and promoting peace and security efforts of the Union.[17]

At the sub-regional level, several initiatives were also put in place to compliment efforts at the continental level.[18] These include the ECOWAS Conflict Prevention Framework, the Protocol on Politics, Defence and Security Cooperation of the Southern African Development Community (SADC), East African Community's Protocol on Peace and Security as well as Conflict Prevention, Management and Resolution Mechanism (CPMR), The Protocol establishing the Council for Peace and Security in Central Africa (COPAX).[19]

Although they did not always lead to the desired results, the multiplicity of regional security arrangements shows that African leaders were alive to the debilitating effects of conflicts and to the need to find regional solutions to regional problems. Together with the OAU Mechanism and the CSSDCA, the regional initiatives constituted the building block of the new pan-African defence and security policy. They directly spurred African leaders to institutionalize common defence and security issues by making relevant provisions in the Constitutive Act and by taking the necessary measures to operationalize them. Two such measures stood out.

The first was the Assembly's decision[20] to incorporate the Central Organ of the Mechanism for Conflict Prevention, Management and Resolution as one of the organs of the African Union in accordance with the provisions of the Constitutive Act.[21] Under the terms of the decision, the Secretary General of the OAU was mandated to undertake a review of the structures, procedures and methods of the Central Organ, including the possibility of changing its name.

The Second was a direct call by the Assembly during the inaugural session of the AU in Durban in July 2002 to operationalize the provisions of the Constitutive Act regarding the Common Defence and Security Policy of African Union.[22] In this regard, the Assembly requested President Thabo Mbeki of South Africa, in his capacity as Chairperson of the Union, to convene an expert meeting to draw up the documentation on the proposed common African defence and security policy. Therefore, one of the main activities of the African Union during the first year of operation was the execution of that mandate.

Although intrinsically peripheral to Africa, the American-led war in Iraq, too, gave greater urgency to the operationalization of the common defence and security arrangement for Africa. It was felt, particularly by the South African Presidency of the Union, that Africa's aspiration for greater multilateralism and a collective response to global problems was being frustrated by the decision to go to war without the mandate of the United Nations. For the Foreign Minister of South Africa, "It can't be right to have one country, whichever country it may be, on issues that affect all of us, wanting to act alone. . . . We do not think it is time to go to war."[23] By implication, the decision to go to war threatened the credibility of the United Nation and, by extension, multilateralism.[24] It also meant that multilateral institutions such as the United Nations could no longer guarantee world peace and that states would have to depend on alternative arrangements such as regional defence alliances for their security. This is why it was felt that weak states such as African countries could face future peace and security challenges only through common and joint initiatives. This accounts for the various processes, instruments and organs that the African Union put in place.[25] These include *the Common African Defence and Security Policy*, the *African Union Peace and Security Architecture*; and the programmes on Post Conflict Reconstruction and Development (PCRD).

THE COMMON AFRICAN DEFENCE AND SECURITY POLICY

The Common African Defence and Security policy was a common understanding among African states about their defence and security challenges and a set of measures they sought to take collectively to respond to those challenges.[26] The Policy was built on a set of notions, principles, objectives and instruments, which both defined it and at the same time constitute its substance.

Notions

Underlying the Common African Defence and Security Policy are the three notions of *defence, security* and *common threats.* The importance of a common understanding of these key concepts to the smooth implementation of the Policy accounts for the attention that member states gave to their definition. In the context of the African Union, therefore, *Defence* was defined broadly to encompass the traditional use by a state and/or any competent public authority of the legally constituted armed forces to protect its national sovereignty and territorial integrity, as well as the less traditional, non-military modes of protecting people's political, cultural, social and economic rights, values and ways of life.[27] Similarly, *Security* was defined as the act and the process of protecting individuals, families, communities as well as their economic, political and social activities.[28] The notion of *common threats* was extrapolated from these broad definitions of defence and security, and hingesd firmly on the principle that the security of each African country was inextricably linked to security of other African countries and the African continent as a whole.[29] Generally, common security threats were threats to one or more member states of the Union, and were grouped under two broad categories: threats that emanated from within the continent and those that were from outside.

Listed among the common internal threats to the continent were inter-state conflicts including situations that threaten national sovereignty and territorial integrity, as well as intrastate conflicts including war crimes, genocide and crime against humanity. Unsettled post-conflict situations, armaments, diseases, and various other crimes all constituted internal threats under the terms of the Common African Defence and Security Policy.[30]

Common external comprised include external aggression against an African country and international conflicts and crises with adverse effects on African regional security. External threats also include terrorism, weapons of mass destruction, narcotic trade as well as the adverse effects of globalization and international trade regimes.

Objectives

The objectives of the Common African Defence and Security Policy were essentially to respond to both internal and external threats effectively. In particular, they were to enhance defence cooperation between and among African states, eliminate suspicion and rivalry between them, enhance the collective defence and strategic capability as well as military preparedness of member states of the Union; facilitate the establishment of a threat deterrence capacity within the AU, integrate and harmonize regional initiatives on defence and security issues; and encourage the conclusion and ratification of non-aggression pacts between and among AU member states.

Principles

These objectives were to be pursued on the basis of various principles. Key among these is the principle of the indivisibility of the security of African countries. Accordingly, any threat, or aggression[31] on one African country was deemed to be a threat or aggression on the others and the continent as a whole. If not a replica of NATO's Article V, the principle certainly drew inspiration from the Alliance's doctrine, which states that an attack on one NATO member will lead to mobilization of the whole Alliance. Sovereign equality and interdependence of African States; respect for colonial borders and peaceful resolution of conflict, and most importantly, the right of the African Union to intervene in any member state in the event of war crimes, genocide and crime against humanity in order to restore peace and stability, were all principles on which the Policy rests.[32]

THE AFRICAN PEACE AND SECURITY ARCHITECTURE

The African Union established the African Peace and Security Architecture (APSA) as a framework for crisis management on the African continent. It was composed of mechanisms such as the Peace and Security Council (PSC), early warning systems of both the AU and the regional economic communities (RECs), Panel of the Wise, the African Standby Force(ASF) and the peace support missions. By the end of the 2011, most of the components of the APSA were operational.

The Peace and Security Council

In general, African countries are themselves responsible for the promotion of the peace and security on the continent. National policies must comply with the principles and objectives of the AU regimes, and actions that contravene its terms are to be treated as potential threats by the entire AU membership. But the immediate responsibility for peace and security lies exclusively with the Peace and Security Council of the African Union. An offshoot of the Central Organ, the PSC was created by the *Protocol Relating to the Establishment of the Peace and Security Council of the African Union*.[33]

The objectives of the PSC, as spelt out in the protocol, include the promotion of peace, security and stability by anticipating and preventing conflict. Where a conflict broke out, the PSC would embark on peace-making and peace-building exercise through mediation, consultation and dialogue. To enable it to carry out its mandate, the PSC was given extensive powers. Besides the promotion of peace and security on the continent, the PSC had the authority to mount and deploy peace support missions, and lay down guidelines for the conduct of such missions.[34] It also had the powers to recommend to the Assembly intervention in member states in pursuance of the provisions of the Constitutive Act regarding war crimes, genocide and crimes against humanity.[35] Furthermore, the PSC imposed sanctions whenever an unconstitutional change of government took place in a member state.[36] Within the framework of its conflict prevention mandate, the PSC was mandated to monitor progress on the continent on matters relating to human rights, democracy, good governance and rule of law.[37] Similarly, it had the authority to take action whenever a member state's sovereignty and independence were being threatened by acts of aggression, including mercenaries.[38]

The Council was composed of 15 members, five of whom were elected for a period of three years, while the remaining ten served for two years. While the terms were renewable, it was felt that the differentiated terms would guarantee a degree of continuity.[39] Membership of the PSC was based on the principle of equitable geographical representation and rotation. And unlike the Security Council of the United Nations, the PSC had no permanent members; neither did any member have a veto power. By 2010, 35 countries had already served on the PSC, with Nigeria being the sole country to have sat on the council since it was established in 2004.

The body operates continuously at the levels of Heads of State and Government, Ministers and Permanent Representatives (Ambassadors) accredited to the African Union. The chairmanship was held in rotation by each member for one month,[40] and decisions were taken by consensus, failing which by voting. Simple majority was required for procedural matters, while a two-thirds majority of members present and voting was required for all other matters.[41] The PSC convened an average of five times per month and by September 2011 had held nearly 300 meetings.

Early Warning Mechanism of the African Union and Regional Economic Communities

One of the lessons that the international community in general and Africa in particular had drawn from the Rwandan genocide was the importance of timely information and the ability to act on that information. The failure of the United Nations and the international community to wake up to the warnings that the field officers were emitting led to what the whole world today recognizes as being a genocide. The effectiveness of Africa's collective security arrangement was therefore dependent to a large extent on the capacity to collect, process and act on information. For this reason, member states deemed it vital to set up a continental early warning mechanism that would collect and analyse data on the basis of "an appropriate early warning indicators mode."[42]

The Panel of the Wise

The Panel of the Wise was established in accordance with the Protocol Relating to the Establishment of the Peace and Security Council of the African Union, and was composed of five distinguished African personalities who had contributed to the cause of peace, security and development on the continent.[43] Members of the panel were chosen according to the principle of equitable regional representation. Their mandate was advisory, mainly in the areas of peace and security, although they had the authority to take actions deemed appropriate to support the PSC and the Chairperson of the Commission in their efforts to prevent conflict. Members could pronounce themselves on issues relating to the promotion and maintenance of peace and security.[44] They were appointed by the Assembly on the recommendation of the Chairperson of the Commission, and served for a period of three years. They were remunerated in accordance with the financial rules and regulations of the Union.[45] The first Panel was appointed in December 2007 and composed of Ahmed Ben Bella of Algeria, who served as chair, Salim Ahmed Salim of Tanzania, Elisabeth K. Pognon of Benin, Miguel Trovoada of Sao Tome and Principe, and Brigalia Bam of South Africa. At the July 2010 Summit in Kampala, Ben Bella and Ahmed Salim were reappointed for another term ending in December 2013 and three new members were appointed: Mary Chinery Hesse of Ghana; Kenneth Kaunda of Zambia; and Marie Madeleine Kalala-Ngoy of the Democratic Republic of the Congo.[46] In addition to undertaking preventive diplomacy, the Panel also addressed electoral related violence and similar crises in Guinea, Guinea Bissau, Madagascar and Zimbabwe. They also addressed impunity, justice and reconciliation issues and the situation of women and children in armed conflict.[47]

African Standby Force

Perhaps the most important and effective elements of the APSA is the military capability of the Union. The Protocol Relating to the Establishment for the Peace and Security Council and the Policy Framework on a Common African Defence and Security Policy constitute the legal framework for such capability[48]. But as we shall see, the military capability was also the Council's liability.[49] The Standby Force, which represented the core military capability of the Union, was composed of civilian, police and military components located in their countries of origin and ready for rapid deployment at appropriate notice. The ASF was to operate in various areas, carry out observation and monitoring missions and other types of peace support operations as well as intervene in a members state in the event of grave circumstances such as genocide, war crime and crime against humanity.

The operationalization of the Africa Standby Force was the subject of extensive debate among military experts and policy makers. The road map was initially charted by a group of consultants, including UN experts. Their output was a document entitled the "Concept Paper on The African Standby Force and the Military Staff Committee, Parts I and II," which was subjected to debate at various fora. These consultations resulted in the final *Policy Framework on the Establishment of the African Standby Force and the Military Staff Committee*. The trust of the recommendation was that the ASF would be based on brigades to be provided by the five regions of the continent: East, West, North, Southern and Central. It was to operate on the following six mission scenarios under the mandate of the African Union.

a. Scenario 1: AU/Regional military advice to a political mission;
b. Scenario 2: AU/Regional observer mission co-deployed with UN mission;
c. Scenario 3: Stand-alone AU/Regional observer Mission;
d. Scenario 4: AU/Regional peacekeeping force for Chapter VI and preventive deployment Missions;
e. Scenario 5: AU peacekeeping force for complex multidimensional peacekeeping missions;
f. Scenario 6: AU military intervention in circumstances such as genocide where the international community fails to act promptly.[50]

The ASF was to be established in two phases: phase 1 running up to mid-2005 and phase 2 ending mid-2010. During which phase I, the Commission of the African Union would develop its capacity to manage Scenarios 1, 2 and 3, while the regions would assemble standby brigade groups, each of which would include a small full-time Planning Element (PLANELM).The regions were also expected to develop capacity to respond to the requirements of scenario 4.[51] During phase II, the Commission was expected to develop its own capacity to manage scenario 5, while the regions were expected to increase their rapid deployment capability.

With regard to the deployment of the ASF, the following recommendations were made: (1) simpler missions should be able to deploy in 30 days; (2) complex missions should be able to complete deployment in 90 days, with the military component being able to deploy in 30 days; and (3) depending on the nature of the situations demanding intervention, it will be important that the AU could eventually deploy a robust military force within 14 days.

To facilitate the management of the military dossier, the Protocol provides for the establishment of the Military Staff Committee as an advisory body to the PSC in all questions relating to the military and security requirements for the promotion and maintenance of peace and security on the continent.[52] It was composed of senior military officers of the members of the PSC, and met at the level of chiefs of defence staff.

Member states were to provide the troops constituting the ASF, while the different RECs were required to provide training for regional brigades. By 2012, the degree of advancement of this process differed sharply from region to region reflecting the discrepancies in the strengths and features of military capabilities between the different member states and RECs. The differences between the individual RECs in the level of advancement of their standby capacity as well as between them and the AU led to a situation where some of them tended towards working via their regional arrangement.

While the ASF was still a number of years away from being operational, the African Union Commission reported some progress during the period under consideration. This included the development of a number of mechanisms such as the ASF Training Plan and strategic Lift Capacity. Support from the United Nations and the European Union also enabled the AU to undertake in October 2010 a simulation exercise labelled "Amani Africa" meant to test the preparedness of the ASF for an AU-led peace mission. The exercise held in two separate locations in Addis Ababa provided opportunities for stock-taking. Lessons learnt were shared in several instances, including during a workshop on Amani Africa held in Dakar, Senegal in February 2011, which, among other things considered the ASF operational road map.[53]

The catalogue of AU legal and institutional frameworks of peace and security arrangements will not be complete without citing instruments dealing with small arms and light weapons (SALW), the security of civilians during peace support operations and maritime security. Although up to 2012, the AU Commission reported on these outside the framework of the APSA, they constitute and integral part of the peace agenda of the continent and must therefore be mentioned even in a cursory manner, because their development is not sufficient to warrant any detailed analysis.

It suffices therefore to indicate that the AU programme on SALW was developed with the initial support of the European Union to fight against the "illicit accumulation and trafficking of firearms in Africa", by raising awareness and knowledge of relevant stakeholders. A steering committee was charged with the management of the programme and worked closely with the Regional Centre on Small Arms in the Great Lakes Region and the Horn of Africa and Bordering States (RECSA).

Regarding the protection of civilians in peace operations, various activities were undertaken, and resulted in the development of the African Union Draft Guidelines for the Protection of Civilians in Peace Support Missions. The overall objective of the guidelines was to serve as a framework for the protection of civilians in coordination with the host country and the local community.

Adopted in Banjul in 2006, the programme on post-conflict reconstruction and development (PCRD) comprised security sector reform as provided for by a decision of the Council in June 2008. However, up to 2012, the AU Policy on Security Sector Reform remained in draft form, despite the fact that the draft policy was discussed at various levels including the UN Security Sector Reform Unit and the Forum on African Perspective on Security Sector Reform.

Existing evidence shows that the African Union was also alive to the challenges that piracy, illegal fishing and illegal dumping of toxic waste posed to maritime security of the continent. Key instruments in this area include Durban Declaration on Maritime Safety, Maritime Security and Protection of the Marin Environment and the Plan of Action on Maritime Transport. There was also the Contact Group on piracy off the coast of Somalia, which the Union set up.

The preceding pages show that there was no shortage of legal and institutional frameworks for the peace and security agenda of the African Union. It is clear however that adopting legal instruments was easier than their practical implementation. Treaties adopted would take on average a decade to enter into force. For example, the African Nuclear Weapon Free Zone Treaty (Pelindaba Treaty), which was signed in 1996, came into force only in 2010, 15 years after it was concluded. As we shall see, when they entered into force they faced other sets of challenges including implementation difficulties, dwindling finances and acute human resource constraints.

THE AU'S PEACE AND SECURITY AGENDA IN PRACTICE

The former Secretary General of United Nations, Kofi Annan, once advised Africans to speak with one voice for the world to listen. "If Africa speaks with a cacophony of confused messages," Annan warned, "few will listen, and none will hear."[54] In my view the various frameworks outlined above constitute Africa's response to Annan's message. In many respect, they represented the determination of the African leaders to take charge of the peace and security agenda of the continent, even though the reality on the ground may suggest differently.

From an analytical perspective, the multiplicity of the frameworks relating to peace and security constitutes a source of confusion. Not only do many of these frameworks have similar scope; their implementation modalities overlap. However, a closer examination will reveal that despite the multiple frameworks, the peace and security agenda of the African Union has only two key components: Conflict Prevention/preventive diplomacy and peacekeeping.

Conflict Prevention and Preventive Diplomacy

Conventionally, conflict prevention refers to processes and activities undertaken to avert crises from escalating to conflicts. However, in his "*Agenda for Peace*," the UN Secretary General Boutros Boutros-Ghali linked conflict prevention to preventive diplomacy, which he defined as "actions to prevent disputes from arising between parties, to prevent existing disputes from escalating, and to limit the spread of the latter when they occur."[55] Dr. Ghali's successor, Kofi Annan, broadened the definition of conflict prevention to cover addressing the structural causes of conflict such as poverty, inequality, and weak governance institutions.[56] While I recognize the validity of a broader definition, I are mindful of the pitfalls of such an approach as just about every other undertaking becomes conflict prevention.[57] The present study therefore adopts a narrower definition of preventive diplomacy as actions that seek to prevent conflicts from happening and to contain and resolve them when they breakout.

Of the various conflicts that broke out in post-independence Africa, few were between states. Between 1960 and 2010, there had been only two interstate wars that rose above the minimum magnitude: the 1978–1979 invasion of Uganda by Tanzanian troops that ousted the Idi Amin regime in Uganda (magnitude 2) and the war between Ethiopia and Eritrea from 1998 to 2000 (magnitude 5).[58] It was internal conflict that accounted for the bulk of the conflicts on the continent, and that were the focus of conflict prevention of the AU and the OAU before it.

By their very nature, internal conflicts are complex and difficult to manage. They invariably involve governments as one of the parties, and most often an insurgency that is armed, secretive, inexperienced in negotiations, with no clear line of authority, and unfamiliar with the norms of international behaviour including international law. This, as Kaplan asserts, makes preventive diplomacy, even though an excellent idea, difficult to carry out in internal conflicts.[59]

The preventive diplomatic efforts of the African Union must be seen against this background. Over the years, the preventive initiatives took several forms including the deployment of special representatives and envoys, mediators, fact-finding missions and election observation missions, international contact groups (ICG) and high-level panels (HLP). Such measures were taken in Kenya in 2007–2008, Madagascar in 2007–2008, Zimbabwe in 2008, Cote D'Ivoire in 2010–2011, Egypt after the fall of Mubarak in 2011, and in South Sudan in 2013.

A review of AU's preventive diplomacy in these countries reveals mixed results. The Union's interventions in Kenya and Madagascar were deemed to be successful, while its efforts in Zimbabwe, Cote D'Ivoire, Egypt and South Sudan were less effective.

In Kenya, the violence that followed the elections in Kenya did not only shock the world, it threatened to reach a level of "crimes against humanity."[60] Supported by the United Nations, Kenya's neighbours, key donors and civil society, the AU embarked upon preventive diplomacy by deploying respected personalities such as Bishop Desmond Tutu and President John Kufour of Ghana as peace makers. Although the intervention of Bishop Tutu and President Kufour had limited impact, it paved the way for the deployment of the Panel of Eminent Africans, under the leadership of Kofi Annan, former Secretary General of the United Nations. Annan's panel arrived in Nairobi in January 2008 and within 40 days was able to reach a breakthrough that human rights observers called a "model diplomatic action under the responsibility to protect principle."[61]

Similarly, AU's role in Madagascar (2009–2013) received a lot of credit. In 2009, a military coup removed Marc Ravalomanana as president of

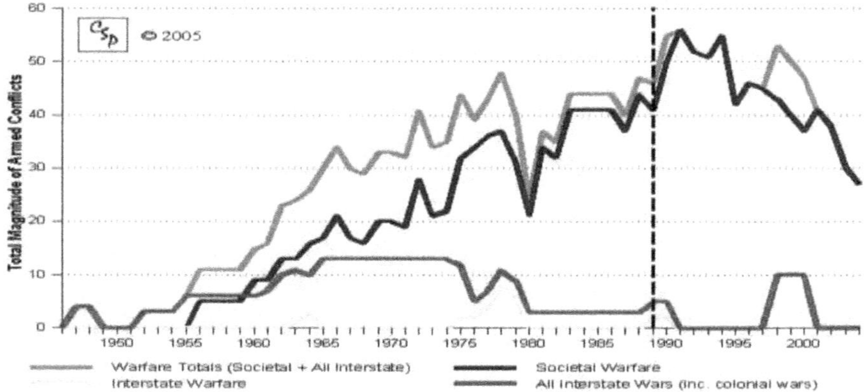

Figure 7.1 Trends in Armed Conflict in Africa, 1946–2004. *Source*: Marc Malan, "Conflict Prevention in Africa."

Madagascar and Andry Rajoelina, untill then mayor of Antananarivo, became president of the "High Authority of the Transition." The AU Peace and Security Council, SADC and COMESA suspend Madagascar's and together with the Organisation Internationale de la Francophonie (OIF), the permanent members of the UN Security Council, the EU, and other interested governments formed an International Contact Group on Madagascar (ICG-M) and jointly pressured the parties to resolve the political crisis.[62] Although it took another three years for elections to be held, AU's intervention was credited for the resolution of the political crises that resulted in the election of Hery Rajaonarimampianina as President of the country in 2014.

Unlike in Kenya and Madagascar, AU's preventive diplomacy in Zimbabwe, Cote D'Ivoire, Egypt and South Sudan was more symbolic than decisive. In Zimbabwe, AU's mediation in the political crises, through the Southern Africa Development Community (SADC), led to a power-sharing government, where President Robert Mugabe maintained the presidency, while Tzangirai became the Prime Minister. Indeed the power-sharing arrangement helped calm the situation temporarily but did not wholly resolve the political crises, as the power-sharing deal collapsed in 2013. In Cote D'Ivoire, and to some extent in Mali, the Union's diplomacy only legitimized processes that ECOWAS and France had initiated. The Ivoirien crises ended when the French-backed forces stormed the presidential palace in Abidjan and arrested Laurent Gbagbo. The violence in the North of Mali was also brought under control by a French military intervention. The impact of the AU high-level panel on the Egyptian political crises 2011–2013 has yet to be fully established. What is clear however is that the crises presented the African Union itself with more challenges. As the AU panel admitted, General Abdel Fattah Sisi's emergence as Egypt's elected president, "who was the head of the army and minister of defence at the time of the unconstitutional change of government, poses a serious challenge to the AU." This was due to the AU rule banning authors of unconstitutional change of governmental from participating in elections held for restoring constitutional rule.[63]

A number of considerations explain the successful outcome of AU's preventive diplomacy in Kenya and Madagascar. First there was the personality factor. Accordingly, Kofi Annan's personality played a crucial role in the resolution of the crises in Kenya. Annan's appointment gave the Kenyan crises a unique international stature, and engendered considerable international pressure for a successful outcome of the negotiations.[64] Second, regional and local players were crowed out in a way that minimized competing negotiation processes and gave Annan's team the opportunity to focus on a single mediation process. Third, Annan was also able to manage an intricate balance between international pressure and the local protagonists' own recognition of the need to accommodate each other. Thus, Annan and party were able to use the international attention on Kenya's instability and the desire of the parties to accommodate each other to broker a peace agreement with which all parties felt comfortable.[65] Flexibility and willingness to accommodate local realities also account for the success of AU's preventive diplomacy in Madagascar.

While AU and SADC jointly condemned the Malagasy coup that brought Rojalina to power, the two organizations differed on how to resolve the crises. As the main regional body, SADC did not only condemn the coup, it also called for an unconditional reinstatement of Ravalomanana and threatened to use force to achieve that objective. Despite having a strong anti-coup framework in place, the African Union adopted a softer position as the army in Madagascar threatened to resist any regional attempt to replace Rajolina as the head of the transitional government, or to reinstate Ravalomana by force. For the African Union, the short-term priority was to prevent a slide into civil war and forge a smooth transition to constitutional normalcy through credible elections. It was not until 2011 when SADC rallied around AU position that sought to build peace on the basis of the local de facto realities. Thus in June 2011, SADC leaders approved the roadmap for ending the crises in Madagascar, which envisaged the formation of an inclusive transitional government and the holding of elections under the UN supervision. SADC also agreed to the "ni-ni" solution that barred both Rajolina and Ravalomanan from running for election.[66] Although it took several months for Madagascar to have a new president, it was clear that the negotiations were successful partly due to the negotiators recognition of the local realities.

Clearly the Kenyan and Madagascar cases show that preventive diplomacy of the African Union had a lot of potential. However, AU's record in other crises shows that the Union had a lot of challenges to address not only with respect to preventive diplomacy, but also in peacekeeping, which constituted the second operational component of the African peace and security agenda.

PeaceKeeping

Besides preventive diplomacy, a major option given to the AU within the context of its peace and security mandate is military intervention to keep the peace.[67] Since the adoption in Cairo in 1993 of the *Declaration on the Establishment, within the OAU, of a Mechanism for Conflict Management and Resolution*, the OAU undertook a number of peace-making missions. The OAU deployed military observer missions in Rwanda (1991–1993), Burundi (1993–1996), the Comoros (1998–2002), the Democratic Republic of the Congo (1999–2000) and Eritrea and Ethiopia (2000–2008). Between 2002 and 2012, the African Union undertook 9 peace support operations that ranged from small operations to complex large-scale peacekeeping operations such as those in Darfur and Somalia.[68]

A number of studies have assessed AU's performance on the peacekeeping front.[69] It will therefore be beyond the scope of the present chapter to provide a detailed assessment of the Union's balance sheet. My objective is limited solely to providing an overview of AU's peace support operations in Burundi, Darfur and Somalia. It will be shown that although there was indeed a strong appetite for peacekeeping operations, the Union's capacity to maintain such operations remained weak. AU peace support operations were either transitioned into United Nations operations or became totally dependent on the United Nations and other partners for funding. Thus in as much as AU's efforts need to be celebrated, it should be recognized that the Union's strength lay in its ability to initiate operation, rather than in sustaining them.

African Union Mission in Burundi

The African Union Mission in Burundi (AMIB) was deployed in 2003 during the Burundi Civil War.[70] It consisted of 2,870 troops mainly from South Africa, Mozambique and Ethiopia. Throughout its operations in Burundi, AMIB had four main tasks: supervise the implementation of the ceasefire agreements that the conflicting parties had agreed on in Arusha in 2003, support disarmament and demobilization initiatives and advise on the reintegration of combatants; create favourable conditions for the presence of a UN peacekeeping mission; contribute to political and economic stability in Burundi. In all four areas, the African Union registered success. The mission was credited for the stabilization of about 95 per cent of the country, and for overseeing the implementation of the ceasefire agreements. AMIB was also able to facilitate the delivery of humanitarian assistance, and provide protection to the designated returning leaders. Within a year, a UN evaluation team concluded that conditions were appropriate for the establishment of UN peacekeeping operations in the country. AMIB was transitioned into the United Nations Peace Keeping Mission in Burundi (ONUB) in June 2004 partly because the conditions were appropriate for the United Nations to take over operations, but also because the AU would not be able to sustain the operations, which was already facing funding difficulties.

For example, the budget for the deployment, operations and sustainment of AMIB was estimated at about US $110 million for the first year. Without adequate funds in its peace fund, the AU had to rely on traditional partners for funding. However, contribution from partners only amounted to US $50 million, and actual donations into the trust fund amounted to just US $10 million, although there were in-kind assistance from the US (US $6.1 million) and UK (US $6 million), to support the deployment of the Ethiopian and Mozambican contingents respectively.[71] With limited resources, the AU had no option other than transferring the mission to the United Nations.

African Union Mission in Sudan (AMIS)

The decision to deploy a peace support mission to Sudan's western region of Darfur was taken in 2004, after several years of conflict that pitched nomadic Arab tribes against the Fur, Maqssaleet and Zagawa tribes. The conflict had claimed thousands of lives[72]

Within a year of AMIS deployment, normal life returned to southern Darfur and witnesses on the ground reported "the effectiveness of African Union peace monitoring troops in the areas where they are operating in Sudan's war-torn region of Darfur."[73] But AU's lack of capacity to sustain the mission and the indifference of the international community was soon to erode the initial gains AMIS was able to realize. AMIS could not deploy in large numbers and therefore could not provide security to all the communities. What is more, the Darfur Peace Accord (DPA), which the AU brokered in May 2006 was short-lived because apart from the Government of Sudan and one rebel movement, most of the rebel movements failed to endorse it. Subsequent peace talks such as those convened in Tripoli in October 2007 also failed.

The international community did not only provide inadequate support, it also passed the responsibility for maintain peace in Darfur to the African Union. This, as Susan Rice, former US Ambassador to the UN, was to admit, was inappropriate. According to Rice,

> The sum of this policy is to pass the military buck to the African Union. The AU guards this buck jealously and has done its best on the ground in Darfur. But the unfortunate truth is this: the African Union's best is not yet enough. Where it has deployed, the AU has performed heroically and greatly increased security for civilians. But the AU force is critically undermanned and has an impossibly weak mandate, limited to monitoring rather than enforcing the nonexistent ceasefire and protecting only those people facing an imminent threat within the force's immediate vicinity.[74]

The limitations of AMIS led to the replacement of AMIS with a joint AU-UN peacekeeping force, the United Nations African Union Mission in Darfur (UNAMID), in 2008. Considered the largest peacekeeping force in the world, [75]UNAMID was mandated to protect civilians, contribute to security for humanitarian assistance, monitor and verify implementation of agreements, assist an inclusive political process, contribute to the promotion of human rights and the rule of law, and monitor and report on the situation along the borders with Chad and the Central African Republic.[76]

The UNAMID may have created a lull in the fighting, but throughout much of the period, the armed resistance groups continued to fight each other. A UN report issued in 2015, identified key issues in Darfur as being "security and humanitarian catastrophe ... which is marked by widespread violence, impunity, and displacement and shows no sign of improving despite the fact that UNMID has been deployed for more than seven years."[77]

African Union Mission in Somalia

The African Union deployed the African Union Mission in Somalia (AMISOM) amidst difficult circumstances.[78] Although Somalia was engulfed in political crises since Said Barre was overthrown in January 1991, it was only the arrival to the Somali political scene in mid-2006 of the Islamic Courts Union (ICU) and the spectre of international terrorism that prompted the first significant international engagement in Somalia since the departure of the United Nations from the country in 1995.[79] The Ethiopian parliament described the ICU as posing a "clear and present danger" to Ethiopia following reports that the ICU leader Hassan Dahi Aweys, had called for Jihad against Ethiopia and for "Greater Somali" to be carved out of the Horn of Africa.[80] The Ethiopian parliament gave Prime Minister Meles Zenawi the authority to use all necessary measures to defend Ethiopia's sovereignty. Ethiopia immediately sent troops in July 2006 to support the Transitional Government of Somalia and within six months the two forces were able to wrest Mogadishu and Kismayo from ICU fighters. Following their initial defeat, the ICU splintered into several different factions, with some of the more radical elements, including Al-Shabaab, regrouping to continue their insurgency against the TFG and the Ethiopian military forces in Somalia.

The deployment of the Ethiopian troops, which preceded AU decision to send troops, took place under the aegis of IGAD, which had planned to send a Peace Support Mission to Somalia (IGASOM). However, IGAD had to abort its plans because of lack of funding and because ICU considered such a mission as being a US and western anti-Islam tool. This, together with the wrangling over the neutrality of the countries contributing troops led to two important outcomes. First, it led to Ethiopia's decision to go it alone until a workable regional solution could be agreed upon. Second, it precipitated the deployment of the African Union Mission to Somalia (AMISOM). The first AMISOM Ugandan contingent arrived in Somalia in March 2007, and was followed by contingents from Burundi, Kenya and Djibouti. Although the Ethiopian troops had earlier dislodged the Islamic Courts Union (ICU) from the capital in early 2007, ICU and the Alshabab fighters continued to engage AMISOM and Somali Government forces for control over Mogadishu. It was not before the latter half of 2011 that AMISOM gained full control of the capital and other important areas such as Kismayo.

Despite the initial difficulties, AU's intervention brought sufficient progress for a political transition and the establishment of a new federal government to take place.[81] For the first time in many years, the Government established its authority over a number of places that were Alshabab strongholds. A new constitution was adopted, a federal parliament was inaugurated and a new president was sworn in. Thus with the support of the UN and other partners, the AU was able to make sufficient progress that moved Somalia from its "non-state" status that it had been in for over two decades. This led many observers to hail AMISOM as a peacekeeping success despite the threat and challenges it continued to face.[82]

Clearly, the implementation of the AU peace and security agenda shows mixed results. The two main operational components of the agenda, preventive diplomacy and peacekeeping, show successes and failures in the different crises situations. As we have seen AU's preventive diplomacy triumphed in Kenya and Madagascar and the continental body successfully initiated peacekeeping missions in Burundi, Sudan and Somalia. A closer look at the peacekeeping cases reveals that the African Union had developed considerable appetite for peacekeeping operations. However, the Union's capacity to sustain such operations remained weak. Missions initiated were either transitioned into United Nations missions (as it was the case in Burundi and Darfur) or became wholly dependent on the United Nations and other donors for funding and other essential supports (as in the case of Somalia). In my view, therefore, an examination of the African Union peace and security agenda cannot be complete without a closer assessment of the Union's relations with the United Nations. These relations were based on the principle of subsidiarity, which also governed AU's relations with the regional economic communities.

Subsidiarity in Practice

As an organizing principle, subsidiarity simply means decentralization. It requires matters to be handled by the smallest, lowest and least centralized competent authority. Accordingly local authority, rather than the central authority, should take political decision at the local level if possible. The principle has been provided for in the Treaty of Rome,[83] and remained central to the function of the European Union. The principle has a number of advantages including lower cost, proximity to the area of intervention, synergies of actors in terms of language and culture, sensitivity to the local environment, local knowledge and politics, inter-operability and self-interest in solving the conflict to avoid spillover effects in the region.[84]

Relations with the United Nations

The subsidiarity principle that underpins UN's relations with regional bodies is implied in Article 53.1 of the United Nations Charter. Accordingly,

> The Security Council shall, where appropriate, utilize such regional arrangements or agencies for enforcement action under its authority. But no enforcement action shall be taken under regional arrangements or by regional agencies without the authorization of the Security Council.[85]

The principle has been fully recognized in the Protocol Relating to the Peace and Security Council of the African Union.[86] The protocol provides that the PSC, in the fulfilment of its mandate in the areas of peace, security and stability, shall cooperate with the Security Council of the United Nations, who bears the primary responsibility for the maintenance of international peace and security as provided for by the Charter of the United Nations.[87] The PSC and the Commission of the African Union were therefore mandated to establish regular contacts with the UN Security Council.

It was within this context that African countries pushed for a more structured relations between the Security Council of the United Nations and the PSC of the AU. The African Union subsequently became the first regional body that met regularly with the members of the UN Security Council.[88] From 2007 members of the two councils met once a year either in New York or Addis Ababa, and the Secretariat of the two organizations also held regular consultations through their Joint Task Force (JTF), and the desk-to-desk meetings that brought together the senior leadership and focal points. Beyond the consultative meetings, the two sides implemented a number of field missions including the joint peace support operation in Sudan. Similarly, the AU's mission in Somalia (AMISOM), which was credited for the relative stability in Mogadishu, benefitted from UN logistical support package, which was funded through assessed contribution of UN member states. Between mid-2008 and mid-2012 AMISOM might have received nearly $800 million from the UN – in addition to the nearly $40 million pledged to the UN's AMISOM Trust Fund between 2009 and 2011. The two institutions also collaborated in various other conflict zones including the DRC, Guinea Bissau, Mali and South Sudan.[89] Notwithstanding AU's dependence on the UN, the two organizations have had a number of differences.

First at a doctrinal level, the two sides disagreed on the type of crises that should trigger the deployment of a peace operation. In particular, they disagreed on whether missions should deploy in the absence of viable ceasefire or a peace agreement. While the UN had been guided by the doctrine of a "peace to keep," the African Union maintained a doctrine according to which peacekeeping must involve enforcement action that establishes peace before keeping it. No where were these differences more pronounced than in Burundi and Somalia operations.

As we have seen, the AU's first peace support operations in Burundi, AMIB, were deployed because UN could not authorize a peacekeeping operations in the absence of ceasefire agreement. Despite the logistical and funding challenges, the AU decided to deploy troops. AMIB succeeded in stabilizing the country, but the mission was quickly transitioned into the United Nations Peace Keeping Mission in Burundi (ONUB) because AU would not be able to sustain the troops on its own.

Similarly, in 2006 the United Nations and the AU disagreed on whether the deployment of a peacekeeping operation was the appropriate response to the situation in Somalia.[90] The UN Security Council resisted calls for a UN peacekeeping mission in Somalia arguing that the circumstances on the ground were not appropriate for such blue helmet mission. On its part, AU stood by its doctrine of establishing peace first and was able to get UN Security Council authorization for AMISOM.

AU's appetite for initiating peace operation on the continent against its inability to sustain the troops on its own constituted another source of disagreement with the UN, especially with respect to the funding modalities of AU's peace operations authorized by the UN Security Council. The disagreement also covered the management of the transition from AU to the UN missions, the alignment of mandates, timetables, standards, and the appropriate division of labour between UN and AU planners, managers, and other key personnel. The AU's peacekeeping operations also gave rise to major criticism against the principle of subsidiarity.

For its critics, the subsidiarity fostered a one sided relations where the African Union designed peace support operations only as interim measures until the United Nations could take over. It also encouraged the AU to be overly ambitious by taking on peace support operations in extremely difficult circumstances before building the relevant security architecture.[91] A reverse argument is that by encouraging regional entities to lead in finding solutions to regional disputes, subsidiarity served as an instrument of passing the responsibility to a lesser-endowed entity.[92] As we have seen, AU's peace support operations demonstrate both criticisms. The Union took on operations which it had no capacity to sustain; it was also forced to take leadership responsibility in Somalia at a time when the United Nations Security Council was reluctant to deploy UN peace keepers. But if subsidiarity led to AU being over-ambitious and the international community being reluctant to assume responsibility, the problem that the principle caused in AU's relations with the regional economic communities was of a different order. I examine those relations in the following section.

Relations with RECs

In addition to the Constitutive Act of the African Union, the framework for cooperation between the African Union and the regional economic communities included the Protocol establishing the Peace and Security Council, the Common African Defence and Security Policy (CADSP) and the Protocol on the Relations between the African Union and the regional economic communities.[93] But the instrument that specifically sought to foster subsidiarity in the relations between the AU and the RECs was the Protocol Establishing the Peace and Security Council. While they assigned the overall political leadership in matters relating to peace and security to the African Union, the PSC Protocol and the CADSP recognized the importance of the RECs in the continent's peace and security architecture. The RECs were to provide troops in the form of regional brigades; and it was the regional bodies that were to facilitate the implementation of the PSC decisions at the regional level. Thus in accordance with the provisions of the PSC Protocolm, the Commission and the RECs concluded in 2008 a Memorandum of Understanding that provides for adherence to the principle of subsidiarity, complementarity and comparative advantage "in order to optimize the partnership between the Union, the RECs and the Regional Coordinating Mechanisms in the promotion and maintenance of peace, security and stability.".[94] It was also within this context that the Commission and the RECs exchanged resident liaison officers to facilitate coordination and cooperation between the AU and the RECs. By the end of 2011, six RECs had opened liaison offices to the AU;[95] the AU Commission established liaison offices at the headquarters of ECCAS, ECOWAS, SADC, and EAC. These liaison offices considerably enhanced coordination as the AU and the RECs were able to hold 10 technical meetings between 2008 and April 2012. These meetings enabled AU and the RECs to coordinate the operationalization of components of the peace and security architecture such as the ASF and the CEWS.[96]

However, even though subsidiarity was implied in the frameworks that govern AU's relations with the RECs, the principle appeared to lack clear legal status especially with respect to preventive diplomacy and peacekeeping. As a result, AU and the RECs maintained different views of the application of subsidiarity. For the AU just as the Union was to seek UN endorsement for its peace support operations, so would the RECs need to obtain AU's endorsement for their enforcement actions and peace support operations. The AU would also be responsible for coordinating and interfacing with the United Nations regarding peace and security support activities in the regions.[97] And funding request from the regions would require the approval of the AU.

For the RECs the subsidiarity principle implied that AU should only assume a coordinating role and leave actual implementation of peace support operations to the region. It was on this basis that SADC sought to play a leadership role in the preventive diplomatic activities in Madagascar, ECOWAS in Guinea Bissau and Mali, and ECCAS in CAR and DRC and IGAD in South Sudan.

In addition to different views about the concept and application of subsidiarity, AU's own limited capacity to coordinate the activities of the RECs effectively strained relations with the RECs. To a certain extent, the liaison offices and the various consultations enabled the AU to harmonized programmes with respect to the operationalization of components of the peace and security architecture such as the ASF and the CEWS of the RECs. But coordination remained weak with respect to other components such as the Panel of the Wise, PSC and the Peace Fund. The application of the subsidiarity principle was also hampered by the disconnect between the PSC of the Union and similar organs in the RECs.[98] The result was that instead of creating synergy, AU and the RECs continued to act as rivals in many instances. For example, the AU disagreed with SADC over Madagascar, with ECOWAS over Cote D'Ivoire, Niger and Togo, and with IGAD over South Sudan and with ECCAS over the Central Africa Republic.

Challenges to the Peace and Security Agenda

Different interpretation of the principle of subsidiarity and its application was not the only factor that beset the effective operationalization of the African Union peace and security agenda. Weak early warning capacity, limited enforcement capability and limited financial and human resources were key challenges that the Union faced throughout the period under consideration.

Weak Early Warning Mechanism

Among the preconditions for effective conflict prevention are the capacity to assess potential conflict situation, the ability to analyses relevant information and the political will to take the right action. These requirements account for the decision to set up the Continental Early Warning System (CEWS) within the Union. At the initial stage, CEWS was made up of the observation and monitoring centre (situation room) at the Commission of the African union, and the observation and monitoring centres of the various regional economic communities, which were to be linked to the AU Centre. The operational framework was elaborated in 2006, but for many years, the Situation Room remained essentially the information centre of the AU. However, support from the UN's Situation Centre in New York and from external donors enabled the Peace and Security Department of the Commission to recruit ten staffers and operate the situation room around the clock. By the end of 2011, the rudiments of the continental early warning system had already been put in place on the basis of the 2006 Framework for the operationalization of the CEWS. With 11 field missions across the continent, the situation room continuously monitored news and collected data from member states and RECs. Collected data was processed by early warning officers and analysts and provided to different actors, both internal and external, in different forms, including:

- daily news highlights based on open media sources and circulated by email internally and to some 2000 external subscribers, including all RECs;
- a variety of internal reports, such as daily and weekly email bulletins as well as incident reports and flash reports (a text message version of internal alerts was developed); and
- in-depth early warning reports containing analysis, scenarios and options.

Although the CEWS improved considerably over time, the improvement was not sufficient to move the AU from being reactive to proactive. As Williams has noted, the Situation Room continued to receive insufficient real time diplomatic reporting and intelligence. And until the establishment of the Liaison Offices at the RECs in 2012, AU had no diplomatic missions in member countries that were mandated to collect information. As a result AU relied on open source journalism or whatever governments chose to share.[99] Another problem that the African Union faced was the difficulty of analysing and using the information to influence decision making within the PSC. For example, the CEWS personnel were unable to generate early discussions within the PSC on the crisis surrounding the Kenyan elections in 2007 or instability in Guinea Bissau in late 2008.[100] Similarly, the Military coup that ousted the President of Mali Amadou Toumani Touré in March 2012 occurred only two days after a ministerial meeting of the PSC was held in Bamako to consider the situation in the Sahel Region and the Tuareg rebellion in Northern Mali. Likewise, the crises in Guinea Bissau in April 2012 occurred when ECOWAS Mediation and Security Council Ministerial Meeting was being held in Abidjan. Thus because AU was unable to act on most conflicts before they broke out, the organization's preventive diplomacy remained for the most part reactive rather than proactive.

Limited Enforcement Capacity

A related problem that stymied the effectiveness of AU preventive diplomacy was the lack of enforcement capacity. In some instances, the AU was able to pick up signals of impending trouble but could not take any adequate measures to prevent problems from degenerating into crises. For example in 2005, the APRM report on Kenya forecasted trouble in the country if Kenya did not urgently undertake institutional reforms and address Kenya's ethnic divisions, corruption and poor governance. The report specifically noted that the country remained polarized along ethnic lines after the referendum, that "the process of national healing and reconciliation is unlikely to proceed as long as society is still polarized" and that "without addressing past crimes, corruption, marginalization and poverty, it is unlikely that reconciliation can be achieved." The Government of Kenya did not publicly object to the conclusions of the report and in fact reported back to the AU Council of Ministers on progress made on the recommendations of the report. The fact that the crises broke out despite early warning signals that the AU picked up is indicative of the limitations of the Union's preventive diplomacy.[101]

Another measure of AU's weak enforcement capacity was the Union's sanctions regime. There was a general agreement to impose sanctions on troublemakers, be they perpetrators of violence, unconstitutional change of government or electoral malpractice. Proposals included travel ban on such individuals and asset freezes, but AU sanctions during the period under consideration consisted mainly of suspension of governments from taking part in African Union gatherings at the various levels.

Inadequate Financial and Human Resources

Perhaps the most important constraint that AU faced in all areas, especially in matters relating to peace, was limited financial and human resources. The Union's preventive diplomatic activities and peacekeeping operations were supposed to be funded from the Peace Fund, which was established to support peace operations on the continent.[102] Since the OAU established the Fund, only 6 per cent or less of the regular budget of the OAU (and later the AU) was allocated to the Fund. Between 1993 and March 2004, for example, the total resources allocated to the Fund were US$67.8 million. Africa itself accounted for only US$23 million, with about US$45 million coming in the form of cash donations and material support from non-African countries and international organizations. In total, therefore, the OAU/AU and member states accounted for 34 per cent of the resources during the period between 1993 and March 2004; while the donor community, including international organizations, accounted for 66 per cent. A further breakdown of the contributions from within the continent indicates that about 79 of the African contributions came from OAU regular budget; contribution from member states of the Organization and other miscellaneous receipts only accounted for 21 per cent of the funds raised within the continent.[103] As table 7.1 shows, between 2004 and 2007, the Peace Fund received close to US$563 million, and spent a little over US$464 million. AU member states contribution to the fund was less than 2 per cent on average. By 2009, the Fund had a negative balance.[104]

The inadequacy of resources prompted a number of appeals for alternative and supplementary resource mobilization strategies. On several occasions, AU experts urged the Commission to organize regular fund raising activities, and seek the participation of African corporate entities in the Peace Fund, as well as urge member states to levy peace tax.

Thus during the Special Summit held in Tripoli in August 2009, and again during the 16th Ordinary Session of the Executive Council of the AU in Addis Ababa in January 2010, AU Member States agreed to increase contribution to the Peace Fund from 6 per cent to 12 per cent of the AU regular budget by 2012. Although the decision was welcomed in many quarters, it was deemed insufficient to fund the Union's peace and security activities,[105] as member states maintained the same low level of contribution during 2008–2011.[106]

The AU therefore continued to rely on outside support for its peace support operations. In addition to financial support, assistance from the outside world included logistical support, mainly from the United States through its Africa Crisis Response Initiative (ACRT), France through its Renforcement des capacité africaines de maintien de la paix (RECAMP), and UK through the African Peacekeeping Training Support Programme (APTSP).[107] Canada, Germany, The Netherlands, Spain, Ireland, Denmark and other Nordic countries also provided capacity building assistance.[108] Although such assistance contributed immensely to AU peace support operations, it came slowly and with conditions that did not provide the organization with the flexibility it required for effective operation.[109] This is one of the reasons that led the UN–AU Panel, set up under the chairmanship of Romano Prodi to review the modalities for strengthening UN support to AU peace operations, to recommend among other things the setting up of a multi-donor trust fund to support AU peacekeeping operations and to finance some peace support operations from assessed contributions of the United Nations.

Members of the Security Council endorsed the recommendation for a strong partnership between the UN and the AU, but differed over the proposal relating to funding AU operations from assessed contribution and from a multi-donor trust fund. Japan, UK and France voiced some opposition to the proposal for the cost of peacekeeping operations to be met from assessed contribution and for a new trust fund to be added to the existing funding structures.[110]

By many counts, the lack of predictable external source of funding and AU's own inability to fund peacekeeping missions from within the continent had a number of consequences. They led to AU peace support operations to be transitions to the UN, or to be fully dependent on external funding. Operations that were transferred to the UN included AMIB (Burundi), AMIS (Sudan), and most recently the peace support operations in Mali (2012 to 2013) , and Central African Republic (2013–2013). According to AU's own report, some of these transitions took place before the conditions for such transitions were ripe.[111]

Table 7.1 African Union Peace Fund 2004–2007 (in thousand US$)

Year	*Contribution from Member States*	*Donors Contribution*	*Total Income Received*	*Member States' Contributions as % of Income Received*	*Actual Expenditure*	*Expenditure as % of Income*
2004	1794	107,652	109,446	1.6	80,541	73.6
2005	2737	122,892	125,629	2.2	104,796	83.4
2006	2786	179,622	182,408	1.5	169,888	93.1
2007	2940	142,350	145,290	2.2	109,082	75.1

Source: Audit of the African Union, 2007

AU did not only lack financial resources, it also lacked material and strategic airlift capabilities (for both personnel and equipment), adequate training facilities, management structures, and qualified staff to sustain even relatively small-scale peace operations.

There was also inadequate capacity at country and regional levels. African states might have participated in peacekeeping operations, which might have given national armies greater exposure and helped to build practical peacekeeping experience and expertise within them. But, such national experience did not provide member states with the capability to undertake peace-keeping missions individually or, in some cases, collectively as a region.[112] Many African governments also failed to invest sufficiently in peacekeeping operations or fund effective bureaucracies to manage existing peacekeepers or existing five centres of excellence to train future ones. For this reason, the AU peace operations continue to depend on the participation of a small handful of main troop-contributing countries.

As Williams has aptly put it, the absence of the necessary capabilities and dependence on external assistance created disjuncture between AU's ambition and capacity. This "ambition-capacity gap" constituted a major risk for African peace support operations not only of failure but also of raising expectations of the people that could not be fulfilled. Worse still, it undermined AU's search for African solutions to African problems.[113]

CONCLUSION

The importance given to peace and security in the overall mandate of the African Union, as well as the priority it has received from policy makers and academics, accounts for the attention given to the subject in this chapter. It has been shown that despite the multiplicity of activities and actors, the AU peace and security agenda consisted of two main components: conflict prevention or preventive diplomacy and peacekeeping. In addition to the nine peace support operations the Union undertook during 2002–2012, there were several preventive diplomatic initiatives carried out across the continent. In both preventive diplomacy and peacekeeping, the African Union registered successes and failures.

Among the success factors of the Union's preventive diplomacy were the personalities and skills of the negotiators, the ability of the negotiators to balance international expectations with the local realities, the willingness of the local protagonists to accommodate each other and the convergence of all negotiations around one negotiating team and one process.

Similarly, the success of AU's peacekeeping missions in Burundi, Sudan and Somalia was largely attributable to the shift in the Union's doctrine – from that of peacekeeping to peace enforcement. But reports of the Union's peacekeeping successes generally tend to mask the real picture. My examination has revealed that the AU did indeed develop considerable appetite for launching peace support operations. However, the Union's capacity to sustain those operations remained weak. The AU either transitioned its operation to the UN (as it did in Burundi and Sudan) or became wholly dependent on UN and international partners for funding (as it was the case for the Somalia mission).

In addition, the implementation of the AU peace and security agenda suffered from weak early warning capability and limited enforcement capacity. Thus, the disjuncture between the Unions ambition and real capacity constituted a major gap in the continental peace and security agenda as it inhibited AU's search for African solutions to African problems.

NOTES

1. Phrase taken from Boutros Boutros-Ghali, *An Agenda for Peace, Preventive Diplomacy, Peace making and Peace keeping* (New York, United Nations 1992).

2. The African Union, Peace and Security Council, 349th Meeting 14 December 2012, Communique PSC/PR/Com/(CCXLIX).

3. Details of such support are provided in, p. 184 and pp.195–196

4. It has been reported that at the founding conference of the OAU in 1963, only the leaders of Uganda and Congo spoke in favour of Nkrumah proposal. See C.O.C. Amate, *Inside the OAU, Pan-Africanism in Practice* (London Macmillan 1986), pp. 37–38.

5. On these preoccupations, see Stephen Wright, "The Changing Contexts of African Foreign Policies" in Idem (editor), *African Foreign Policies* (Boulder, Col.: Westview 1999), pp.13–18.

6. See Opening Address by Emperor Hale Selassie to the Conference of African Heads of State and Government, Addis Ababa, 23 May 1963, in Organization of African Unity, *Proceedings of the Conference of the Independent African States* Vol. I (Addis Ababa: 1963);

7. Report of the Secretary General to the 5th Ordinary Session of the Assembly of Heads of State and Government, cited in OAU Secretariat, *Resolving Conflicts in Africa: Implementation Option* (Addis Ababa, nd)

8. For more on this, see Colin Legum, "The Role of the Organization of African Unity in Dealing with Violent Conflicts," in Colin Legum et.al. *Africa in the 1980s: A Continent in Crises* (New York: McGraw-Hill Book Company, 1979). pp. 38–43.

9. Ibid.

10. Kofi Annan, "The Causes of Conflict and Promotion of Durable Peace and Sustainable Development in Africa," Report of the Secretary General to the UN Security Council 1998 (A/52/871-5 1998/318).

11. Article 3 (2) of the Charter of the OAU.

12. The only exception was the Angolan civil war which broke out at a time when there was no recognized government. The OAU's approach to the crises was to give equal recognition to the three warring factions before the external intervention of the Soviets and the Cubans on the side of the MPLA and the intervention of South Africa and some Western countries on the side of UNITA and the FNLA prompted two-thirds of OAU member states limiting their support to the MPLA

13. Earnest Harsh, "Africa Builds its Own Security," *Africa Recovery*, Vol. 17, 3 (2003), p. 15. For more on the shifting dynamics of African politics, see, Crawford Young, "The End of the Post-Colonial State? Reflections on Changing African Political Dynamics," *African Affairs* vol. 103, 410 (2004) pp. 23–49, Hussein Solomon and Maxi Van Aardt, *"Caring": Security in Africa,* Institute of Security Studies Monograph Series No. 20 (Pretoria: ISS, 1998).

14. The Cairo Declaration was the concretization of a decision taken a year earlier in Dakar to set up such a body.

15. Paragraphs 12 and 15 of the Declaration.

16. See table 7.1 p. 194.

17. The African Leadership Forum, *The Kampala Documents: Towards a Conference on Security, Stability, Development and Cooperation in Africa,* (Lagos: 1991), especially the security and stability calabashes, pp. 9–19; and Olusegum Obasanjo and Felix G.N. Mosha (editors), *Africa: Rise to Challenge – Towards a CSSDCA* (Lagos: Africa Leadership Forum 1993); and African Union, "Concept Paper on the Establishment of a Common African Defence and Security Policy"(2003), pp. 20–21.

18. For a detailed assessment of the regional initiatives, See www.iss.co.za/regional organizations, or their CDROM entitled *African Regional Organisations: From Unity to Union* (2001). Harsh, "Africa Builds its Own Security," p. 18; Mark Malan *SADC and Sub-regional Security;* and Eric G. Bernman and Katie E. Sams, *Constructive Disengagement: Western Efforts to develop African Peace Keeping*, Institute of Security Studies Monograph Series No. 33 (Pretoria: ISS 1998), p. 8.

19. For more on the regional peace and security arrangements, see F. Söderbaum, and R. Tavares (eds), *Regional Organizations in African Security*, London: Routledge 2010.

20. Decision AHG/Dec.168 (XXXVII) adopted by the 37th Session of the Assembly in Lusaka, Zambia, in July 2001.

21. In particular Article 5(2).

22. Articles 3(b and f) and 4(d).

23. See "South Africa Opposes US War on Iraq" www.africacrisis.org 19 December 2002; see also "South Africa Tries to Avert War in Iraq," *Mercury*, 27 January 2003.

24. See South Africa Regrets Iraq War, www.bbc.co.uk 20 March 2003.

25. See Opening Statement by Dr N.C. Dlamini-Zuma, Foreign Minister of South Africa, at the meeting of Experts on Common African Defence and Security Policy, Randburg, South Africa, 27 March 2003.

26. For more on this, see Omar A. Touray, 'The Common African Defence and Security Policy" *African Affairs* No. 417 (Oct 2005), pp. 635–654.

27. African Union Commission, "Policy Framework for the Establishment of the African Standby Force and the Military Staff Committee (Part I) Exp/ASF-MSC/2 (1) May 2003, paragraph 5.

28. Ibid., para 6.

29. Ibid.

30. For an exhaustive list of the threats, see Framework for the Common Africa Defence and Security Policy.

31. This term was the subject of a lengthy debate during the various meeting. The original wording was "*unprovoked attack*," and most delegations felt that this phrase was a contradiction in terms. It was only during the last attempt by the Ministers of Defence in Sirte to resolve the remaining issues (the bracketed items) that the Tunisian delegation suggested the replacement of the term "*unprovoked attack*" with the word "*aggression*." See the African Union, "The Report of the First Meeting of African Ministers of Defence and Security on the Establishment of African Standby Force and the Common African Defence and Security Policy," MIN/Def.&Sec/Rpt(1) Original: English, p. 4.

32. For an exhaustive list of the principles, see Framework for Common African Defence and Security Policy, paragraphs 11 and 12.

33. Adopted in Durban in 2002 and entered into force in December 2003.

34. Art. 7c of the Protocol;

35. Article 7e of the Protocol. And Article 4h of the Constitutive Act.

36. Article 7g of the Protocol. For a list of countries sanctioned, see chapter 8, pp. 155.

37. Article 7c and m.

38. Article 8 (10).

39. By December 2006, the PSC was composed of the following states: For *three-year term*: Gabon, Ethiopia, Algeria, South Africa, Nigeria; for *two-year term*, Cameroon, Republic of Congo, Kenya, Sudan, Libya, Lesotho, Mozambique, Ghana, Senegal and Togo. Membership rotated several times so that by 2012 members of the council were Angola, Egypt, Republic of Guinea, Cameroon, Cote Ivoire, Republic of Congo, Djibouti, Tanzania, the Gambia, Lesotho, Libya, Equatorial Guinea, Kenya, Nigeria and Zimbabwe.

40. Article 8 (6).

41. Article 8 (12), and Rule 29 of *The Rules of Procedure of the Peace and Security Council of the African Union.*

42. Article 12 (1a). Details of the Continental Early Warning System is provided below, pp.130–131.

43. Article 11 *Protocol Relating to the Establishment of the Peace and Security Council of the African Union.*

44. Article 11(4).

45. Article 11 (8).

46. UN Security Council, "Special Research Report No. 2: Working Together for Peace and Security in Africa: The Security Council and the AU Peace and Security Council" available at http://www.securitycouncilreport.org/special-research-report/lookup-c-glKWLeMTIsG-b 6769467.php

47. Paul D. Williams, The African Union's Conflict Management Capabilities, Working Paper, Council on Foreign Relations (October 2011).

48. African Union *Protocol Relating to the Establishment of the Peace and Security Council of the African Union*; Art.19

49. For reactions to the initial proposals for an ASF, see Eric G. Berman and Katie E Sams, *Constructive Disengagement,* pp. 6–8.

50. See African Union, Policy Framework for the Establishment of the African Standby Force and the Military Staff Committee (Part I) Exp/ASF-MSC/2 (1) May 2003, p. 3.

51. Ibid.

52. African Union, *Protocol Relating to the Establishment of the Peace and Security Council of the African Union.* Article 13 (8)

53. UN Security Council, "Special Research Report No. 2: Working Together for Peace and Security in Africa: The Security Council and the AU Peace and Security Council available at http://www.securitycouncilreport.org/special-research-report/lookup-c-glKWLeMTIsG-b 6769467.php

54. Secretary General Kofi Annan's address to the Central Organ of the OAU Mechanism for Conflict Prevention, Management and Resolution, Lome 26 March 1997 (SG/SM/6192).

55. United Nations, *An Agenda for Peace: Preventive Diplomacy, Peacemaking and Peace-keeping*, Report of the Secretary-General Boutros Boutros-Ghali A/47/277 – S/24111, 17 June 1992. See also Mark Malan, "Conflict Prevention in Africa: Theoretical Construct or Plan of Action," *KAIPTC Paper* No... February 2005, available at http://www.kaiptc.org/Publications/Occasional-Papers/Documents/no_3.aspx.

56. United Nations, "Report of the Secretary-General on the Causes of Conflict and the Promotion of Durable Peace and Sustainable Development in Africa," (1998) A/52/871-S/1998/318, par.20.

57. See United Nations Development Programme, "Conflict Prevention Thematic Guidance Note," *NHDR Occasional Paper No 3, 2004* available at http://hdr.undp.org/sites/default/files/nhdr_conflict_gn.pdf.

58. Monty G Marshal, *Conflict Trends in Africa, 1946–2004: A Macro-Comparative Perspective, October 2005*, available at http://www.systemicpeace.org/africa/AfricaConflictTrendsMGM2005us.pdf

59. Mark Malan, "Conflict Prevention in Africa: Theoretical Construct or Plan of Action," *KAIPTC Paper No. 3 February 2005,* available at http://www.kaiptc.org/Publications/Occasional-Papers/Documents/no_3.aspx. pp. 3–19.

60. For the background and detailed account of the crises, see Peter Kagwanya and Roger Southall (editors), *Kenya's Uncertain Democracy: the Electoral Crises of 2008* (Oxford: Routledge 2010) various chapters; Johannes Langer, "The Responsibility to Protect: Kenya's Post-Electoral Crises" *Journal of International Service* (Fall 2011) available at www.american.educ/sis,

61. Human Rights Watch, 67, (2008), cited in Johannes Langer, *the Responsibility to Protect*, p. 11.

62. For more on the background and the mediation processes, see Lauren Polch and Nicolas Cook, "Madagascar's Political Crises", *Congressional Research Services*, June 18 2012, available at https://www.fas.org/sgp/crs/row/R40448.pdf; for OAU's role in an earlier crises in Madagascar see, Richard Cornwell, "Madagascar: First test for the African Union", *African Security Review* 12(1) 2003, pp. 41–53. For more on AU's intervention in Madagascar and other countries, see Martin Rupiya, *A review of the African Union's experience in facilitating peaceful power transfers: Zimbabwe, Ivory Coast, Libya and Sudan: Are three Prospects for Reform,* Africa Journal of Conflict Prevention, Vol 12, 2 (2012) pp. 161–183.

63. For more on this, see Solomon Dersso, "Egypt Vs African Union: A mutually Unhappy Ending" *Aljazeera* 14 July 2014, available at http://www.aljazeera.com/indepth/opinion/2014/07/egypt-vs-african-union-mutually-u-2014714687899839.html

64. For more on this see, G. M. Khadiagala, "Regionalism and Conflict Resolution: Lessons from the Kenyan Crises" in Peter Kagwanya and Roger Southall (editors), *Kenya's Uncertain Democracy: the Electoral Crises of 2008* (Oxford: Routledge 2010), pp.171–182.

65. G. M. Khadiagala, " Regionalism and Conflict Resolution," p. 182.

66. For more on this see, Laurie Nathan, "Mediating in Madagascar by Bypassing the AU Ban on Coup Legitimization," *Kujega Amani,* 5 November 2013, available at www.ssrc.org.

67. Article 3 (f), article 4 (j) of the Constitutive Act; and Article 6 and of the Protocol Relating to the Establishment of the Peace and Security Council of the African Union;

68. The peace support operations are the AU Mission in Burundi (AMIB) 2003–2004, AU Military Observer Mission in Comoros 2004–2008; AU Mission in Sudan Darfur (AMIS) 2004–2007; Special Task Force in Burundi 2006–2009; AU Mission for Support to the Elections in the Comoros (AMISEC) 2006; AU Electoral and Security Assistance Mission on to Comoros MAES 2007–2008; Democracy in Comoros 2008; AU UN Hybrid Operation in Darfur (UNAMID) 2007–present; AU Mission in Somalia (AMISOM) Since 2007.

69. "See G. M. Khadiagala, "Regionalism and Conflict Resolution."

70. See Festus Agoagye, "The African Mission in Burundi: Lessons Learned for the First African Union Peace-Keeping Operation," available at https://www.issafrica.org/uploads/CT2_2004%20PG9-15.PDF

71. Festus Agoagyye, The African Mission in Burundi: Lessons learned from the first. African Union Peacekeeping Operation (Pretoria: Institute for Security Studies 2004) available at https://www.issafrica.crg/uploads/CT2_2004%20PG9-15.PDF

72. Peter Kagwanja, Patrick Mutahi, "Protection of Civilians in African Peace Missions. The Case of the African Union Mission in Sudan, Darfur" *ISS Paper 139*, May 2007, Tim Murithi, "The African Union's Evolving Role in Peace Operations: the African Union Mission in Burundi, the African Union Mission in Sudan and the African Union Mission in Somalia," *African Security Review* 17 (1) 2008, pp. 70–82.

73. Adam Mynott, (2005) "Darfur Peacekeeping Challenge," *BBC News*. Of 22 August 2005. Cited in Roba Sharamo, The African Union's Peacekeeping Experience in Darfur, Sudan, *Conflict Trends*, 3 (2006),pp. 50–55 available at http://www.isn.ethz.ch/Digital-Library/Publications/Detail/?lang=en&id=104124, Arvid Ekengard, "The African Union Mission in Sudan (AMIS). Experiences and Lessons Learnt," *FOI Report*, August 2008.

74. Quoted in Sharamo, "The African Union's Peacekeeping Experience in Darfur," pp. 50–55 available at http://www.isn.ethz.ch/Digital-Library/Publications/Detail/?lang=en&id=104124

75. UNAMID initially had 19555 military personnel, 6432 police personnel and a significant civilian component. Resolution 2173 of the Security Council of 27 August 2014 reduced the size of the military and police components to 15845 and 3403, respectively. The budget stood at 1.15 billion in 2014–2015.

76. Security Council Resolution 1769 of 31 July 2007.

77. See *Security Council Report*, Monthly Forecast March 2015 available at www.securitycouncilreport.org.

78. For a quick overview, see Tim Murithi, "The African Union's Evolving Role in Peace Operations," pp. 70–82.

79. Cedric Barnes and Harun Hassan " The Rise and Fall of Mogadishu's Islamic Courts" available at https://www.chathamhouse.org/sites/files/chathamhouse/public/Research/Africa/bpsomalia0407.pdf

80. For more on this see, Bill J. Roggio, The Rise and Fall of the Islamic Courts: An Online History January 4, 2007, The *Long War Journal*, available at http://www.longwarjournal.org/archives/2007/01/the_rise_fall_of_som.php

81. For more on this, see Matt Freear and Cedric de Coning, Lessons from the African Union Peace Mission for Somalia for Peace Operation Mali", in M.J. Ramos et al., *Stability: International Journal of Peace and Stability* (June 2013) available at www.stabilityjournal.org.

82. See Cecilia Hull Wiklund, *The Role of the African Union Mission in Somalia*, Stockholm, Ministry of Defence 2013.

83. Article 36.

84. Ricardo De Real, P De Sousa, "The African Peace and Security Architecture (APSA): subsidiarity and the Horn of Africa: The Inter-Government Authority on Development (IGAD)" in Alexandra Magnolia Dias (editor) *State and Societal Challenges in the Horn of Africa* (Lisbon: Centre for African Studies 2013), pp. 59–77.

85. It is to be recognized that the charter makes exceptions to this rule. See Charter of the United Nation.

86. Article 17 of the Protocol.

87. The Charter of the United Nations, article 21 (1).

88. For more on the Security Council's relations with other regional bodies, see Mauricio Artinano, Peace Operations Partnerships: The UN Security Council and (Sub)-Regional Organizations, Policy Briefing (Berlin Centre for International Peace Operations (ZIF) March 2012).

89. For more on the specific nature of the collaboration, see Commission of the African Union, "Report of the Chairperson on the African Union-United Nations

Partnership: The Need for Greater Coherence, 24 September 2013 available at www.peaceau.org /en/article/Report of the Chairperson.

90. Arthur Boutellis and Paul Williams, "Peace Operation, the African Union and the United Nations: Toward More Effective Partnerships" (New York: International Peace Institute, April 2013) p. 7 and 9.

91. Paul William, The African Union Conflict Management Capability, p. 17.

92. Ricardo De Real, P De Sousa," The African Peace and Security Architecture (APSA): subsidiarity and the Horn of Africa, p.61; Samuel M. Makinda, F. Wafula Okumu, David Mickler, *The African Union: Addressing the challenges of peace, security, and governance* (London: Routeldge 2016), pp. 97–136.

93. See African Union, Decision on the Protocol on the Relations between the African Union and the Regional Economic Communities, Assembly/AU/Dec 166 (IX) 2007.

94. African Union, Memorandum of Understanding on Cooperation in the Area of Peace and Security Between the African Union and the Regional Economic Communities and the Coordinating Mechanisms of the Regional Standby Brigates of Eastern and Northern Africa (2008) Article IV Paragraph iv.

95. The RECs that had established liaison offices at the AU by 2012 were COMESA, EAC,ECCAS,ECOWAS,SADC and IGAD.

96. See Alhaji Sarjoh Bah, Elizabeth Choge-Nyangoro, Solomon Dersso, Brenda Mofya and Tim Murithi, *The African Peace and Security Architecture: A Handbook* (Addis Ababa: Friedrich-Ebert-Stiftung, 2013). p. 48.

97. African Union Commission, *Road Map for the Operationalization of the African Standby Force*, 2005.

98. African Union, *African Peace and Security Architecture 2010 Assessment Report*, p. 19 paragraph 17.

99. Paul D. Williams, *The African Union's Conflict Management Capabilities*, p, 9.

100. Ibid., pp. 9–10.

101. For more on this see, Karuti Kanyinga and Sophie Walker "Building a Political Settlement: The International Approach to Kenya's 2008 Post-Election Crisis", *International Journal For Security and Development*, Vol 2 Issue 2 July 2013, available at http://www.stabilityjournal.org/articles/

102. The peace fund is made up of financial appropriations from the regular AU budget, part of the arrears of contributions, voluntary contributions from member states, the private sector, civil society and individuals as well as through appropriate fundraising activities.

103. African Union Commission, "Resource Mobilization for the OAU/AU Peace Fund" Background Paper presented to the Third African Peace and Security Agenda Brainstorming Retreat, Cape Town, 1–5 May 2004; African Union Commission, "Peace and Security Department at a Glance" available at http://www.peaceau.org/uploads/au-booklet.pdf

104. African Union Commission, Moving Africa Forward: The African Peace and Security Architecture, 2010 Assessment Study, p. 59.

105. United Nations Secretary General, "Support to African Union Peace Keeping Operations," Report, par 51, cited in Paul Williams, "The African Union's Conflict Management Capabilities," p. 12.

106. Raymond Gilpin and Michelle Swearingen, "Financing and Refocusing the African Union Peace Fund," *International Network for Economics and Conflict,* (June 24, 2013), available at https: //www.swp-berlin.org/ fileadmin /contents/products/ comments/2012C29_vrr.pdf

107. For more on this see, Eric G. Berman and Katie E. Sams, *Peacekeeping in Africa: Capabilities and Culpabilities*, (Geneva UNIDIR and Prestoria: ISS 1999), pp. 265–375.

108. Ibid., also Earnest Harsch, "Africa Builds its Own Security," *Africa Recovery*, Vol. 17 No. 3 (2003), p. 1 and pp.14–18.

109. African Union, "Resource Mobilization for the OAU/AU Peace Fund"; African Union, "Policy Framework for the Establishment of the African Standby Force and the Military Staff Committee, Part II – Annexes, Exp/ASF-MSC/2(1), May 2003. p. B6; see also Roger Middleton: "The EU and the African Peace and Security Architecture," *Estrategia*, available at www.davidmlast.org/.../Middleton- EU%20 and%20african%20security%20architecture.pdf

110. United Nations Security Council, "Support for AU peace Keeping", *Updated Report* No. 3, 22 October 2009, available at www.securitycouncilreport.org.

111. African Union Commission, "Report of The Chairperson Of The Commission On Follow-Up Steps On The Common African Position On The Review Of United Nations Peace Operations," PSC/AHG/3.(DXLVII), 26 September 2015. Paragraph 10.

112. African Union Commission, "Policy Framework for the Establishment of the African Standby Force," p. B3.

113. Paul William, The African Union Conflict Management Capability, 2011.

Chapter 8

Some "Larger Freedom"[1]

A Catalogue of Human Rights and Governance Norms in Africa

African politics has evolved considerably since independence. The leaders who led their countries to independence were relatively receptive to political pluralism, and in fact temporarily succeeded in instituting democracy or a semblance of it. But the arrival of the military and one-party regimes to the African political scene brought an end to Africa's "romantic period," and shattered the hopes for freedom and development that gave the decolonization struggle the momentum it so much required. Except for a handful of countries, the majority of African countries lived under military or one-party civilian dictatorship for much of the post-independence period. The Cold War, which these regimes exploited, enabled dictatorship to thrive by confining security to state security alone.

The attendant human rights abuses and other forms of political repression that the dictatorial rule inflicted upon the population played an important role in increasing the continent's civil war propensity. Until the 1990s, single-party civilian regimes and military dictatorships in most African countries made coups d'états and attendant violence the only means through which transfer of power could be achieved. This led many observers to conclude that Africa would discourage civil wars only through a combination of greater political rights, improved standard of living and diversified economies.[2]

The demise of the Cold War brought about preference shift on the continent. At the political level, the concept of security was broadened beyond state security to encompass human security. One of the implications of this is that the support that dictators enjoyed during the Cold War waned and considerable emphasis was placed on democracy and popular participation. These effects could be seen from within the states and at the continental level. By the second half of the 1990s, a large number of African countries had transitioned from single-party and military dictatorship to multiparty democracies.[3] Many others had adopted constitutions providing for political pluralism and guaranteeing the political rights of minority groups in the political process. They had also put in place legal frameworks such as independent electoral commissions that facilitate, if not guarantee, smooth electoral processes. The emergence of vocal civil society organizations and the non-governmental organization considerably strengthened this trend. But the most recent human rights and good governance initiatives are better appreciated when seen against their noteworthy antecedents, all of which combined to occasion a preference shift on the continent. In cataloguing these frameworks, this chapter will show not only how the political preference of African leaders shifted over time but also how AU institutions and norms had transformational effect on African political and military leaders.

PROTECTION OF HUMAN AND PEOPLE'S RIGHTS

African conflicts and economic plight have always had a devastating impact on the human rights situation on the continent. It was however the atrocities committed by Idi Amin in Uganda during 1971–1979, Bokassa in Central Africa during 1966–1979 and Nguema in Equatorial Guinea in 1969–1979, and Apartheid and white-minority regimes that galvanized the continent into action.[4] These crises gave momentum to the various human rights initiatives and expedited the process of institutionalizing the protection of human beings on the continent. Thus, between 1961 and 1979 several meetings on human rights, rule of law and political pluralism took place[5] that culminated in the adoption of the African Declaration on Human Rights in Monrovia in September 1979.[6] Three years later, the Assembly of the heads of state and government adopted the African (Banjul) Charter on Human and People's Rights in Nairobi in 1981. The charter entered into force in October 1986.

The Banjul Charter was the third regional human rights instrument to take effect. It reflects internationally recognized fundamental rights in its four sections. The first substantive part covers those inalienable individual rights such as the right to life, prohibition of torture and ill-treatment, prohibition of arbitrary arrest or detention; right to a fair trial and freedom of conscience, expression, association and assembly,[7] people's right, which include the right to self-determination and development; the duties of individuals, which include the duty towards the family, society and the state, and the international communitys;[8] and state duties, which include the duty to promote and ensure awareness of and respect for rights guaranteed in the charter through teaching, education and publication, and the duty to guarantee the independence of the courts.[9]

The charter also provides for an African Commission on Human and Peoples' Rights to be composed of 11 commissioners with competence in the field of human rights and chosen to serve in their personal capacities. The commission has been assigned with the task of promoting human and people's rights and ensuring their protection.[10] Since its creation, the commission has been pursuing this dual mandate. And in order to reinforce protection of human rights, the OAU Assembly of heads of state and government adopted a resolution in Tunisia in 1994, which required the convening of a meeting of senior government experts to examine, with the Commission on Human and People's Rights, ways to boost the efficiency of the African Commission, and in particular to examine possibilities of creating an African Court on Human and People's rights.[11]

In accordance with that resolution, three expert meetings were held in Cape Town, South Africa, in September 1995, in Nouakchott in April 1997 and in Addis Ababa in December 1997. The draft protocol on African Court on Human and People's Rights, which was drawn up by the experts, was adopted by the Assembly in June 1998.[12] The protocol entered into force in 2004 following ratification of the required number of 15 member states. The protocol was to be replaced by the protocol on the Statute of the African Court of Justice and Human Rights, adopted in 2008. The new protocol provided for the merger of the African Court of Justice and the African Court of Human Rights and ensured that adequate resources were available for an effective operation of the court.

An associated instrument was the African Charter on the Rights and Welfare of the Child. Adopted in July 1990 and enforced in November 1999, the African Charter on the Rights and Welfare of the Child provides for the protection of the child. In particular, the Charter guarantees the protection of the rights of the child, including the rights to enjoy sound physical, mental and spiritual health. The provisions of the Charter also protect right to education, life and protection against sexual exploitation, drug abuse, trafficking and abduction were also protected. The charter provides for an African Committee of Experts on the Rights and Welfare of the Child. In addition to these instruments was the Protocol to the African Charter on Human and People's Rights on the Rights of Women, which I have discussed above.[13]

The wind of change that swept the post-Cold War world did not only underline the need for greater human rights protection, it also brought to the fore the need for greater democratization on the continent. This shift of preferences was marked by two measures. The first was the continent's move to mainstream constitutional governance by outlawing coup d'états and other unconstitutional routes power. The second was a move to give greater role to the OAU and the African Union in the promotion of democracy through election monitoring and observation.

CONSTITUTIONAL GOVERNANCE

The first formal decision to outlaw coup d'états in Africa was taken by the OAU Council of Ministers during their 64th ordinary session held in Yaounde, in July 1996. The decision followed timid attempts to foster democracy on the continent through the adoption of a number of frameworks. These include the *Cairo Agenda for Action on Re-launching African Economic and Social Development,*[14] which stressed the importance of good governance through popular participation on the basis of respect for human rights and dignity, free and fair elections, as well as respect for freedom of the press, of speech, association and conscience. The military takeover that took place in Sierra Leone in 1997 was perhaps the first test of the OAU's resolve to promote democracy and good governance on the continent. The coup, that took place at a time when OAU Council of Ministers were meeting in Zimbabwe, gave the African leaders the opportunity to show a collective resolve to democratize the continent. For the first time, African leaders collectively condemned a coup d'état. The ministers went beyond condemnation and pledged not to tolerate unconstitutional change of government within member states. But the Harare spirit was cast into a formal instrument only two years later. In one of the decisions[15] taken during its 35th ordinary session held in Algiers in July 1999, the Assembly formally recognized the importance of democracy and rule of law in ensuring good governance, and issued an ultimatum to all the governments that came to power unconstitutionally after 1997 to return to constitutional rule within one year or face sanctions. The leaders strengthened their position further with a declaration on the framework for an OAU Response to Unconstitutional Changes of Government adopted in Lomé in 2000.[16] The Declaration called for the adoption of democratic constitutions on the basis of generally accepted principles of democracy and for respect for the constitution and adherence to provisions of the law and other legislative enactments adopted by parliament. In particular the leaders called for a clear separation of powers and the independence of the judiciary. The declaration further stressed the OUA's attachment to the following common values and principles of democratic governance:

- political pluralism and other forms of participatory democracy and the role of the African civil society, including enhancing and ensuring gender balance in the political process;
- the principle of democratic change and recognition of the role for the opposition;
- free and regular elections, in conformity with existing legal texts;
- freedom of expression and freedom of the press, including freedom of access to the media for all political stakeholders;

- constitutional recognition of fundamental rights and freedom in conformity with the Universal Declaration of Human Rights of 1948 and the African Charter on Human and People's Rights of 1981.

Besides the declaration, the leaders adopted two key documents that institutionalized democracy as the basis of governance on the continent. The first was the solemn declaration on the Conference on Security, Stability, Development and Cooperation in Africa (CSSDCA). Originally the brainchild of Olusegun Obasanjo, then chairman of the African Leadership Forum, the CSSDCA was launched in 1990, but it was only after the return of Obasanjo to power in Nigeria that the CSSDCA was accepted by African leaders as a programme of the OAU.[17] Among other things the CSSDCA emphasized the role of democracy and good governance in the promotion of political and social stability in individual African countries.[18] It sets performance indicators in several areas. Within the CSSDCA framework members states tasked themselves to adopt as a common African position by 2004 fundamental tenets of democracy such as a constitution, free and fair elections, and independent judiciary, freedom of expression and subordination of the military to legitimate civilian authority; rejection of unconstitutional changes of government. They undertook to implement these principles by 2005.[19]

They also undertook to elaborate by 2004 principles of good governance based on commonly agreed set of indicators to be included in national legislations, including decentralization of administration and effective transparent control of state expenditure. By 2003, all African countries were expected to enact legislation to provide for the impartiality of the public service, the independence of the judiciary and the necessary autonomy of public institutions such as the Central Bank and the office of the auditor general. Member states further undertook to adopt by 2005 a commonly derived code of conduct for political office holders that provides for limits to term of office that cannot be violated. They also made the commitment to sign and ratify the OAU Convention on Combating Corruption and to establish by 2004 in each African country an independent anti-corruption commission, with an independent budget that must annually report to the national parliament on the state of corruption in the country. Other measures they agreed upon include

- the establishment of independent national electoral commissions by 2003 in all African countries and other appropriate mechanisms and institutions that ensure free and fair elections.
- the adoption and standardization by 2003 of guidelines for independent and effective observations of elections in the AU member states, with the provision of an effective electoral unit within the AU Commission. The guidelines must include provisions for strengthening civil society and

local monitoring groups in individual African countries and the continent as a whole to support the process of ensuring free and fair elections. The commission should be gradually equipped and funded to conduct independent election observation by 2003. The reports of the various election observation teams of the AU should be made public.[20]

- the conclusion by 2004 of appropriate arrangements for the institution of campaign finance reform, including disclosure of campaign funding sources and for the proportionate state funding of all political parties, to ensure transparency and accountability in electoral contests.
- the conclusion by 2004 of appropriate arrangements, including electoral reforms, for the institution of more inclusive systems of government. There was also the requirement to implement the provision of the charter for popular participation in the development and transformation of African, adopted by the Assembly of heads of state and government in 1990, by creating more enabling environment for increased participation of women, youth and civil society organizations.
- the adoption by 2004 of enabling legislations on the formation and operation of political parties to ensure that such parties are not formed and operated on ethnic, religious, sectarian, regional, racial basis and to establish a threshold of voter support as criteria for public funding without compromising freedom of association and the principle of multiparty.[21]

The advent of the African Union and NEPAD strengthened African leaders' resolve and commitments towards democracy and good governance enunciated in the CSSDCA. According to the Constitutive Act of the African Union, one of the objectives of the African Union is the promotion of democratic principles and institutions and popular participation and good governance.[22] And one of the principles on which the union is based is the respect of democratic principles, human rights, the rule of law and good governance,[23] as well as the rejection of unconstitutional change of government.[24]

Under the Democracy and Political Governance Initiative of the NEPAD, African leaders also recognized that true democracy, respect for human rights and good governance promote development. They consequently undertook to respect the global standards of democracy, the core components of which include political pluralism that creates space for political groups and labour unions and fair, open and regular democratic elections.[25]

Their objective under the NEPAD initiative was therefore to strengthen the political and administrative framework of participating countries, in accordance with the principles of democracy, transparency, accountability, integrity, respect for human rights and promotion of the rule of law.[26] The initiative consists of the following elements:

- A series of commitments by participating countries to create or consolidate basic governance processes and practices;
- An undertaking by the participating countries to take the lead in supporting initiatives that foster good governance;
- The institutionalization of commitments through the leadership of NEPAD to ensure that participating countries abide by the core values of the initiative.

The participating countries undertook to meet the basic standards of good governance and democratic behaviour, and to support each other's institutional reform agenda. To this end, a series of capacity-building initiatives were programmed. It was further decided that the Heads of State Forum of NEPAD would serve as a mechanism through which the leadership of NEPAD would periodically monitor and assess the progress made by African countries in meeting their commitment towards achieving good governance and social reforms. The forum was to provide a platform for countries to share experiences with a view to fostering good governance and democratic practices.[27]

Perhaps the most profound commitment to democracy and rule of law and which constitutes the major mandate of the union was the declaration on the principles governing democratic elections in Africa adopted during the AU summit in Durban in July 2002. In that document, African leaders once again underscored their commitment to democracy by confirming that genuine democratic elections were the basis of the authority of any representative government. They asserted that elections constitute a key element of the democratization process and therefore were essential ingredients for good governance, the rule of law, the maintenance and promotion of peace, security, stability, and development. They also viewed democratic elections as an important dimension in conflict prevention, management and resolution, and agreed that elections were to be conducted freely and fairly under democratic constitutions, as well as other supportive legal and judicial instruments, and under a system of separation of powers that ensured in particular the independence of the judiciary. They also agree that elections would be held at regular intervals, and managed by impartial all-inclusive and competent electoral institutions.[28] The declaration was not only a mere statement of principles but it also committed member states of the African Union in various ways: it committed them to take all the necessary measures to ensure the scrupulous implementation of the principles enshrined in the declaration in accordance with the constitutions of the individual member states. It also showed the leaders' commitment to the following:

- estabilishing appropriate mechanisms where issues such as codes of conduct, citizenship, residency, age requirements for eligible voters, compilation of voters registers could be addressed;

- estabilishing impartial, all-inclusive, competent and accountable national electoral bodies and effective constitutional courts to arbitrate in the event of electoral disputes;
- safeguarding the human and civil liberties of all citizens including the freedom of movement, assembly, association, expression and campaigning as well as access to media on the part of all stakeholders during electoral processes;
- promotion of civic and voters' education about the democratic principles and values in close cooperation with the civil society groups and other relevant stakeholders;
- adoption of all necessary measures and precautions to prevent fraud, rigging or any illegal practices throughout the whole electoral process, in order to maintain peace and security;
- ensuring the availability of adequate logistics and resources for carrying out democratic elections;
- ensuring adequate security for all parties participating in the elections;
- ensuring the transparency and integrity of the entire electoral process by facilitating the deployment of representatives of political parties and individual candidates at polling and counting stations and by accrediting national and international observers and monitors;
- encouraging the participation of African women in all aspects of the electoral process in accordance with the national laws.[29]

In addition to these commitments, the declaration further accorded individual citizens certain electoral rights. Accordingly, every citizen shall have the right to participate freely in the government of his or her country, either directly or through freely elected representatives in accordance with the provisions of the law. Citizens shall also have the right to fully participate in the electoral process of the country, including the right to vote or be voted for, according to the laws of the country and as guaranteed by the constitution, without any kind of discrimination. They shall have the right to association and assembly in accordance with the law. Furthermore, every citizen shall have the freedom to establish or to be a member of a political party or organization in accordance with the law. Individuals and political parties shall have the right to freedom of movement, to campaign and to express political opinions with full access to the media and information within the limits of the laws of the land. They shall have the rights to appeal and obtain timely hearing against all proven electoral malpractices to the competent judicial authorities in accordance with the electoral laws of the country. Similarly, candidates or political parties shall have the right to be represented at the polling and counting stations by duly designated agents or representatives. And no individual or political party shall engage in any act of violence or hinder others from exercising the constitutional rights and freedoms. All stakeholders should refrain from using abusive language and hate speech, false or defamatory allegations and provocative language. These acts should be monitored and sanctioned by designated electoral authorities.

Stakeholders are to renounce the practice of granting favours, gifts or any inducements to the electorate for the purpose of influencing the outcome of elections, and every candidate and political party shall respect the impartiality of the public media by refraining from any act that might constrain or limit their electoral adversaries from using the facilities and resources of the public media to air their campaign messages.

Individuals and political parties participating in elections shall recognize the authority of the electoral commissions or any statutory body empowered to oversee the electoral process and accordingly render full cooperation to such an agency / body in order to facilitate their duties. And every citizen and political party shall accept the results of elections proclaimed to have been free and fair by the competent national bodies as provided for the national constitution and other electoral laws.

Africa's collective drive to promote democracy and enhance governance received a bigger boost in later years by two new mechanisms: the African Peer Review Mechanism of NEPAD and the African Charter on Democracy, Election and Governance.

Considered the most innovative dimension of NEPAD, the African Peer Review Mechanism constituted Africans' own means of monitoring compliance with national, regional and international norms of political, economic and corporate governance. As such, the mechanism was supposed to replace the intrusive role that donors increasingly played in promoting economic and political reforms.

The review process would begin with a support mission to a country. This was a pre-country review phase, in which members of the review panel, assisted by the mechanism secretariat and NEPAD strategic partner institutions (AU, ECA, ADB, UNDP) would assess the preparedness and capacity of the country to participate in the African peer review process, particularly to undertake self-assessment and prepare a national programme of action. The missions would also ascertain the robustness of the mechanism instruments, including the degree of participation of major stakeholders in the national process. At the end of the support missions, each participating country would be expected to undertake a self-assessment with a view to preparing the preliminary national programme of action. A country's self-assessment was the first of the five stages of the peer review process. It would be followed by a country review visit by the panel, which would then prepare a country review report. The overall aim of the country review, and more generally of the peer review itself, was to help countries identify institutional, policy and capacity weaknesses; suggest remedial measures to such shortcomings and seek support for that effort. By the end of 2012, the number of countries that had subscribed to the mechanism rose to 30, suggesting the growing appeal of the APRM's voluntary approach and African ownership and leadership of the process.

The African Charter on Democracy, Election and Governance came into effect in 2012. It aims at encouraging state parties to adhere to the universal values and principles of democracy, respect for human rights, rule of law and constitutional order, which include the independence of the judiciary. In this regard, it enjoins state parties to reaffirm their commitment to regular, transparent, free and fair elections. The African Union's role in this process was important. Through its Democracy and Electoral Assistance Unit and Democracy and Electoral Assistance Fund, the African Union provided various forms of assistance to state parties, ranging from advisory services to assistance to electoral institutions.

On governance, the charter obliges state parties to promote the fight against corruption in conformity with the provisions of the OAU Convention on Preventing and Combating Corruption. To this end, state parties were obliged to strengthen the oversight role of parliament and other legal bodies, enhance the capacity of public institutions and foster strong partnership between the government, civil society and the private sector.

Perhaps the greatest innovation offered by the charter was the criminalization of unconstitutional change of government and the broadening of the definition of acts that constitute an unconstitutional change of government. Accordingly, acts that constitute unconstitutional change of government are in three categories:

- putsch or coup d'état, intervention by mercenaries, armed dissidents against a democratically elected government;
- refusal by a sitting government to relinquish power to the wining party or candidate after free and fair elections;
- any amendment or revision of the constitution or legal instrument, which is an infringement on the principles of democratic change of government.

In addition to the sanctions provided for by earlier instruments, such as the suspension of the unconstitutional government from participating in the activities of the union, the charter provides that the perpetrators of the unconstitutional change of government shall not be allowed to participate in elections held to restore democratic order or hold any position of responsibility in political institution of their state. Most importantly, the perpetrators may also be tried before the competent court of the union or of a state party.

Indeed, human rights and democratic governance might be in their infancy in Africa, but the plethora of legal instruments that aim at promoting these values suggest that African leaders were alive to the need to improve governance on the continent. The various instruments were subsequently integrated into a single framework: the African Governance Architecture. Adopted in 2012, the African Governance Architecture constituted an overall political and institutional framework for the promotion of democracy, governance and human rights in Africa, and constitutes the main reference framework for governance on the continent.

Parallel to the establishment of continent-wide frameworks for democratic governance was the direct involvement of the OAU and the African Union in elections in member states for which a number of guidelines were drawn.[30]

ELECTION OBSERVATION AND MONITORING

Until the end of the 1980s, the OAU strictly adhered to Article 3 of its charter, which provided for the non-interference in the domestic affairs of member states. For the OAU, the focus was on the elimination of the vestiges of colonialism and white-minority rule on the continent. The OAU's involvement in national elections of member states was a corollary and a practical expression of the new drive to foster democracy on the continent. Thus, the organization first got involved in election monitoring during the independence election of Namibia in 1989 and the elections in Comoros in February 1990.[31] But the OAU's involvement in these elections was at an informal level because neither did the organization have any formal mandate to play that role nor did member states recognize its role in this area. It was during its 26th Ordinary Session in Addis Ababa in 1990 that the Assembly of heads of states adopted a declaration in which they confirmed that in order to facilitate the process of socio-economic transformation and integration of the continent, it was necessary to promote popular participation in the processes of government and development. The declaration further stated that a political environment that guarantees human rights and the observance of the rule of law also ensures higher standards of probity and accountability particularly on the part of those who would hold public office. In addition, people-centred political process would ensure the involvement of all including women and youth in the development efforts. The declaration also stressed the leader's commitment to deepen the democratization process and to consolidate the democratic institutions across the continent. Similarly, the leaders reaffirmed the rights of the countries to determine, in all sovereignty, their system of democracy on the basis of their sociocultural values and the realities of each of the countries.[32]

As the democratization process deepened on the continent, and member states' demands on the OAU increased, a consensus was built around the leadership role that the OAU could play in the promotion of democracy. However, it was not clear what the leadership role that the member states expected the OAU to assume in the monitoring of elections, as there were no formal decisions or resolutions specifying the goal and objectives to be achieved through that exercise.[33] As a result, the organization was confronted with a number of difficulties in this area. Unclear mandate, ineffective policies and weak institutional capacity were cited as constituting some of the constraints. Because of this, election monitoring and observation could not be standardized and continued to be carried out in an ad hoc manner and upon request by member states.

The challenges the OAU had faced served as lessons learnt for the African Union and informed provisions of the Declaration on the Principles Governing Elections in Africa, as well as the Guidelines for AU Electoral Observation and Monitoring Missions, both adopted in Durban in July 2002. Under these frameworks, the observation and monitoring of election shall be undertaken on the basis of a memorandum of understanding between the African Union Commission and the host country in accordance with the principles enshrined in the Durban Declaration and the laws of the host country. Second, the election observers were to observe guidelines of the commission, which were to be based on the Durban Declaration, specific terms of reference determined by the individual cases and the laws of the country. Third, election observation and monitoring would be carried out only upon invitation, and such invitations were to be made at least two months before the date of the elections. The African Union reserved the right to decline any such invitation. Apart from the cost of air travel and daily subsistence allowance that the African Union paid out to monitors and observers, member states were to ensure that the whole process were free of charge.[34] By 2012, the OAU and the AU had observed 250 elections across the continent.[35]

THE BALANCE SHEET

The assessment shows that the African Union frameworks for human rights and democratic governance were too many to be exhausted in a single chapter. However, the following general conclusions can be drawn from them.

During the period under consideration, a lot of progress was made with respect to human rights protection. However, while the role of national frameworks and institutions (constitutions, laws and parliaments) in the area of human rights must be recognized, the extent to which continental frameworks contributed to greater human rights protection remains unclear. What is clear however is that they remained hanging over the heads of policy makers and could not therefore be completely ignored, especially as the African Commission on Human and People's Rights and the regional human rights bodies continued to hear human rights cases. To that extent, therefore, I can support the argument of the constructivist students that institutions have transformative effects on national elites. But the plethora of the challenges that human rights institutions faced reduced their effectiveness considerably. The institutions created in the context of the various frameworks were not sufficiently empowered to enforce human rights protection at the national level. But although created by member states, the institutions were invariably seen as agents with foreign agenda or being outright hostile. The institutions were also seen to be too many, scattered and largely uncoordinated.

Regarding constitutional governance, there is clear evidence to suggest that African Union governance frameworks and institutions have had some transformational effects on African civilian and military elites.[36] The African Union regime on unconstitutional change of government played a decisive role in reducing the incidence of military coups on the continent, and had been an enhancing factor in the continent's experiment with democratic pluralism. Between 1952 and 2012, 88 successful military coups took place in Africa. Of these, 63 took place before 1990 and only 10 occurred after the adoption of the Lomé declaration in 2000.[37] The implementation of the declaration took the form of routine suspension since the mid-1990s of all governments that came to power through unconstitutional means from participating in the activities of the African Union. Countries suspended include Central African Republic (March 2003–June 2005); Togo (February 2005–May 2005); Mauritania (August 2005–April 2007); Mauritania (August 2008–June 2009); Guinea (December 2008–December 2010); Niger (August 2009–March 2011); Madagascar (March 2009–today); and Côte d'Ivoire (December 2010–April 2011).[38] To a large extent, the suspension, together with the sanctions that the donor community routinely imposed on unconstitutional governments, was an undeniable contributor to the reduction of coups on the continent.[39]

African Union's engagement in elections observation and monitoring produced mixed results. By observing and monitoring elections, the AU was not only fostering democracy on the continent, it was also engaged in preventive diplomacy. In most instances, AU's association, just like the participation of other regional and global observers, enhanced the integrity, transparency and credibility elections, thereby reducing the risks of election-related violence. But the AU continued to face a number of challenges including inadequate financial and human resources. For much of the period under consideration, the level of funding did not match the additional responsibility given to the organization in the area of election monitoring. Member states were reluctant to allocate sufficient resources for election monitoring, and the general scepticism about elections on the continent accounted for the Secretariat's inability to raise extra-budgetary resources from non-African sources.[40] The result was that OAU/AU teams had often been too small to cover national territories or other important activities such as the voters' registration, campaign and ballot counting. What is more, members of the OAU observers at times went to mission areas without appropriate insurance despite the inherent risks.[41]

The African Union's involvement in elections on the continent also came under strong criticism especially from outside the African continent. The charges included the fact that the number of regular multiparty elections did not make these elections contributory factors to building and sustaining democracy.[42] And the spate of election observation activities did not correspond to improvement of electoral processes and democracy as a whole.[43] What is more, the AU and the RECs may have developed important frameworks that establish benchmarks for credible elections, but the experience in Africa showed that different missions had arrived at divergent conclusion on the same elections.[44]

Thus, while the progress made in the area of governance should be celebrated, it must be recognized equally that the gains remained modest and fragile. As the African Development Bank concludes, only a handful of African countries had reached a point where the peaceful transfer of power through elections was routine. For many, elections posed considerable risks for election-related violence; for the others, the playing field was not only unlevelled but it was stacked in favour of the incumbent.[45]

NOTES

1. Adapted from the report of the United Nations' Secretary General entitled *In Larger Freedom: Towards Development, Security and Human Rights for All*, launched in 2005

2. World Bank, *Can Africa Claim the 21st Century*, p. 60.

3. For more on this see, Leonardo A. Villalon and Peter Von Doepp (editors), *The Fate of Africa's Democratic Experiment: Elites and Institutions* (Bloomington: Indiana University Press, 2005), Especially, Chapters 1 and 12; Victor T. Le Vine, "The Fall and Rise of the Constitutionalism in West Africa," *Journal of Modern African Studies*, 35, 2 (1997), pp. 207–229.

4. Gino J. Naldi, *The Organization of African Unity,: An Analysis of its Role* (London: Mansell, 1989), p. 108.

5. Gino J. Naldi, *The Organization of African Unity* pp. 108–110; and also Ian Brownlie (editor), *Basic Documents on Human Rights*, 2nd Edition (Oxford: Clarendon Press, 1981). p. 21; Omar A. Touray, *The Gambia and the World: A History of the Foreign Policy of Africa's Smallest State, 1965–1995,* Hamburg African Studies Series Vol. 9 (Hamburg: Institute of African Affairs, 2000), pp. 161–64.

6. Zdenek Cervenka and Colin Legum, "The Organization of African Unity in 1979," in *Africa Contemporary Record* (1979–1980), p. A66.

7. *The African Charter on Human and Peoples Rights*, Articles 2–18.

8. Ibid., Articles 19–24.

9. Ibid., Articles 25–26.

10. Ibid., Article 30.

11. Resolution AHG/Res. 230 (XXX) adopted in Tunisia in 1994.

12. African Union, *Rapport intérimaire sur la création d'une cour Africaine des droits de l'homme et des peuples* MIN/CONF/HRA/9 (11), May 2003

13. Chapter 6.

14. Adopted in Cairo in 1995.

15. Decision AHG/Dec.142 (XXXV)

16. OAU Secretariat, Document AHG/Decl.5. (XXXVI)

17. African Union, "Report on the Conference on Security, Stability, development and Cooperation in Africa," EX.CL/74 (IV), March 2004. For more on the CSSDCA, see, Francis M. Deng and I William Zartman, *A Strategic Vision for Africa: The Kampala Movement* (Washington DC: Brookings Institution, 2002)

18. Report of the Secretary General on the Implementation of the CSSDCA C/2255 (LXXVI), Rev. 1 Original English.

19. See Memorandum of Understanding on Security, Stability, Development and Cooperation in Africa, annexed to The Report of the Secretary General on the Implementation of the CSSDCA, p. 16.

20. Ibid., p. 17.

21. Ibid., p. 18.

22. *The Constitutive Act of the African Union*, art. 3 (g)

23. Art. 4 (m)

24. Art. 4 (p).

25. *The New Partnership for Africa's Development, Paragraph* 79.

26. Ibid.

27. Ibid. paragraphs 84–85.

28. African Union, Declaration on the Principles Governing Democratic Elections in Africa AHG/Decl.1 (XXXVIII) July 2002; pp. 2–3.

29. Ibid.

30. Ibid.

31. African Union, Report of the Secretary General on Strengthening the Role of the OAU/AU in Elections, Observations and Monitoring and the Advancement of the Democratization Process in Africa, CM/ 2257 (LXXVI) July 2002.

32. OAU, Declaration of the Assembly of Heads of State and Government of the Organization of African Unity on the Political and Socio-Economic Situation in Africa and the Fundamental Changes Taking Place in the World, July 1990.

33. Ibid. Paragraph 16.

34. Ibid.

35. See Shubana Karuma and Eleanora Mura, "Reflections on African Union Election Assistance and Observations," IDEA, The Integrity of Elections: The Role of Regional Organizations, 2012, pp. 21–38, available at ... See also Report

of the Secretary General on Strengthening the Role of the OAU/AU in Elections, Observations and Monitoring and the Advancement of the Democratization Process in Africa, CM/ 2257 (LXXVI) July 2002 Annex I

36. Chapter 5.

37. For more on this, see Issaka K Souaré, "The African Union as a 'Norm Entrepreneur' on Coups D'Etat in Africa, 1952–2012: An Empirical Assessment," *Journal of Modern African Studies*, Vol 52, 1 (2014) pp. 69–94.

38. Konstantinos D. Magliveras: The Sanctioning System of the African Union: Part Success, Part Failure, 2011 available at http://www.academia.edu/1103678/

39. See Ernest Harsch, "Africa Defends Democratic Rule," African Renewal, April 2010, available at http://www.un.org/africarenewal/magazine/april-2010/africa-defends-democratic-rule

40. For more on this see, Judith Kelley, "Watching the Watchmen: The Role of Election Observers in Africa," available at www.thinkafricapress.com May 2013.

41. Ibid.

42. D.K Leonard, Election and Conflict in Africa: An Introduction, *Journal of Elections*, Vol. 8,1 (2009), pp. 1–15.

D Kadim, "An Overview" Compendium of Elections in Denis Kadim and Susan Boayse (editors) *Southern Africa 1989–2009: 20 Years of Multiparty Democracy* (Johannesburg: Electoral Institute of Southern Africa 2009).

43. EISA Two Decades of Elections Observation in Africa: Lessons Learned, Role, Performance and Impact on Democracy Building, available at www.eisa.org/event/symposium 2.html

44. H. Ogune, "Appraising Election Monitoring and Observation in Africa: The Case of the Democratic Republic of Congo's 2011 Presidential Elections," sited in www.eisa.org.za

45. African Development Bank et al, *African Economic Outlook 2013*, p.16.

Chapter 9

The Policy Organs

The Assembly, the Council and the PRC

Structurally, the African Union was like a pyramid. At the apex was the Assembly of heads of state and government of the 53 member states. Below the Assembly was the executive council of foreign ministers. Slightly parallel to the executive council were the specialized technical committees that brought together other sectoral ministers. Although it took a long time before these ministers could constitute themselves formally into specialized technical committees, they met under the umbrella of the African Union and deliberated on issues that fell within their purview. Under the ministers was the group of ambassadors of member states accredited to the union as permanent representatives. At the same level was the commission of the union, the Pan African Parliament, the Courts of Justice and Human Rights and the Financial Institutions. Below these organs were the Economic and Social Council (ECOSOC) consisting of non-governmental organizations, diaspora organizations, grassroots and other civil society bodies.[1]

Although it might be beyond the scope of this chapter to examine all these organs, the importance that Institutionalists (including rational choice advocates and Constructivists) attach to institutions requires that we look at some of them in order to provide a more comprehensive assessment of the African Union. This chapter therefore looks at the Assembly of heads of state and government, the executive council of foreign ministers, and the Committee of Permanent Representatives (PRC). The Commission of the African Union and the Pan African Parliament are looked at in the two subsequent chapters.

THE ASSEMBLY

In accordance with the provisions of the Constitutive Act, the Assembly was the supreme organ of the union. It composed of heads of state and government and until 2005 met only once a year in an ordinary session as provided for in the Constitutive Act.[2] From 2005, the Assembly met twice a year in ordinary sessions in January and July. All the January sessions were held at the headquarters of the Union (Addis Ababa). At the request of any member state or at the proposal of the chairperson of the Assembly, and upon approval by a two-thirds majority of member states, the Assembly met in extraordinary sessions.[3] The office of the chairperson of the Assembly was held for a year by a head of state or a head of government. Although the Constitutive Act provided for the election of the chairperson of the Assembly, the position was filled by selection after consultation, rather than by election. Up to 2005, the chairmanship automatically went to the country that hosted the ordinary session of the Assembly. However, during its 4th ordinary session in Abuja in 2005, the Assembly decided to break with tradition in two respects: (a) it took the decision that all the January sessions would henceforth be held at the seat of the organization (except that of January 2006; (b) it also took the decision that the chairperson of the Assembly, and by extension of the council and the PRC, would be elected during the January session. The implication of the decision was that while the chairmanship changed during the only ordinary session of the year and while the chairmanship invariably went to the country hosting the session, henceforth the chairmanship would be decided at the seat of the union and would therefore be open to competition. However, up to 2012, the position of chairperson of the union had been decided by consensus. The chairperson of the union was assisted by four vice chairpersons, who were selected on the basis of equitable geographical distribution.[4] Previously, this number was 14, but the rules of procedure of the Assembly was amended to provide for only four vice chairpersons.

Table 9.1 Chairpersons of the African Union 2002–2012

Jan 2012 to Jan 2013	Thomas Yayi Boni, Benin
Jan 2011 to Jan 2012	Teodoro Obiang Nguema Mbasogo, Equatorial Guinea
Jan 2010 to Jan 2011	Bingu wa Mutharika, Malawi
Feb 2009 to Jan 2010	Muammar Gadhafi, Libya
Jan 2008 to Jan 2009	Jakaya Mrisho Kikwete, UR of Tanzania
Jan 2007 to Jan 2008	John Kufuor, Ghana
Jan 2006 to Jan 2007	Dénis Sassou N'Guesso, Congo
July 2004 to Dec 2005	Olusegun Obasanjo, Nigeria
July 2003 to July 2004	Joaquim Alberto Chissano, Mozambique
July 2002 to July 2003	Thabo Mbeki, South Africa

The Assembly's powers are stipulated in Article 9 of the Constitutive Act. Accordingly, the Assembly determined the common policies of the Union; received, considered, and took decisions on reports and recommendations of the other organs of the Union; considered requests for membership of the Union; established organs of the Union; monitored the implementation of the decisions and policies of the Union, as well as ensured compliance by all member states; adopted the budget of the Union; gave directive to the Executive Council on the management of conflicts, war and other emergency situations and restoration of peace; appointed and terminated the appointment of the judges of the court of justice; appointed the chairperson and the vice-chairperson(s) of the commission and determined their functions and terms of office.

The powers of the Assembly, broadly outlined in the Constitutive Act, were spelt out in greater detail in the rules of procedure of the Assembly. Within the context of the African Peace and Security Architecture, and in accordance with the provisions of the protocol establishing the Peace and Security Council of the African Union, the Assembly was empowered to decide on intervention in a member state both at the request of that state and in respect of grave circumstances, namely war crimes, genocide and crimes against humanity.[5] It could also determine the sanction to be imposed on any member state for non-payment of assessed contributions, violations of the principles enshrined in the Constitutive Act and the rules of procedure of the Assembly, non-compliance with the decision of the Union and unconstitutional changes of government. While the Constitutive Act provided that the Assembly shall appoint the chairperson and deputy chairperson of the commission, the rules of procedure went further by giving the Assembly the right to terminate the appointment of these officials and that of the commissioners. The rules also gave the Assembly the authority to appoint the judges of the African Court of Justice. The Assembly held all its sessions at the headquarters of the Union, except when a member state invited the Assembly to meet on its territory. In that case, the country would bear the extra expenses incurred by the commission as a result of the session being held outside the headquarters.[6] The member state hosting the session of the Assembly must not be under any sanctions imposed by the Union.

The Executive Council was responsible for the preparation of the Assembly's agenda, which normally comprised (a) items that the assembly itself decided, at a previous meeting to place on its agenda, (b) items proposed by the Executive Council, (c) items proposed by other organs of the Union that did not report directly to the Executive Council, (d) items proposed by a member state and submitted 60 days before the opening of the session and the supporting documents and draft decisions relating thereto communicated to the chairperson of the commission at least 30 days before the opening of the meeting. In the past, items from member states proved to be problematic because they led to decisions that were hasty and eventually difficult to implement. With the amendments to the rules of procedure, the Assembly examined the items proposed by member states on the recommendation of the Executive Council, although the Assembly reserved the right to decide differently from the recommendation of the Executive Council. An example was the decision by the Assembly to set up a committee of heads of state and government to examine the Libyan proposal for the creation of posts of ministers at the continental level. The Executive Council had recommended that in as much the proposal was desirable and consistent with the long-term objectives of the Union, it was premature and therefore ought to be shelved.

Generally, items on the Assembly's agenda were grouped under two categories: (2) those that were for adoption without discussion. These were items on which the Executive Council had reached agreement and for which the approval of the Assembly was possible without discussion; (2) items that were for discussion before decision. They were generally those on which the Executive Council had not reached agreement. The agenda of an extraordinary session comprised only items communicated to member states at the time the extraordinary session was being proposed.

With regard to decision-making, the Constitutive Act provided that the Assembly shall take its decisions by consensus or, failing which, by two-thirds majority of member states of the Union.[7] Decisions on procedural matters were taken by a simple majority. Voting on substantive issues was by secret ballot and that on procedural matter could be taken by any other method as might be determined by the Assembly.

The original mover of a proposed decision or amendment could at any time withdraw the decision or amendment. Any member state had the right to reintroduce the proposed decision or amendment that had been withdrawn. A proposal was considered as an amendment to a text if it modified it by adding a part to it or removing a part from it.

The decisions of the Assembly were issued in the forms of regulation, directives, recommendation, declaration, resolution and opinion. Decisions that came in the form of regulation were applicable in all member states, which were required to take all necessary measures to implement them. Directives were addressed to all member state, to undertakings, or to individual. They bound member states to the objectives to be achieved but left governments to determine implementation modalities.[8] Failure to implement regulations and directives would normally attract appropriate sanctions in accordance with Article 23 of the Constitutive Act. Such sanctions could include denial of transport and communication links with other member states and other measures of a political and economic nature to be determined by the Assembly. The assembly was authorized to assign any of these functions to the executive council of foreign ministers, which was the second most important decision-making organ of the Union.

EXECUTIVE COUNCIL

Composed of the foreign ministers of member states, the Executive Council was endowed with executive authority and grappled with the day-to-day operation of the Union on behalf of the Assembly. In a more general manner, the Executive Council prepared the session of the Assembly; determined the issues to be submitted to the Assembly for decision; coordinated and harmonized the policies, activities and initiatives of the Union in areas of common interest to member states. It also monitored the implementation of the policies, decisions and agreements adopted by the Assembly; elected the commissioners to be appointed by the Assembly; elected members of the African Commission on Human and People's Rights and the African Committee of Experts on the Rights and Welfare of the Child; and submitted the list of the elected officials to the Assembly for appointment. The council was also authorized to take appropriate action on issues referred to it by the Assembly; examine the programme and budget of the Union and submit them to Assembly for consideration; promote cooperation and coordination with the regional economic communities, the African Development Bank (ADB), other African Institutions and the United Nations Economic Commission for Africa (UNECA); determine policies for cooperation between the Union and Africa's partners and ensure that all activities and initiatives regarding Africa were in line with the objectives of the Union; decide on the dates and venues of its sessions on the basis of criteria adopted by the Assembly; appoint its chairperson and other office bearers in conformity with the bureau of the Assembly; receive, consider and make recommendations on reports and recommendations from other organs of the Union that did not report directly to the Assembly; set up such ad hoc committees and working groups as it might deem necessary; consider the reports, decisions, projects and programmes of the committees; approve the rules of the committees; oversee, monitor and direct their activities; consider the staff rules and regulations and the financial rules and regulations of the Commission and submit them to the Assembly for adoption; approve the headquarters agreements, and other organs and offices of the Union; consider the structure, functions and statutes of the commission and make recommendations thereon to the Assembly; determine the conditions of service including salaries, allowances and pensions of the staff of the Union; ensure the promotion of gender equality in all programmes of the Union. The Executive Council was also mandated to implement sanction regimes approved by the Assembly in respect of various situations, including (a) arrears of contributions, (b) non-compliance with decisions and policies of the Union, and (c) unconstitutional changes of government, as specified in rules 35, 36 and 37 of the rules of procedure of the Assembly.[9]

The Executive Council, like the Assembly itself, met in ordinary sessions twice a year, and the sessions normally preceded the sessions of the Assembly. The council's agenda generally contained the report of the commission, the report of the Committee of Permanent Representatives, items that the Assembly had referred to it, items that the council itself decided at a previous session to place on its agenda, the draft programme and administrative budget of the union, and items proposed by other organs of the Union. The council also considered items proposed by a member state, provided that the proposal was submitted 60 days before the opening of the session and the supporting documents and draft decisions had been communicated to the chairperson of the commission at least 30 days before the opening of the session. The Executive Council considered such items only on the recommendation of the Permanent Representatives Committee.

The agenda of the Executive Council was generally divided into two parts. the first part grouped those items on which the Permanent Representatives Committee had reached agreement and therefore could be adopted by the Executive Council without discussion. The second part contained items on which the PRC could not reach agreement and therefore required debate by the Executive Council before a decision was taken.

Like the Assembly, the Executive Council too held extraordinary sessions at the instruction of the Assembly, or at the request of the chairperson of the council or the commission or any member state, provided two-thirds of member states gave their approval for the session to be convened.[10]

With regard to decision-making, the Executive Council took all its decisions by consensus or, failing which, by a two thirds majority of the member states eligible to vote. Decisions on questions of procedure were taken by a simple majority of member states eligible to vote. And decisions on whether a question was a matter of procedure were taken by a simple majority of the states eligible to vote.

Decisions of the Executive council were issued in the following forms[11]:

a. *Regulations:* these were binding and applicable in all member states and national laws and shall, where appropriate, be aligned accordingly; The non-implementation of regulations and directives could attract appropriate sanctions in accordance with Article 23 of the Constitutive Act.
b. *Directives:* these were addressed to any or all member states, to undertakings or to individuals. They bound member states to the objectives to be achieved while leaving national authorities with powers to determine the form and the means to be used for their implementation;
c. *Recommendations, declaration, resolutions* and *opinions*: these were not binding and were intended to guide and harmonize the viewpoints of member states.

Decisions adopted by the Executive Council were required to be authenticated by the signature of the chairperson of the Executive Council and the chairperson of the commission, and were published in all the working languages of the Union in the official journal of the African Union within 15 days of the signature and transmitted to all member states. However, the practice was different from the legal provisions. While the texts of the decisions were ordinarily printed and circulated to member states through their missions in Addis Ababa, they were neither signed nor published in the official journal of the Union. The council could delegate any of its functions to the Committee of Permanent Representatives.

PERMANENT REPRESENTATIVES COMMITTEE (PRC)

Composed of permanent representatives and ambassadors accredited to the African Union and other duly accredited plenipotentiaries of member states, the PRC was placed directly below the Executive Council in the decision-making structure of the African Union. Although most permanent representatives were based at the seat of the Union (Addis Ababa), there were countries that were represented on the PRC by non-resident representatives.[12] The rules of procedure also provided that until a country could establish a resident representative in Addis Ababa, it could designate another country from its region to represent it on the committee.[13]

The Permanent Representatives Committee served as an advisory body to the Executive Council.[14] It was required to prepare the meeting of the Executive Council, including the agenda and draft decisions; make recommendations on areas of common interest to member states, particularly on issues on the agenda of the Executive Council; facilitate communication between the commission and capitals of member states; consider the programme and budget of the Union as well as other administrative, budgetary and financial matters of the commission and make recommendation to the Executive Council;[15] consider the financial report of the commission and make recommendation to the Executive Council; consider the report of the board of external auditors and submit written comments to the Executive Council; consider report on the implementation of the budget of the union; propose the composition of the bureaux of the organs of the Union ad hoc committees and subcommittees; consider matters relating to the programme and projects of the Union, particularly issues relating to the socio-economic development and integration of the continent and make recommendations thereon to the Executive Council; consider reports on the implementation of the policies, decisions and agreements adopted by the Executive Council; participate in the preparation of the programme of activities of the Union; participate in the preparation of the calendar of meetings of the Union; carry out any other assignment that may be assigned to it by the Executive Council.[16]

To facilitate its work in the various areas, the PRC established twelve sub-committees as provided for by the rule of procedure.[17] Each of these sub-committees reported directly to the PRC, which was the committee of the whole. The body held its sessions at the headquarters of the Union at least once a month, but sessions preceding the session of the Executive Council were held where the Executive Council was convened. The quorum was constituted by two-thirds of the entire membership of the Union. Like the Executive Council and the Assembly, the sessions of the PRC were closed, although it could decide to hold open sessions.[18] The sessions were chaired by the permanent representative whose country held the chairmanship of the Assembly. The chairperson was assisted by three vice chairpersons and a rapporteur whose countries were members of the bureau of the Assembly.

As it was the case with the Executive Council, the PRC took all its decisions by consensus or, failing which, by a two-thirds majority of member states eligible to vote. Decisions on questions of procedure were taken by a simple majority of the member states eligible to vote, and decisions on whether or not a question was one of procedure were also decided by a simple majority of member states eligible to vote. All decisions by the PRC remained recommendations until when they were adopted by the Executive Council.

Of all the three organs, the Permanent Representatives Committee was the most engaged in the daily operation of the Union. It dealt directly with the commission on a daily basis and was regularly seized with matters relating to the Union. In other words, the permanent representatives of the Union were the foot soldiers of member states with regard to continental integration. For this reason, the PRC had won the admiration of member states.

But the committee had also attracted the displeasure of a few member states who saw the committee as little more than a group of bullies and saboteurs of the integration process through their incessant wrangling over issues and constant confrontation with the commission. Such perception led to the proposal by leaders such as Ghaddafi of Libya to remove the PRC from the structures of the Union.[19] Although that proposal failed to gain sufficient support, it raised questions about the role of the permanent representatives in the whole process of the African Union.

EU AND THE AU: A COMPARATIVE ANALYSIS

Indeed, a case for the permanent representatives in a study like this might suggest the author's biases, having served on that committee for several years. However, an overview of the *Comité Des Représentants Permanents*

(COREPER) of the European Union will demonstrate the importance of the role that permanent representatives play in international affairs.

The most important task of the EU COREPER was the preparation of the meeting of council of ministers and carrying out other tasks assigned to it by the council. When the commission's proposal or memorandum was submitted to the council, the latter entrusted its examination to either the COREPER or, in the case of agriculture issues, to the special committee on agriculture. As the pivot between the technical and political levels, COREPER was assisted by several working parties which examined and reported each issue to it. COREPER itself held sessions in two parts: COREPER part 1, which was composed of Deputy Permanent Representatives, examined technical questions on the whole, and COREPER part 2, which was composed of the ambassadors themselves, dealt with political questions on the whole. The purpose of discussion in the working groups and in the COREPER was to identify in precise details the points of agreement and discord on any proposal, and to try to resolve any remaining disagreement so that the council could focus on the major points of dispute. Once a point had been settled at a lower level, the presidency would try to avoid opening it at a higher level. This was why the council's agenda was often divided into A and B points, the former being issues that had been satisfactorily concluded at a lower level. In both cases, the council's work was much lighter owing to the intervention of COREPER. This was why observers of European affairs argue that COREPER's influence was often greater than that of the formal meeting of the council that it prepared.

The council's General Secretariat, headed by the Secretary General, assisted COREPER and the working parties in carrying out their tasks, and the European Commission participated in all the meetings to explain its position.

The conclusion drawn from the above overview is that despite their proximity to Brussels and the frequency of their meetings, the member states of the European Union depended heavily on their permanent representatives in Brussels on matters relating to European integration. The frequency of the council's meetings (on average 80 per year) also attest to the significance of the intergovernmental process to Europe's match towards the union. The same process was required to push the African Union forward. But Africa's conditions differed markedly from Europe's. Besides the large expanse of the continent, Africa was also confronted with communication difficulties that complicated travelling within the continent. An implication of this was that the Executive Council of the AU could not meet as frequently as its EU counterpart did. Therefore, the intergovernmental process, which lay at the heart of the African Union, needed to be carried out at a different level. Thus, if the Addis Ababa-based permanent representatives did not exist, they would have to be invented. The dissolution of the PRC, as proposed, would have seriously jeopardized the intergovernmental process that lends credibility to the Union and confers legitimacy to its action.

A further glance afield would also reveal that permanent representatives constitute vital instruments of the multilateral processes under way in various fora. The majority of the life or death and peace or war resolutions of the United Nations Security Council were taken at the level of Ambassadors of Security Council members. And the all-important international trade regime that had shaped lives was worked out largely at the level of permanent representatives and other plenipotentiaries of WTO member state. The African Union therefore had to recognize that the objectives set out in the Constitutive Act could be achieved through the same intergovernmental dialogue alone and that the PRC had a vital role to play in that process.

The European Union did not offer parallel to the PRC alone. A close examination of the African Union and the European Union shows considerable similarities between the two institutions. Structurally, both Unions had the heads of state and government at the apex of their structures. They played similar roles: to provide a political direction to the Union and resolve problems that had proved intractable at the level of ministers.[20] However, the Assembly of the African Union was the principal decision-making body within the African Union; it was the Council of Ministers of the European Union that served as the principal decision-making body within the European Union.[21] The European Council's role was limited largely to providing political direction and resolving intractable problems.

While the European Council was required to meet at least twice a year, the Assembly of the African Union was required, under its rules of procedure, to meet at least once a year until 2005.[22] From 2005, the Assembly met twice a year in ordinary sessions. However, both bodies met in extraordinary sessions as frequently as required. Participation in the meetings of the leaders was different. The European Council meetings was open to member states' delegation (led generally by the head of state or government), the Commission of European Union was represented by its president, and only commissioners directly dealing with the subject of the summit were invited to attend. The president of the European Parliament was invited to address the meeting, but was not entitled to attend the proceedings. Similarly, the finance and economic ministers were also invited to meetings at which matters relating to the Economic and Monetary Union (EMU) were discussed.[23] The proceedings of the Assembly of the African Union were less restrictive. While the gatherings were in principle for heads of state and government, they were open to ministers other than foreign ministers, ambassadors and other senior government officials, provided they were included in the official list of delegation of member states. All the eight commissioners attended the proceedings of the Assembly alongside the chairperson and the deputy chairperson. Participation was also opened not only to the president of the Pan African Parliament but also to the chief executive officers of the various regional economic communities. And more often, all the senior officials of the commission attended the summits. However, at times, matters of sensitive nature (such as the chairmanship of the Union) were discussed in closed doors at which participation was limited to only the head of delegation and one member of the national delegation. Observers did not attend and the commission was represented by its chairperson.

The outcomes of discussions at meetings of the European Council were expressed in the form of "conclusions of the presidency." However, these were supplemented by declarations embodying more detailed agreements on substance. These declarations had no legal force, but could have great political importance as pointers to future legislative action.[24] As we have seen, the outcome of the deliberations of the Assembly of the African Union, however, took several forms: regulation, directives, recommendation, declaration, resolution and opinion.[25] Decisions that come in the form of regulation were applicable in all member states, which were required to take all necessary measures to implement them. Directives were addressed to all member state, to undertakings or to individual. They bound member states to the objectives to be achieved but left national authorities to determine implementation modalities.[26] The non-implementation of regulations and directives could normally attract appropriate sanctions in accordance with Article 23 of the Constitutive Act. Such sanctions may include denial of transport and communication links with other member states and other measures of a political and economic nature to be determined by the Assembly. Both the Assembly of the African Union and the European Council took decisions by consensus, but both institutions had provisions for voting.

The Council of Ministers of the European Union and the Executive Council of the African Union bore some resemblance, but were different in one important respect. The EU Council of Ministers had more powers because it was the principal decision-making organ of the Union. Yet both councils operated in a similar fashion. They both took decisions and conferred implementing powers on their commissions or the permanent representatives. Both bodies were composed of representatives of members states at the ministerial level, but the EU rules went further by providing that the representative on the council should have the authority to commit the government of that member states. The African Union rules took this authority for granted. Another difference between the two organs was that the European Union operated a qualified majority voting system,[27] whereas the African Union operated a one-member-one-vote system. In practice, however, both institutions took decisions largely by consensus.

The EU Council of Ministers divided its work into several distinct subject-based Councils that operated in parallel. The senior council within this structure was the council of Foreign Ministers (officially called the General Affairs Council), and the Foreign Minister of each member state was its lead representative on the council.

The Foreign Affair's Council normally met monthly, as did the Councils of Agriculture Ministers, and of Economic and Finance Ministers. There were regular, but less frequent, meetings of the industry, environment, research, transport, social affairs, fisheries and budget councils. Less frequent still were meetings of ministers of development, energy, justice, consumer affairs, regional affairs, culture education and health. From time to time, joint or "jumbo" councils were arranged to discuss cross-cutting issue.[28]

The structure of the African Union was modelled on the European Union structure where the Executive Council, consisting mainly of foreign ministers, was the most senior body after the Assembly; the other sectoral ministers formed the specialized technical committees. But AU Executive Council and other Specialized Technical Ministerial Councils met less frequently.

CONCLUSION

Clearly, the African Union was not designed in a vacuum. The architects of the continental body drew considerable inspiration not only from the OAU but also from extra-continental organizations, such as the European Union. Considering that the EU was Africa's main development partner and that EU had reached a level of integration that pan-Africanists over the years have dreamt for Africa, it was only natural that the AU was modelled on the European Union. The similarities between the EU and the AU carry many advantages. The AU drew inspiration from EU experience in many areas and sought to emulate many best practices, but also fell into the pitfalls that beset the European integration efforts since the Treaty of Rome in 1957.

NOTES

1. *Constitutive Act of the African Union*, Article 5. There are provisions for additional organs that the Assembly may decide to establish.
2. Article 6.3.
3. Article 6.3.
4. In the African Union's context, an equitable geographical distribution meant the allocation on the basis of the size of regions. West Africa, having the largest number of countries invariably got the largest number of shares, although this understanding had increasingly been challenged by other regions. For example, where 15 positions were to be allocated, 4 went to West Africa (with 15 members); 3 to each of Central Africa, East Africa and Southern Africa; and 2 to North Africa.

5. Rule 4 of the Rules of Procedure of the Assembly, Document Assembly/AU/2/(1)-aRev.1, July 2002.

6. Rule 5:2 of the Rules of Procedure of the Assembly.

7. Article 7.

8. Rule 33 of the Rules of Procedure of the Assembly.

9. Rule 36 of the Rules of Procedure of the Executive Council.

10. The general procedure for convening an extraordinary session was as follows: the chairperson of the commission would receive the request for the convening of an extraordinary session. He or she would notify all member states within seven days of the receipt of such a request and invite them to communicate, in writing, their response within a specified period. If the specified period lapsed and the required two-thirds majority had not been attained, the Chairperson of the Commission would notify member states that extraordinary session would not take place. This procedure was at times ignored. In 2005, the Chairperson of the Commission had ruled that since the two-thirds majority could not be attained on the specified date, the proposed extraordinary session scheduled to take place in Abuja in 2005 could not be held. The following day, the Commission advised member states that the Chairperson of the Assembly had instructed that the session would be held, because on the basis of his consultations, the quorum would be attained. The quorum was attained and the meeting went ahead.

11. Rule 34 of the Rules of Procedure of the Executive Council.

12. Member states had taken steps to be represented in Addis Ababa, as required by the Constitutive Act of the African Union. However up to 2012, Guinea Bissau, Sao Tome and Principe, Seychelles Central African republic, and Comoros remained without a resident mission in Addis Ababa.

13. Rule 3.2 of the Rules of Procedure of the Permanent Representatives Committee.

14. Rule 4.

15. Rule 4.

16. Rule 4.

17. Rule 4.2. These were subcommittees on administrative, budgetary and financial matters; programmes and conferences; refugees; contribution; scale of assessment; emergency assistance; structures; headquarters and host country agreements; NEPAD; trade and economic affairs; and multilateral cooperation.

18. Rule 9 of the Rules of Procedure of the Committee of Permanent Representatives.

19. One of the proposed amendments to the Constitutive Act tabled by Libya in 2003 provided for the removal of the PRC from the structure of the union. Ghadafi felt that members of the PRC were scuttling his plans to transform the African Union as he would like to. The Libyan proposal was, however, rejected.

20. Maastricht Treaty (Article D). *Constitutive Act of the African Union*, Article 9.

21. Timothy Bainbridge, *The Penquin Companion to the European Union* (London: Penguin Books, 1998), p. 98

22. However, in 2004, the Assembly took a decision to meet in ordinary sessions twice a year, although a number of countries felt that was not necessary.

23. Timothy Bainbridge, *The Penquine Companion to the European Union*, p. 192.

24. Ibid., p. 114. This section has benefited from the insights of Ambassador Tim Clark, Head of the European Commission Office in Addis Ababa and Carmen de La Pena Corcuera, Ambassador of Spain to Ethiopia.

25. See Section on the Assembly above.

26. Rule 33 of the Rules of Procedure of the Assembly.

27. Until the most recent expansion of the European Union to include the former Eastern European countries, the QMV system was as follows: France 10, Germany 10, Italy 10, United Kingdom 10, Spain 8, Belgium 5, Greece, 5, Netherlands 5, Portugal 5, Austria 4, Sweden 4, Denmark 3, Finland 3, Ireland, 3 Luxemburg 2 (Total 87). For details of this intricate system, see Timothy Bainbridge, *The Penguine Companion to the European Union,* pp. 410–415.

28. In the year 2000, for example, the council held 85 sessions in 16 groups: General Affairs Council: 14 sessions; Agriculture: 10; Finance and Economic Affairs: 13; Environment: 5; Transport and Telecommunication: 8; Labour and Social Affairs 6; Fisheries: 3; Energy and Industry: 3; Justice and Interior: 5; Tourism and Consumer Affairs: 5; Research 2; Budget: 2; Culture: 3; Development: 2; Education and Youth: 2; Health: 2. See Geneviève Bertrand, *La Prise de decision dans l'union européenne*, 2e edition (Paris: la documentation francaise 2002), pp. 38–44.

Chapter 10

The Voice of the People

The Pan African Parliament

The idea of a Pan African Parliament has a fairly recent origin. African leaders neither listed it as one of the organs of the OAU nor mentioned it anywhere in the OAU charter. Indeed, at that time, it was inconceivable that a body of this nature could be entertained at the continental level. Thus, for so many years, the OAU took decisions on behalf of the African people without any attempt to associate African people directly. This undoubtedly epitomized the intergovernmental thesis about integration. It was the Abuja Treaty that made the first concrete attempt to promote popular participation in African integration process. As one commentator puts it, the wind of change that swept across the continent in the late 1980s and early 1990s weakened resistance to multiparty democracy in many parts of the world. At the level of the African continent, the OAU was also forced to show that it was more than a club of governments. The Abuja Treaty, which was adopted in 1991, provided that in order to ensure that the peoples of Africa were fully involved in the economic development and integration of the continent, a Pan African Parliament should be established.[1] The treaty went further by providing for a protocol that defined the composition, function, powers and organization of the Pan African Parliament.[2] Despite the enthusiasm that greeted the conception of the African Economic Community, it took member states ten years to operationalize the treaty provision relating to the Pan African Parliament. After several sessions of lengthy discussions at the levels of experts, ambassadors and ministers, member states of the OAU were able to adopt during their meeting in Sirte, Libya in March 2001 the protocol to the Treaty Establishing the African Economic Community Relating to the Pan African Parliament.[3] The Constitutive Act of the African Union subsequently recognized the Pan African Parliament as one of the key organs of the African Union.

According to the protocol, the Pan African Parliament shall represent all the peoples of African. Its ultimate aim was to evolve into an institution with full legislative powers, whose members were to be elected by universal adult suffrage.[4] However, it was stated clearly that until such time, as member states decided otherwise by an amendment to the protocol, the Pan African Parliament shall have consultative and advisory role only,[5] and its members were to be appointed in accordance with the provisions of the protocol. Accordingly, during the interim period, member states shall be represented in the parliament by five members, at least one of whom must be a woman; and the representation of each member state must reflect the diversity of political opinions in each national parliament or deliberative organ from which the representatives were chosen.[6]

The term of office was regulated by Article 5 of the protocol. The term of a member of the Pan African parliament ran concurrently with his or her term in the National Parliament or other deliberative organ.[7] His or her seat became vacant if the Parliamentarian died, resigned, or was physically or mentally incapacitated, was removed on grounds of misconduct, ceases to be a members of his national parliament, was recalled by his or her national parliament, or his or her country withdrew from the African Union.[8]

The objectives of the Parliament as spelt out in Article 3 of the protocol included the following:

1. facilitate the effective implementation of the policies and objectives of the OAU/AEC and, ultimately, the African Union;
2. promote the principles of human rights and democracy in Africa;
3. encourage good governance, transparency and accountability in member states;
4. familiarize the people of Africa with the objectives and policies aimed at integrating the African continent within the framework of the African Union;
5. promote peace, security and stability;
6. contribute to a more prosperous future for the peoples of Africa by promoting collective self-reliance and economic recovery;
7. facilitate cooperation and development in Africa, strengthen continental solidarity and build a sense of common destiny among the peoples of Africa;
8. facilitate cooperation among regional economic communities and their parliamentary fora.

To fulfil these objectives, the protocol provides that the Parliament shall be vested with legislative powers. It was envisaged that during the first five years of its existence, the Pan African Parliament would play advisory and consultative role only. More specifically, its immediate functions during the initial five years were to:

1. examine, discuss or express an opinion on any matter, either on its own initiative or at the request of the Assembly or other policy organs and make recommendations it may deem fit relating to, inter alia, matters pertaining to respect for human rights, the consolidation of democratic institutions and the culture of democracy, as well as the promotion of good governance and the rule of law;
2. discuss its budget and the budget of the community and make recommendations thereon, prior to its approval by the Assembly;
3. work towards the harmonization or coordination of the laws of member states;
4. make recommendations aimed at contributing to the attainment of the objectives of the OAU/AEC and draw attention to the challenges facing the integration process in Africa as well as strategies for dealing with them;
5. request officials of the AU Commission to attend its sessions, produce documents or assist in the discharge of its duties;
6. promote the programmes and objectives of the OAU/AEC in the constituencies of the member states;
7. promote the coordination and harmonization of the policies, measures, programmes and activities of the regional economic communities and other parliamentary fora in Africa;;
8. adopt its rules of procedure, elect its own president and propose to the Council and the Assembly the size and the nature of the support staff of the Pan African Parliament;
9. perform such other functions as it deems appropriate to achieve the objectives of the Union.

It was expected that exercising these functions, the Pan African Parliamentarians would enjoy the immunities and privileges extended to representatives of member states under the General Convention on the Privileges and Immunities of the OAU and the Vienna Convention on Diplomatic Relations.[9] More specifically, a member of the Pan African Parliament shall not be liable to civil or criminal proceedings, arrest, imprisonment or damages for what was said or done by him or her within or outside the Pan African Parliament in his or her capacity as a member of the Pan African Parliament in the discharge of his or her duties.[10] However, the Pan African Parliament would decide to waive the immunity of a member in accordance with its rules of procedure.

The protocol allowed the parliamentarians to adopt their rule of procedure (by a two-thirds majority), but offered a detailed guidelines as to how the body would operate as well as on how the officers would take charge of the daily operations of the Parliament. Accordingly, the officers of the Pan African Parliament who were to include the president and the vice presidents would be responsible for the management and administration of the affairs and facilities of the Pan African Parliament and its organs. They were to be assisted by a clerk, two deputy clerks and such other staff and functionaries as deemed necessary for the proper discharge of their function. The rules gave the president the authority to presided over all parliamentary proceedings except those held in committee, and the office of the president or that of the vice president would be deemed vacant in the event of their death or resignation, or if they suffered physical or mental incapacity, ceased to be a member of national parliament, or withdrew by national parliament or their country withdrew from the African Union.

Decisions in the house were to be taken by consensus or by a two-thirds majority of members present and voting. However, like in most African Union organs, procedural matters were to be decided by simple majority of members present and voting.[11]

THE FORMATIVE PERIOD

The first session of the Pan African Parliament was convened in Addis Ababa on 18 March 2004 amidst considerable pomp and fanfare. In attendance were the chairperson-in-office of the Union, President Joaquim Alberto Chisasano of Mozambique, President Girma Wolde-Giorgis and Mr Meles Zenawi, respectively, President and Prime Minister of Ethiopia, and Professor Alpha Oumar Konare, Chairperson of the Commission of the African Union, 202 parliamentarians from the 41 countries that had already deposited their instruments of ratification of the protocol. In accordance with the provisions of the protocol, Ambassador Gertrude Mongela of Tanzania was elected the first chairperson of the parliament. Four other parliamentarians were elected as first, second, third and fourth vice chairpersons. At the same session, the members of Parliament set up three committees dealing with rules, budget and credentials.

The Parliament held its second ordinary session in South Africa, the seat of the Parliament. Among the items that the proceedings covered were the adoption of the rules of procedure and the setting up of ten other committees.[12].

In addition to the setting up of committees and administrative structures, PAP's activities centred on the implementation of its first strategic plan 2006–2010. The main objective of the strategic plan was the gradual institutional transformation of the Pan African Parliament from its consultative and advisory role to a body with full legislative powers. In order to achieve those objectives, the strategy laid out activities in two areas: institutional development and promotion of political agenda. Activities envisaged under institutional development include:

a. development of a resource mobilization plan and strategy;
b. share and transfer of knowledge, skills and expertise from other parliamentary institutions;
c. identification and mobilization of potential supporters on the African continent and beyond;
d. establishment of a unit within PAP to be responsible for resource mobilization and management;
e. encouragement of national parliaments to create a dedicated budget line for PAP activities; and
f. consolidation of the PAP Trust Fund to finance extra-budgetary activities.

The political agenda consisted of the following measures:

a. representation of the voices of the peoples of Africa so as to create unity and dignity of Africa;
b. promotion, protection and defence of the principles of human rights, gender parity, democracy, peace and security;
c. enhancement of the oversight capacity of PAP;
d. promotion of the harmonization of continental, regional and national laws to foster continental integration;
e. support for inter-institutional and other deliberative organs; and
f. transformation of PAP from advisory and consultative body to a full legislative organ.

According to PAP's own reports, members of the parliament pursued the political agenda by contributing to debates on key issues facing the African continent, such as the New Partnership for Africa's Development (NEPAD), the African Peer Review Mechanism (APRM) and migration. Within the context of its political agenda, the PAP also attempted to show some independence by adopting independent positions on certain issues, especially as they relate to governance and human rights. For example, in 2006, PAP adopted a resolution calling for the unconditional release of Dr Kizza Besigye, an opposition leader in Uganda. It also called on African governments to repeal laws that were deemed to stand against media freedom.[13] Additionally, the PAP issued many recommendations and resolutions on a range of issues such as the peace and security and AU funding. It also dispatched fact-finding missions to conflict zones and observed elections in member states.[14] Participation in various consultative fora was also reported in the annual reports.

Table 10.1 Budget Appropriations of the Pan African Parliament 2004–2012

Year	*Operations*	*Programmes*	*Total*
2014	10,891,000	3,400,000	14,300,000
2013	10,372,000	120,000	10,493,000
2011	9,586,223	2,286,000	11,872,223
2010	9,129,736	5,019,514	14,149,250
2009	9,535,477	3,943,477	13,478,924
2007	6,406,959	—	6,406,959
2005	5,600,000	—	5,600,000
2004	5,000,000	—	5,600,000

Source: African Union, Various Decisions of the Assembly and the Executive Council

A closer assessment of the Pan African Parliament will reveal a disjuncture between PAP's ambitions and the resources put at its disposal as well as the powers that member states ceded to it. As Table 10.1 shows, the regular operational budget of the Pan African Parliament grew steadily from US$5 million in 2004 to US$9.5 million in 2011 and to US$10.9 million in 2014. Although there was no budget for programmes before 2009, the Assembly approved a total of 8 million for programmes between 2009 and 2013, even if much of this was coming from partners.[15] Programme budget rose from 3 million in 2009 to US$5 million in 2010, before it dropped to USD2.2 million and to a paltry US$120,000 in 2013.

In 2009, the Assembly asked the African Union Commission to initiate the review of the protocol establishing the Pan African Parliament. The revised protocol was examined by government legal experts and approved by the Ministers of Justice in May 2012. However, controversial provisions relating to the legislative and oversight functions of the parliament kept the amended draft from being accepted at the level of the Executive Committee.

In essence, the controversy revolved around the proposed powers and functions of the Parliament. The revised protocol provided that the Pan African Parliament shall be the legislative organ of the African Union, and shall exercise legislative powers to be defined by the Assembly. It might propose draft laws to the Assembly, which shall determine the subject area of such proposed draft laws. Article 8.2 further provided that the Pan African Parliament shall have consultative and oversight powers to:

a. receive and consider annual reports on the activities of all the other organs of the AU, including audit reports and any other reports referred to it by the council and make recommendations thereon to the council;
b. debate and adopt the budget of the AU for the approval of the Assembly;
c. establish any committee, determine its mode and prescribe its procedures;
d. discuss all questions relevant to the AU including the Constitutive Act and make recommendations thereon to the council;

e. discuss any matter and make recommendations thereon to the Assembly;
f. make proposals to the council on the size and number of the support staff of the Secretariat of the Pan African Parliament taking into account the specific needs of a continental Parliament;
g. request the attendance of officials of the other organs of the AU at its sessions.

Other controversial provisions relate to the proposal for PAP to receive and consider annual reports of other AU organs, adopt the AU budget approval by the Assembly, as well as to summon officials of the various organs to the sessions of PAP.

Proponents of the new proposal contended that having legislative functions would not automatically mean that PAP could legislate supranational laws for member states without those laws being adopted by the Assembly and ratified by the national authorities.[16] With respect to the oversight functions, the supporters of the amendment maintained that Article 8.2 of the draft amendment was just a repetition of the provisions of paragraphs 1, 2 and 5 of Article 11 of the existing protocol. As a result, the Assembly that invariably acted on the recommendation of the Executive Council decided to subject the draft text for further consultation. Arguably, the length of time that parallels like the European Parliaments took to obtain legislative authority gave the "gradualist" additional ammunition.

Among the four institutions provided for under Article 7 of the 1951 Treaty of Paris establishing the European Coal and Steel Community (ECSC) was a Common Assembly, to be composed of representatives of the peoples of the states brought together in the community.[17] It was given supervisory powers, and its members were nominated by the national parliaments from among their own members in accordance with procedures laid down by each member state. Thus, the European Parliament did not achieve legislative authority overnight, and its members were not directly elected by universal adult suffrage even though it was foreseen that the MEPs would one day be directly elected rather than nominated.[18]

It was the treaties establishing the European Economic Community and the European Atomic Energy Community (Euratom) that brought the first important changes to the status and composition of the Assembly. Because these two treaties provided for each community to have an Assembly, the ECSC Assembly was expanded to cover all three communities under the European Convention on certain institutions common to the European Communities' signed in Rome at the same time as the EEC and the Euratom Treaties. Thus, the number of MEPs was increased from 78 to 142, but members were still nominated by their national parliaments: Belgium had 14, France 36, Luxembourg 6, Italy 36, The Netherlands 14 and West Germany 36.[19] Under the new dispensation, the powers of the Parliament remained largely the same, except that in addition to its supervisory role, as provided for under the ECSC Treaty, it also exercised advisory functions. With the expansion of the EEC in 1973 to include Demark, Ireland and the United Kingdom, the number of MEPs was further increased from 142 to 198.[20] Discussion about direct elections to the European Parliament begun in earnest in 1974, when at a meeting in Paris, the European Council decided that direct election should be held as soon as possible. During its meeting in Rome in the following year, the European Council decided that the direct election should be held in May or June of 1978. However, direct election took place only in 1979. While taking the decision on direct election, the European Council also opted to extend the competence of the European Parliament in the community's legislative process.[21] This was gradually granted. Therefore, it took some 27 years for the MEPs to be directly elected and an equal length of time for the institution to acquire appropriate legislative authority. The MEPs' decision to reject the community's budget in 1980, only a year after the community-wide elections in 1979, was another consideration that might not be too far from the mind of those calling for the gradual empowerment of the Pan African Parliament. In addition to the fact that African states still maintained firm grips on their sovereignty, PAP's own balance sheet did not help matters.

The PAP may have held debates on wide-raging issues, sent missions of different kinds, taken independent positions on important issues and issued recommendations on various topics. There was, however, little evidence that decisions taken by the Executive Council or the Assembly during 2004–2009 acknowledged or reflected any of the PAP's recommendations as contained in the various reports the body issued.[22] This led one independent assessment of PAP's performance to conclude that "PAP has had little impact on substantive issues of significance to the Continent."[23]

At the institutional level, relations between PAP and other organs such as the African Union Commission and the Permanent Representatives Committee remained poor. As a result, invitations that PAP extended to other AU organs, such as the African Union Commission, the Secretariat of NEPAD and the African Peer Review Mechanism (APRM) to present reports to the parliament, remained largely unanswered.[24] The overall effect of these problems was that the PAP lacked an effective voice in AU's decision-making processes.[25]

With regard to its oversight functions, PAP's performance had been equally poor. On several occasions, PAP complained that inadequate financial resources had reduced its ability to carry out its mandate and to implement projects.[26] The budget of the Pan African Parliament might have been inadequate in the eyes of its members, but its growth followed the pattern of growth of the regular budget of the commission of the African Union.

Between 2004 and 2012, the budget of both the parliament and the commission grew by 50 per cent. For PAP's critics, the problem was not inadequate financial resources; it was PAP's inability to achieve effective supervision of its own budget. Allegations as well as reports of financial misappropriation and mismanagement of funds were unearthed by PAP's own internal investigations and confirmed by an audit process that led to sanctions by the Executive Council. This and similar shortcomings not only reduced PAP's influence, it also strengthened the resistance of member states to give PAP a more supranational authority. This was reflected in an interview with one of PAP's own members.[27]

The size of the Pan African Parliament was another challenge that was not readily recognized. While the European Parliament started as a body of three and then six member states, the Pan African Parliament begun as a full-fledged continental body, with challenges and tribulations that large organizations face.

CONCLUSION

Just like the African Union itself, the inception of the Pan African Parliament attracted varied comments. In most quarters, it was hailed as another example of Africa's determination to break with the past and move forward, particularly in the area of governance. The ultimate objective was to have the parliamentarians elected by universal adult suffrage and the parliament itself to evolve into an institution with full legislative powers that would subsequently take precedence over national legislatures. The consultative role was to be phased out within a period of five years.[28] But the reluctance of Executive Council and the Assembly to accept the revised protocol suggested that governments were not fully prepared to give the PAP full legislative powers.[29] The sense of sovereignty was still strong on the continent, and continued to inhibit moves to give supranational status to the Pan African Parliament. As Colin Legum has aptly put it, whereas other illusions and institutions were shattered by the disorder and the turmoil that characterized Africa's post-independence period, the importance and the need for sovereign nation state is the only idea that has endured.[30] In addition to this, PAP's low impact on continental issues, weak oversight capacity, charges of financial indiscipline and poor relations with sister AU institutions all combined to inhibit PAP's evolution into a full-fledged legislative body.

Notwithstanding these challenges, the Pan African Parliament had an important role to play in Africa's match towards integration. The Parliament could have been an effective tool for outreach to the population of the continent that still looked at the African Union as a remote and distant entity.

The Parliament could also have advanced the integration agenda by having a strong bearing on the ratification process that stalled the implementation of several African Union treaties. Out of the various treaties concluded by AU member states, only half were in force by 2012; and much of the slow implementation of the treaties was blamed on the slow ratification process. Thus, an AU-sensitive national legislature would have certainly helped speed up ratification and implementation of the AU treaties. In sum, therefore, the Pan African Parliament faced considerable challenges, but also held considerable prospects in Africa's integration process.

NOTES

1. Article 14. paragraph 1.
2. Art.14.2 of the Treaty Establishing the African Economic Community.
3. Protocol to the Treaty Establishing the Abuja Treaty relating to the Pan African Parliament, Article 2 Paragraph, 3.
4. Protocol to the Treaty Establishing the African Economic Community, Abuja 1991.
5. Ibid.
6. Ibid. Art. 4, paragraphs 2 and 3.
7. Ibid. Art. 5, paragraph 3.
8. Ibid. Art. 5, paragraph 4 and Article 19.
9. Article 8, paragraph 1.
10. Article 9, paragraph 1.
11. Article 12, paragraph 12.
12. These were the committee on Rural Economy, Agriculture, Natural Resources and Environment; the Committee on Monetary and Financial Affairs; the Committee on Trade, Customs, and Immigration Matters; Committee on Cooperation, International Relations and Conflict Resolution; the Committee on Transport, Industry, Communications, Energy, Science and Technology; the Committee on Health Labour and Social Affairs; the Committee on Education, Culture, Tourism and Human Resources; the Committee on Gender, Family, Youth and People with Disability; the Committee on Justice and Human Rights; and the Committee on Rules, Privileges and Discipline.
13. See Pan African Parliament Resolution Press Freedom for Development and Governance: Need for Reform: Resolution PAP/P/(3)RES/08/(1); see also "Pan-African Parliament Calls on African Countries to Repeal Oppressive Media Laws", available at http://mediarightsagenda.net/pan-african-parliament-calls-on-african-countries-to-repeal-oppressive-media-laws/
14. Countries where fact-finding missions were sent include Chad, Côte d'Ivoire, Sudan (Darfur), Mauritania, Rwanda, the Sahrawi Arab Democratic Republic, South Sudan and Mali. Election observers were sent to Angola, Democratic Republic of

Congo (DRC), Kenya, Zimbabwe, Senegal, Gambia, Congo, Libya, Burkina Faso, Sierra Leone, Ghana, Djibouti, Kenya.

15. Executive Council Decision No EX.CL/Dec 455(XIV)

16. Report of the Pan African Parliament for the period July 2012–May 2013.

17. The other three were High Authority (later the European Commission), a Special Council of Ministers and a Court of Justice. For more on this see Bainbridge, *The Penguin Companion to European Union*, pp. 218–241.

18. Article 21.3 of the Treaty of Paris, cited Bainbridge, *The Penguin Companion to European Union* p. 218.

19. Bainbridge, *The Penguin Companion to European Union*. p. 219.

20. The additional seats were distributed as follows: Demark 10, Ireland 10 and the United Kingdom 36. Ibid., p. 220.

21. Ibid., p. 222.

22. Ogochukwu Nzewi, "The Challenges of Post-1990 Regional Integration in Africa: The Pan African Parliament," *Policy Brief 57* (Johannesburg: Centre for Policy Studies 2009), p. 10; available on

23. See High Level Panel, *Audit of African Union 2007*, p. 80, para 224.

24. See Ogochukwo Nzewi, "Rapid or Incremental Change: Assigning Greater Legislative Powers to the Pan African Parliament," *Research Report 123* (Johannesburg: Centre for Policy Studies 2010), p. 18.

25. See, "Zuma: PAP is Voiceless," in *News 24*, 26 October 2009, available on http://www.news24.com/Africa/News /Zuma-PAP-is-voiceless.

26. See High Level Panel, *Audit of the African Union 2007*, and Report of the Pan-African Parliament for the Period July 2012–May2013; and Jakkie Cilliers and Prince Mashele, The Pan-African Parliament: A Plenary of Parliament, Essay 2004.

27. Ogochukwo Nzewi "Rapid Or Incremental Change."

28. African Union Commission Press Release No. 093 /2003 Addis Ababa, 14 November 2003.

29. See Klaas van Walraven. "From Union of Tyrants to Power to People? The Significance of the Pan-African Parliament for the African Union," *Afrika Spectrum*, 39, 2 (2004), pp. 197–221.

30. Colin Legum, *Africa Since Independence*, pp. 72–73.

Chapter 11

The Continental Bureaucracy

The Commission of the African Union

There was hardly any institution that was more central to the operations of the African Union than the commission. Combining both administrative and executive functions, the commission was the centrepiece of the Union and the locomotive of the whole integration process. As such, it constituted a perfect barometer of the state of the Union. This chapter offers a brief survey of the background, the composition and the mandate of this important organ as well as the challenges and constraints it faced.

Like all the major organs of the Union, the commission of the African Union was established under Article 5 of the Constitutive Act, and its functions and structure broadly outlined in Article 20. While endowed with some executive authority, the commission played the role of the Secretariat of the Union.[1] According to the Constitutive Act, it shall be composed of the chairman, his or her deputy or deputies and other commissioners. It was the statute of the commission, as adopted by the Assembly of heads of state and government during its first session in Durban in July 2002, that specified the structure, the mandate and the composition of the commission. It was composed of ten members: the chairperson, the deputy chairperson and eight commissioners.[2] The choice of a ten-member commission was accounted for by the size of the mandate assigned to the commission and the need to have all five regions of the continent represented equally at that level.[3] In order to give more face to the principle of gender mainstreaming that the Assembly adopted during its first ordinary session in Durban in 2002, it was decided that at least one of the commissioners from each region shall be a woman.[4]

The actual establishment of the commission might have taken place in 2003, but the process began immediately upon the entry into force of the Constitutive Act. Activities undertaken prior to the establishment of the commission include a study the ILO had undertaken in order to determine the appropriate structure that would be put in place to make the commission of the African Union dynamic and effective. In addition to the structure of the commission, the study also looked at the conditions of service that would motivate existing personnel and attract new and competent staff. For the following 12 months, these issues occupied centre stage in the activities of the Secretariat and the deliberations of the Permanent Representatives Committee.

The ILO study and consultation with the various stakeholders formed the basis of a report of the interim commission that identified 13 tasks that had to be accomplished prior to the establishment of the commission. These included the establishment of an appropriate structure of the commission, determining the conditions of service and computing the financial implications of the structure.[5]

The Interim Commission's report was the subject of lengthy discussion first at the level of the PRC subcommittee on structures and subsequently in the plenary. The final recommendation of the PRC was adopted by the Executive Council during an extraordinary session held in Sun City, South Africa, from 19 to 24 May 2003. The broad terms of the recommendations include a structure with a staff compliment of 749 and a salary scale based on the pay scale of the Southern African Development Community (SADC).[6]

Thus, as Figure 11:1 shows, the commission of the African Union is divided into 10 units: the office of the chairperson, the office of the deputy chairperson and the offices of the eight commissioners, called departments.

The commission's function was spelt out in Article 3 of the Statute of the Commission. It included representing the Union and defending its interest; initiating and submitting proposals to member states, implementing decisions taken by other policy organs; acting as custodian of the Constitutive Act and other legal instruments of the Union; assisting member states to implement the programmes of the Union, tabling draft common positions and coordinating the action of member states in international negotiations, preparing and submitting budget estimates to member states; collecting and managing the budgetary and other financial resources of the Union; managing the assets and liabilities of the Union; promoting integration and socio-economic development as well as peace, democracy, security and stability on the continent. It was also required to provide operational support to the various organs of the Union, develop, promote, coordinate and harmonize the programmes of the Union with those of the regional economic communities, as well as undertake administrative duties such as preparing and submitting to member states, standing orders, rules and regulations of the Union and keeping the books of the Union.

The individual responsibilities of the chairperson, the deputy chairperson and other members of the commission were provided for in Article 8 of the statutes.

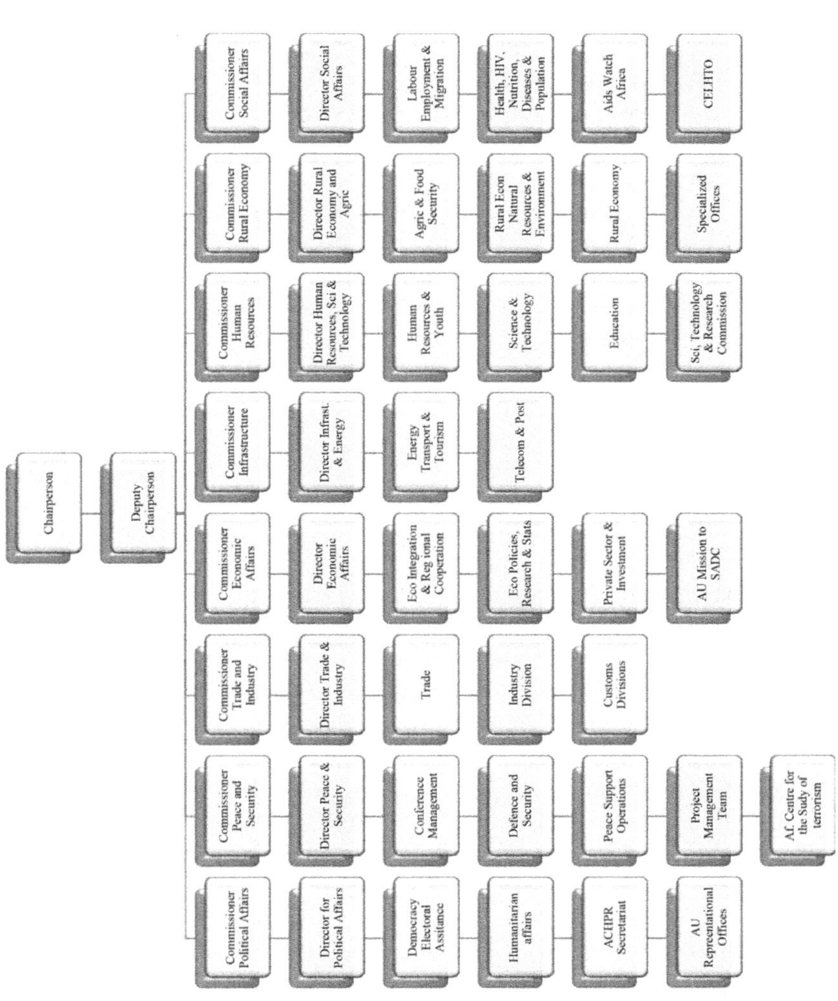

Figure 11.1 Organigramme of the Commission of the African Union

Among other things, the chairperson was required to undertake the following functions:

1. chair all meetings and consultation of the commission;
2. promote and popularize the objectives of the Union;
3. promote cooperation with other organizations;
4. keep records of the deliberations of all the organs of the Union;
5. report to the other organs of the Union;
6. prepare staff rules, audited accounts and programmes of work;
7. act as depository of the legal instruments of the Union as well as the instruments of ratification of member states;
8. receive and safeguard copies of international agreements entered into between or among members states;
9. receive and circulate to all member states the notification of member states that may desire to renounce their membership;[7]
10. in conjunction with the Committee of Permanent Representatives, and upon the approval of the Assembly, create or abolish any administrative or technical office as may be deemed necessary for the adequate operations of the commission;
11. appoint the staff of the commission in accordance with the provisions of the Article 18 of the Statutes of the Commission;
12. assume overall responsibility for the administration and finances of the commission;
13. carry out diplomatic representation of the Union and such other functions as may be determined by the assembly or the Executive Council.

As for the deputy chairperson, in addition to such other function that the chairperson might delegate to him, he is required to

1. assist the chairperson in the exercise of his or her duties;[8]
2. be in charge of the administration and finance of the commission;
3. act as chairperson in case of death or permanent incapacity of the latter, pending the appointment of a new chairperson.[9]

Commissioners were responsible for the implementation of decisions, policies and programmes in respect of the portfolio for which they had been elected; and they were accountable to the chairperson.[10]

The term of office of members of the commission was four years. They were eligible for re-election for another term of four years. The Assembly of the Union had the powers to terminate the appointment of the chairperson, the deputy chairperson or any other commissioner.[11] During their term of office and in the performance of their duties, members of the commission and other staff were required did not seek or receive instructions from any government or from any other authority external to the Union. They were to refrain from any action that might reflect adversely on their position as international officials responsible only to the Union.[12] They were not allowed to engage in any other occupation, whether gainfully or not. In the event a member of the commission breached his or her obligations, the Assembly could, on the recommendation of the Executive Council or the Commission, determine the disciplinary measures to be applied. In the event that other staff members of the commission breached their obligations, the provisions of the staff rules and regulations were to apply, but the staff member was given the right of appeal to the African Court of Justice after exhausting all the internal administrative remedies.[13]

ESTABLISHMENT OF THE COMMISSION

Notwithstanding the fact that the African Union succeeded the OAU, which had its own management team composed of a Secretary General and several deputy secretary generals, the selection of the first management team of the new commission proved considerably delicate. The selection modalities, as provided for in the Statute of the Commission, were too elaborate to be covered here in any exhaustive manner.[14] What I have provided here is just a brief description of the selection of the first college of commissioners that served under Professor Oumar Konare in order to give the reader a sense of what many saw as a major power politics on the continent.

The first stage involved the pre-selection of the candidates, and this was left to regional groupings. Individual country nominations were submitted to the regional bodies that treated applications in accordance with their own procedures. The regions were required to nominate two candidates, including a woman, for each portfolio. The candidates selected at the regional level formed part of the continental pool, which went through a central pre-selection process.

The central pre-selection process was conducted by a ministerial panel,[15] consisting of two ministers from each of the five regions. The panel was assisted by a team of independent consultants, whose mandate included assisting the Ministerial Panel to analyse, evaluate and ascertain the academic qualification and the relevance of the work experience. For each portfolio, the panel submitted a list of candidates, ranked according to scores ranging from 50 to 100. During this phase of the exercise, the decision that proved most delicate was in relation to the division of the portfolios along gender lines. The Departments of Social Affairs, Political Affairs, Trade and Industry and Human Resources, Science and Technology, Rural Economy and Agriculture were assigned to women, while the position of chairperson, deputy chairperson were reserved for men, and so were the departments of economic affairs, infrastructure and energy and peace and security. The criticism that was levelled against this distinction was that in as much as the union required gender mainstreaming, the decision was arbitrary because it meant that the best women candidates fell off the list of candidates applying for portfolios reserved for men, and vice versa. The reason given by the ministerial panel was that some of the portfolios had no female applicant. The panel could not therefore give such portfolios to women. After a series of consultations, and a heated debate during an extraordinary session in Sun City, South Africa, the Executive Council endorsed the recommendation of the ministerial panel regarding the assignment of the various portfolios along gender lines. By the time the Assembly was convened in Maputo in July 2003, 20 women and 14 men were in line for the ten positions. By the time the summit was over eight of the ten members of the commission were elected.[16] The two remaining commissioners were elected during the subsequent session of the Council in Addis Ababa in February 2004.[17]

Some of the difficulties encountered in 2003 were resolved by 2008, when the second commission that served under the chairmanship of Jean Ping of Gabon was elected. However, new problems emerged in 2012 that made the election of the third commission a more eventful process.[18]

The term of the second commission came to an end in December 2011. Thus, when the AU Assembly met in its 18th Ordinary Session in Addis Ababa in January 2012, the main item on the agenda was the election of the chairperson and other members of the commission. The incumbent Chair of the Commission Jean Ping of Gabon was challenged in the position by Dr Nkosazana Dlamini-Zuma, former Minister of Foreign Affairs of South Africa.

Despite South Africa's weight on the continent, Mr. Ping was expected to be re-elected for a second term, as he was assured of the support of French-speaking countries from both Central and West Africa and that of other West African states, including demographic giant and South Africa's rival for a permanent seat on the UN Security Council, Nigeria.

However, Mr. Ping was unable to convince African leaders to grant him a second term. After three consecutive rounds of voting, where he held a slight lead over his challenger, Jean Ping missed the necessary two-thirds majority votes of 36 (winning 32 votes) in a solitary fourth round. A last-minute compromise entrusted him with the chairmanship of the commission for the next six months. When the elections were conducted again in July 2012, Dr Dlamini-Zuma secured a simple majority in the first three rounds of the elections before securing victory in the fourth and final round.

Dr Zuma election was a subject of intense analyses. The debate revolved around the reasons why Dr Dlamini-Zuma gained more than 60 per cent of confidence votes from the AU member states after the deadlock in January. Many observers saw Zuma's victory as an outcome of South Africa's and Southern African Development Community's (SADC) persistent diplomatic efforts. But a more objective analysis that Cilliers and Okeke have undertaken shows that it was only necessary for two or three countries that had voted for Mr. Ping in January to vote for Dr Zuma for her to win. In any event, her election shows that the AU member states could transcend some of Africa's colonial divisions, especially those along linguistic lines.

The Statutes of the African Union Commission provided that the college of ten commissioners were to be assisted by a corps of suitably qualified men and women. These were to be recruited by a recruitment board, comprising the members of the commission, the head of human resources, the legal counsel and a representative of the staff association.[19] However, on the recommendation of the Permanent Representatives' Committee, the Executive Council endorsed a recruitment process where an independent team of consultants was hired to screen and shortlist candidates for each position. The commission selected candidates on the basis of the consultant's recommendation, taking into account the requirement for an equitable geographical balance, the quota system[20] and the principle of gender mainstreaming. Thus, the staff strength of the African Union Commission varied over time. Between 2003 and 2007, the overall number of staff increased dramatically from 284 to 617 personnel. By mid-2011, the figure of actual staff compliment was estimated at around 700, although 912 staff compliment was approved in 2011.

To enhance its human resource management, the African Union Commission put in place a number of measures, including the introduction of performance management, and the setting up of human resources roster. But most significantly, the commission undertook major reforms that allowed departments to spearhead the whole recruitment process from the drafting of job description to shortlisting of candidates. The Appointment and Promotion Board (APROB) too was revived and this facilitated the recruitment process in such a way that the commission was able to recruit 65 new staff in 2011 alone.

Despite these advances, a number of challenges remained. The AUC quota system, though desirable for the sake of equity and fairness, proved debilitating as it delayed recruitment considerably in various instances.[21] These difficulties led to a situation where positions were filled with temporary short-term contract holders or foreign-funded consultants.[22]

FINANCING THE COMMISSION OF THE AFRICAN UNION

For many years, the African Union had one budget (the recurrent budget), which was assessed to member states on the basis of a laid-down scale of

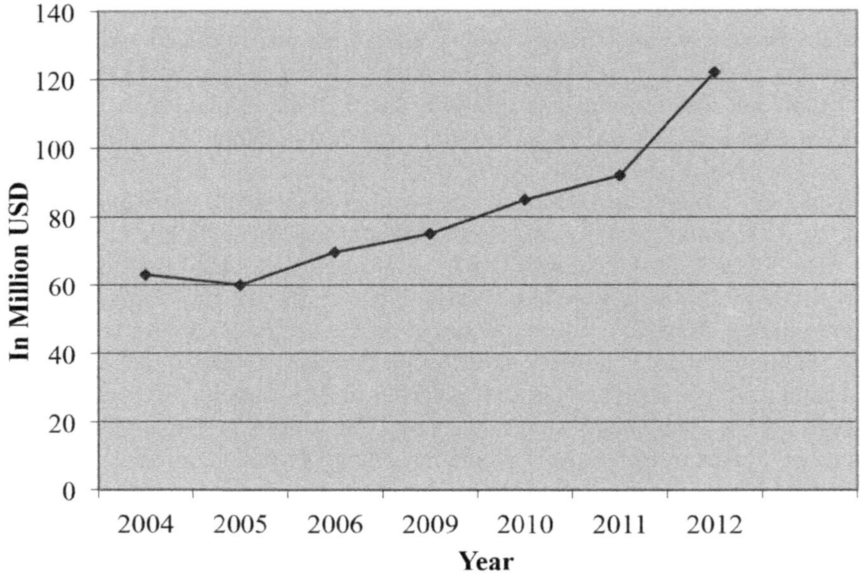

Figure 11.2 Operational Budget of the African Union Commission 2004–2012

assessment, similar to the one used in most international organizations. The Union also had a number of funds which received voluntary contribution from member states and the international donors. However, from 2004, attempts were made to divide the budget into the recurrent budget and programme budget. The programme budget was to be raised through voluntary contribution from member states and the international community. At the end of 2004 financial year, only Ethiopia, South Africa and Nigeria made any voluntary contribution to the programme budget.[23]

During the period 2004–2012, African Union budgetary appropriation rose from USD158 million to USD 274 million. As Figure 11.2 shows, operational budget rose from 63 million in 2004 to 75 million in 2009 and to 122 in 2012. Programme budget went from around USD63 million in 2009 to around USD152 million in 2012. Together, the programme and operational budget rose from 137.85 million in 2009 to 274 million in 2012, making a total of 877 million, almost 10 per cent higher than the amount initially estimated for the full implementation of the strategic plan 2009–2012.

The problem AU faced in the area of budgetary resources was in two forms. First, member states were less supportive of AU's development budget. Although member states accounted for the entirety of the operational budget, they accounted for less than 10 per cent of the programme budget. As Figure 11.3 shows, partners accounted for over 90 per cent of the programme

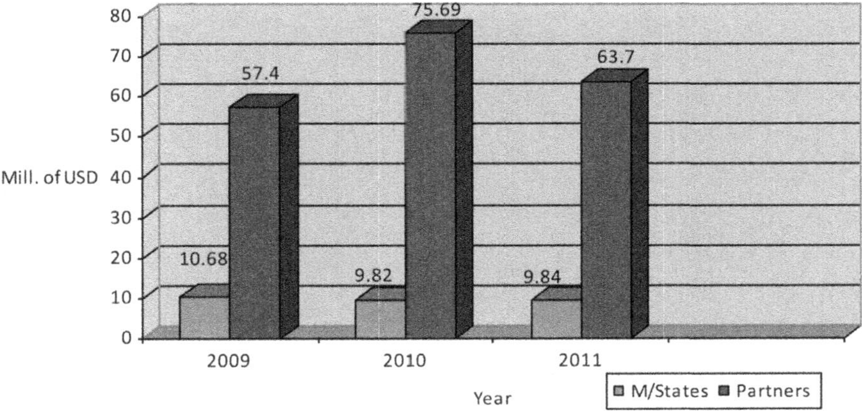

Figure 11.3 Member States and Partners Contribution to AU Programme Budget

budget. Even for the operational budget member states contribution could still be enhanced. For example, the recurrent budget for the 2006 financial year was set at US$69.4 million. By June 2006, only US$31.7 million, representing about 46 per cent, was paid.[24] Compared to the previous years, this seemingly poor performance was in fact the best performance by member states in several years. At the same period of the preceding year, only 24 per cent of the 2005 recurrent budget of US$60 million was received. The financial report of the commission in June 2005 indicated that member states owed about US$90 million, comprising arrears of about US$44 million and an unpaid assessed contribution of US$46 million for the current year.[25] Thus, of the total of 53 members, only 5 members were current with their contribution; 28 were in arrears of one or more years, [26] and seven countries were placed under sanction for owing more than two years of contribution. Even the good performance in 2006 could be attributed to a single factor: the new scale of assessment, which made five big countries to account for 75 per cent of the Union's recurrent budget,[27]and which brought the assessed contribution closer to the capacity-to-pay of the member states.

The disjuncture continued for much of the period under study. For example, by June 2011, only 9 countries had fully paid their assessed contributions for 2011; 16 countries had no arrears but had yet to pay for the current year, while two had cleared their arrears and paid part of current year assessment; 26 had arrears, with two of these already under sanctions. Thus, the total contributions from member states by mid-2011 amounted to US$43.8 million, which represented 35.7 per cent of the total assessed contribution for the year.

The second problem relates to the African Union's Commission absorptive capacity of the budgetary resources. As Figure 11.4 shows, while the

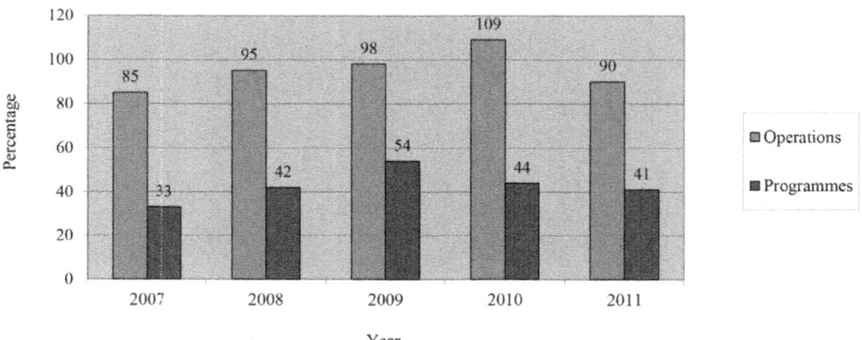

Figure 11.4 Budget Utilization Rates of the African Union Commission 2007–2011

absorptive capacity of the commission with respect to the operational budget was high, it was definitely low for the programme budget. The AUC blamed the Union's budget process for the low budget implementation rate.[28] However, partners and member states alike blamed the low budget implementation rate on AUC's low absorptive capacity, as both programme and operational budgets were determined at the same time.

THE BALANCE SHEET

In addition to shortage of funds, the commission of the African Union was beset with difficulties of a different order. No doubt the commission of the African Union produced a substantial amount of results since its inception in 2003. The enthusiasm of the various chairpersons of the commission as well as the changed international environment gave the African Union unprecedented international exposure. It also won the African Union a lot of good will as demonstrated by the international community's willingness to recognize AU's leadership in the management of contemporary African problems. To a large extent, this translated into great advances in the area of peace and security, with the African Union sending its first major peace-keeping operations to Burundi, Sudan and Somalia.[29] The commission also pushed for the adoption of several initiatives in the area of agriculture, peace and security as well as in science and technology.

But like any complex bureaucracies, the commission was faced with organizational problems that student of management call *want-got-gaps*. Accordingly, this problem exists when a gap or *deviation* exists between what a manager or a staff thinks ought to be occurring and what is actually occurring. A series of discussion with the commission management and staff as well as management reports reveal that these problems were both intra-departmental and interdepartmental.[30]

At the interdepartmental level, there was a problem that the consultancy firm, Ernst &Yung, called *territoriality*. This refers to a situation where staff of one department ignored what they consider to be outside their areas of competence, or they prevented others from dealing with or know about their work. Thus, team spirit was either totally lacking or seriously impaired. Complaints also included the lack of adequate information, late communication of information, marginalization, lack of transparency and various forms of intrigue. To address this problem, the African Union Commission put as one of the objectives of its 2009–2012 Strategic Plan the enhancement of interdepartmental cooperation. A review of 2009–2012 Strategic Plan shows that interdepartmental cooperation improved at the top level (the level of the commission).[31] Between 2008 and end of 2011, the commission held over 155 such meetings, under the leadership of the chairperson or, in his absence, that of the deputy chairperson. The weekly meeting of the Commision facilitated dialogue and interdepartmental harmonization among commissioners. However, the problem persisted at the lower operational levels.

Although the commission had established the office of the Secretary General of the commission with a mandate to coordinate interdepartmental collaboration, departments continued to work in silos. Lack of information about other departments' activities made coordination difficult. In their response to the questionnaires circulated by the Strategic Planning Directorate, the Gender Directorate, for example, reported the lack of understanding of gender issues as the main cause of the difficulty of the gender directorate working with other directorates. The Citizens' Directorate (CIDO) also reported lack of understanding of the work of CIDO as a major obstacle to interdepartmental collaboration. Others, such as the Office of the Legal Council (OLC), cited short notices for meetings and the failure of other department to take account of OLC's own programme of work as being part of the difficulties of interdepartmental collaboration. Finance Department reported that other departments do not consider planning/budgeting, reporting and monitoring of budget execution as being part of their responsibility.

Intra-departmental coordination and collaboration was also lacking in some instances. While several departments seemed to enjoy a lot of intra-departmental cohesion, many other hardly convene intra-departmental meetings. As a result, work was done on a day-to-day basis, if not haphazardly, and long-term planning was not optimal.[32]

The commission's problems were not limited to internal difficulties; they loomed large in the body's relations with the Committee of Permanent Representatives (PRC) of member states, the sole organ with which the commission had to interact on a daily basis in Addis Ababa.

For the PRC, the independence that the commission sought to assume had no legal foundation. The commission was accountable to member states for both its financial management and administration. A general feeling within the PRC was that the commission did not have any supranational authority; and until it was given such powers, the body must act on the instruction of the policy organs composed of member states, which the permanent representatives represented in Addis Ababa. The PRC also complains about financial indiscipline in the commission. They saw members of the commission as being more interested in overseas trips than in doing work in Addis Ababa. They cited instance where all ten elected officials were out of Addis Ababa at the same time, and instances where none was available to attend the deliberations of the PRC at the commission headquarters, while they were all readily available to attend the PRC meetings held outside Addis Ababa. They also cited as an example of financial mismanagement the unauthorized spending of US$7 million on the Conference of Intellectuals in Dakar in October 2004.[33] This scandal shocked not only member states, it also amazed the chairperson of the commission, who publicly disowned and denounced such financial indiscipline during the session of the Executive Council in Banjul in July 2006.

On its part the commission complained about the PRC tendency to micromanage the commission, and to interfere in the daily business of the commission in such a manner that threatened authority within the commission and thereby upset the smooth operation of the body. Their political interference also accounted for the behaviour of certain staff members, who were too often ready to seek both the diplomatic and political protection of their missions.

Thus, one of the strategic objectives of the commission for 2009–2012 was to develop and enhance the framework for regular dialogue and exchange with member states. Within the context of this objective, the commission established dialogue with member states representatives and convened special retreats to enhance such dialogue. These efforts and the physical presence of diplomatic representations of almost all African countries improved relations to some extent, but did not remove all the misgivings the two sides had towards each other. Up until the end of 2012, member states complained about financial indiscipline and lack of transparency and accountability in the commission. Other charges include the commission's failure to implement audit recommendations, budgets that were based on guesswork rather than on professional budgeting, insensitivity to the economic realities of member states, incomplete programme proposals that did not show the legal and financial implication of proposed activities, inadequate and poor quality of conference documentation, staff being more attentive to overseas travels than to work at hand in duty stations. The commission on its part continued to complain about the PRC's bullying tendencies, and about instances where some PRC members (especially junior staff of the missions) were disrespectful to commissioners, most of whom were senior officials in their home governments and deserve on their own rights due respect and consideration from representative of member states. The commission also charged that PRC had the tendency to compare the conditions of work at the national level with the conditions of work at the commission.

It might indeed be beyond the scope of this chapter to cover in an exhaustive manner the difficulties that surfaced during the first ten years of the commission's existence. However, it should be realized that such difficulties were not unique to the African Union Commission. In 1979, the *Spierengurg Report* identified similar problems within the European Commission. These range from low motivation among commission officials, over-elaborate hierarchies of authority, inflexible responses to changing priorities as well as the usual rivalry and intrigue associated with international bureaucracies in relation to appointments and promotions.[34] And the mass resignation in 1999 of the European Commissioners, under the leadership of Jacques Santer of Luxemburg on charges of corruption is indicative of the fact that the European Commission too was not immune from financial and administrative problems.

The European Commission also had its rough days with member states. President Charles De Gaulle, for instance, took exceptions to what he saw as the commission's pretensions (such as the Commission President Walter Hallstein's insistence on receiving the credentials of foreign diplomats accredited to the European Communities). De Gaulle used the commission as a target for his dislike of supranational institutions in general and denounced it in a number of well-publicized statements.[35] Despite all these initial difficulties, the European Commission has evolved into a relatively open bureaucracy by comparison with most national civil services, and has been active in encouraging greater transparency with the EU institutions. Thus, the solution to the AU Commission's problems was not beyond reach. What was required was to determine the *action levers* or a menu of possible actions by identifying the *source problem.*

It is my contention that the source problem was the very nature of the commission of the African Union. As an interstate body, the commission was staffed with people of deferent backgrounds, culture, training and psychological make-up. These differences translated into different *assumptions, perceptions, conclusions, feelings* and *behaviour.* The source of conflict between an elected official and director might have been the assumption each might have about how the other got to the position he or she occupied. This assumption naturally coloured the perception of each of them, which in turn led to a certain conclusion on the part of each one of them. That conclusion engendered certain feelings and behaviour. This problem was compounded by the fact that none had any power over the other.

With regard to the interdepartmental problems, these were attributed to departmental *values*. The perceived differences in values led to interdepartment rivalries and other undesirable practices. According to experts in organizational behaviour, differences in values can be corrected by shifting emphasis on *goal congruence*, or similarity of objectives or complementarity. Indeed, goal congruence among individuals of an organization makes the group more productive because it convinces all of them that they are all aiming for the same objective. Instilling goal congruence within departments may also help smoothen relations within the same department. Thus, the initiative launched by the commission, which aimed at instilling and promoting *shared values*, was a step in the right direction, if only it was taken seriously by both the management and staff. And, finally, with respect to relations with member states, a strengthened dialogue between the commission and the PRC would have gone a long way to enhancing relations. But during much of the period under consideration, relations between the commission and the PRC remained largely conflictual, as the time the PRC took to examine and approve the 2012 budget proved.[36]

CONCLUSION

Clearly, the African Union was confronted with challenges at various levels and in various areas. In addition to political and socio-economic challenges, there were bureaucratic challenges that affected the Commission of the African Union. The intra-departmental and interdepartmental problems that are routinely associated with complex organizations were running side by side with charges of financial indiscipline and administrative gaps. Compounding these problems was inadequate funding, and sore relations with the PRC. To a large extent, the internal difficulties and the poor relations that existed between the commission and the PRC were indicative of the problematic nature of principal–agent relations that the Institutionalists have advanced. The European Union and regional organizations elsewhere faced similar problems. The African Union Commission only needed to tap in to the experience of these organizations, implement the various recommendations and regain the confidence of member states and other stakeholders. By 2012, a number of steps were taken in that direction.

NOTES

1. *Constitutive Act of the African Union*, Art. 20.1.
2. *Statute of the Commission of the African Union*, Article 2.

3. This meant that each region was entitled to two seats in the college of commissioners. Ibid. Article 6 (2); and Rules of Procedure of the Assembly, Rule 39 (1);

4. Statute of the Commission, Article 6 (3).

5. See the African Union, *Introductory Note to the Report of the Interim Chairperson of the Commission of the African Union,* Report Presented to the 2nd Ordinary Session of the Executive Council, Njamena, Chad, 3–4 March 2003, especially Part II, A, Paragraphs 21–31.

6. Initially, the pay scales of South African Foreign Service, Botswana Foreign Service and the SADC were examined. After considerable discussion, it was decided to apply the "noble mère" principle, whereby the AU being the main continental body should not offer conditions lower than a smaller regional organization. Thus, SADC scale was found to be the highest among the regional organization. It was therefore adopted by the PRC. See African Union, *Report of the Third Ordinary Session of the Executive Council*, Maputo July 2003 Doc. EX/CL/Rpt (III).

7. As provided for by Article 31 of the Constitute Act.

8. Article 9 of the Statutes of the Commission.

9. The deputy chairperson shall also act as the chairperson in the absence or in case of temporary incapacity of the substantive chairperson. In accordance with Article 9 (2), in case of absence, death, temporary or permanent incapacity of the deputy chairperson, the chairperson shall, in consultation with the chairperson of the Assembly, appoint one of the commissioners to act as the deputy chairperson, pending the return of the incumbent or the appointment of a new deputy chairperson.

10. It is important to note that although the commissioners were accountable to the chairperson of the commission, the chairperson could not personally and directly terminate their appointments.

11. Rule 4 (1)(m) of the Rule of Procedure of the Assembly.

12. Article 4 of the Statutes of the Commission.

13. Ibid. Article 4 (5).

14. See Articles 13, 14, 15 and 16.

15. The panel included the foreign ministers of Burundi, Congo, Djibouti, Mauritius, Mozambique and South Africa, Ghana and Cape Verde.

16. Professor Alpha Oumar Konare (Mali) was elected as Chairperson of the Commission, Patrick Masimhaka (Rwanda) Deputy Chairperson; Elizabeth Tankeu (Cameroon) Commissioner for Trade and Industry (elected as a single candidate following the automatic elimination of her rivals on account of regional representation); Rusbud Kurwijila (Tanzania) Commissioner for Agriculture and Rural Economy (elected as a single candidate following the automatic elimination of her rivals on account of regionalism); Julia D. Joiner (The Gambia) Commission for Political Affairs (obtained two-thirds majority at the fifth round); Gawanas Bience Philomina (Namibia) Commissioner for Social Affairs (obtained two-thirds majority at the 3rd round), Bernard Zoba (Republic of Congo), Commissioner for Infrastructure and Energy (obtained two-thirds majority at the third round); Said Djinit (Algeria) Commissioner for Peace and Security (obtained two-thirds majority at the first round).

17. Maxwell Mkawezalamba (Malawi) Commissioner for Economic Affairs, elected out of two Malawian candidates; and Professor Nadia Mohammed Essayed (Libya) Commissioner for Human Resources, Science and Technology, elected as a single North African candidate. Professor Nadia replaced the Tunisian candidate Mr. Said Agrebi, who was elected as a single candidate, but did not take up the position.

18. For more on the election of the Third Commission, see Jakkie Cilliers and Jide Martyns Okeke, "The Election of Dr Dlamini-Zuma as AU Chairperson: Towards Pan Africanism and African Renaissance?" *Policy Brief* No. 33 (South Africa: Institute for Security Studies, July 2012), available at http://dspace.africaportal.org/jspui/bitstream.

19. *Statute of the Commission*, Article 18. It should be pointed out that the actual recruitment of staff was done differently.

20. The quota system was linked to the scale of assessment. Countries on the floor of the scale of assessment were entitled to 4 places and those at the ceiling were entitled to 17 positions. The rest fell in between. Excluded from the quota system were elected officials, staff on special appointments and staff in the general service category.

21. The quota system led to positions being re-advertised because either the best candidates were from countries whose quotas were full or the shortlisted candidates did not respect gender considerations and the need to distribute senior's positions equitably.

22. For example, up to 2013, the African Union Commission was working with less than 55 per cent of staff capacity. See Cilliers and Okeke, "The Election of Dr. Dlamini-Zuma as AU Chairperson," p. 3.

23. Ethiopia's contribution was US$100,000, South Africa's was US$ 11 million and Nigeria US$ 10 million.

24. African Union, *Mid-Term Report on the Budget Performance of the AU Commission for the Period 01 January to 30 June 2006*, p. 1.

25. African Union, Statement of Contribution of Member States to the African Union Budget as at 10 May 2005, May 2005.

26. Ibid.

27. These were Algeria, Egypt, Libya, Nigeria and South Africa.

28. Until 2010, the budget process begun in September of the preceding year and approval done in January of the budget year. Member states were informed about their assessed contribution between February and March, and first payments would come in around April. From 2010, this process was reversed, so that the budget was prepared and approved during the first half of the preceding year.

29. For more on AU's peace support operations see chapter 7, supra.

30. There were instances where the problems between commissioners and their directors were sufficiently serious to disrupt the smooth operation of the department. Insubordination, incompetence and at times sheer madness, divide and rule tactics, lack of transparency were all charges that senior managers traded, sometimes publicly.

31. Review Report on the Implementation of the African Union Commission Strategic Plan 2009–2012.

32. Ibid.

33. The convening of this conference was approved by the Assembly on the condition and the understanding that it would have no financial cost to the African Union. It turned out that not only did it have financial implications for the commission, but it actually cost the continental body more than what a ministerial or the session of heads of state would cost.

34. See Bainbridge, *The Penguin Companion to European Union*, pp. 184.

35. Ibid., p. 183.

36. Existing evidence suggest that the difficulty of convening the meeting of the PRC Sub-committee on Finance and Administration account for some of the finance and budget management difficulties. Virements and supplementary budget appropriations could not take place in time because of the difficulty of convening PRC Sub-committee in time to look at these exigencies. See Review Report on the Implementation of the AUC Strategic Plan 2009–2012.

Chapter 12

Conclusion

The argument I advanced at the beginning of this study is that despite their strength, the analytical frameworks of the Intergovernmentalists and Institutionalists cannot on their own offer a comprehensive explanation of international integration. The limitation of the individual approaches accounts for my proposal for *fusionism*, an integrated framework that amalgamates Intergovernmentalists and the various strains of Institutionalist theoretical school. My analysis of the first ten years of the African Union has been based on such an integrated approach. The empirical evidence presented in the study validates fusionism in many ways. It shows that integration is indeed an intergovernmental process that involves preference formation and international negotiation; it equally involves the creation of institutions that influence preferences and also regulates principal–agency relations, by determining the degree of agency autonomy. The evidence also demonstrates the transformational effects of institutions and norms on national elites and ordinary citizens. In this chapter, I recapitulate the main findings of the study in a bid to remove any residual misunderstanding that the reader may have about my thesis.

THE AFRICAN UNION AS AN INTERGOVERNMENTAL INSTITUTION

From the outset, I have shown that the African Union was the product of a lengthy intergovernmental process that lasted for several years. Since the idea of a new continental organization was first mooted in Algiers in July 1999 up to the launch of the African Union in Durban in July 2002, African governments held several consultations aimed at building consensus on the nature and mandate of the African Union. The intergovernmental process did not end with the formation of the African Union; it continued throughout the period under consideration. The heated debate on the proposals for the Union Government and the United States of Africa that raged between 2005 and 2012 was not only a clear testimony of the continued intergovernmental process, but it also substantiated my argument that the African Union was not a pet project of the former Libyan leader Ghaddafi.

While the liberal intergovernmentalists rightly maintain that integration is essentially an intergovernmental process that involves preference formation and bargaining, they tell us little about what shapes particular preferences. And the institutionalists' answer that institutions shape preferences is hardly sufficient. My own position, supported by empirical evidence, is that among the determinants of state preferences are the socio-economic realities, geography, politics, history and the idiosyncrasies of the individual leaders. Thus, in order to understand AU's preferences, I have reviewed the continent's political and socio-economic conditions at the turn of the century. It has been shown that Africa not only accounted for the bulk of the world intrastate conflicts, the continent started the twenty-first century as the poorest, the most indebted and the most marginalized region. These challenges, together with history and geography, gave rise to a number of preferences for independence, peace and security, good governance, and socio-economic development. The AU and the OAU pursued these objectives with a varying degree of success.

DECOLONIZATION AND POLITICAL LIBERATION

The study shows that in the immediate aftermath of independence, the most pressing preference of African leaders was the political liberation of the entire continent. President Nkrumah's well-publicized statement that "the independence of Ghana is meaningless unless it is linked up with the total Liberation of Africa" reflects Nkrumah's worldview. But most importantly, it shows the importance that African leaders attached to the liberation of the continent. The Liberation Committee set up within the OAU to coordinate support to the liberation struggle exemplified the collective stance on political liberation. The fact that the number of OAU/AU member states rose from 32 in July 1963 to 53 in July 2002 is indicative of the success of the decolonization struggle.

The decolonization agenda was pursued simultaneously with other preferences such as socio-economic development and conflict resolution. To achieve these objectives, African leaders adopted about 24 treaties between 1963 and 2002 on areas as diverse as peace and security, agriculture, health, industrial relations, trade and economic development. Some 14 of these treaties were in force by 2002. But if Africa was successful on the decolonization front, the continent remained faced with daunting political and socio-economic challenges. Africa not only accounted for the bulk of the world's intrastate conflicts, the continent started the twenty-first century as the poorest, the most indebted and the most marginalized region of the world. I have argued that the OAU's limited success in addressing the political and socio-economic difficulties of the continent does not offer sufficient justification for the sweeping claim that the organization had actually failed. The organization was endowed and structured in a manner that best served the mandate of decolonization originally assigned to it. Additional mandate in the area of intrastate conflict resolution, socio-economic development, and good political and economic governance require greater autonomy not only in the form of legal frameworks but also in the form of additional human and financial resources. But the Cold War and Realist politics that characterized much of the period of OAU existence thwarted attempts to empower the OAU in these areas.

With the end of the Cold War, collective approach to common challenges became a more realistic and feasible project. This accounts for the decision to replace the erstwhile OAU with the AU and to give the new organization a broader mandate in matters relating to *peace and security* as well as in *governance* and *socio-economic development.*

PEACE AND SECURITY

In the area of peace and security, I have shown that although collective security was a long-standing preoccupation of African leaders, it was taken more seriously only in the aftermath of the Cold War. It was in this period that the African leaders adopted a large number of legal frameworks on peace and security and initiated peace support operations. I maintain that despite the multiplicity of the legal frameworks and activities, AU peace and security agenda consisted of two main components: *preventive diplomacy* and *peacekeeping.*

The preventive diplomatic efforts took several forms and were deployed in Kenya in 2007–2008, Madagascar in 2007–2008, Zimbabwe in 2008, Cote D'Ivoire in 2010–2011, Egypt in 2011, and in South Sudan from 2013. The study shows that AU's preventive diplomacy in these countries yielded mixed results. The Union's interventions in Kenya and Madagascar were deemed to be successful, while its efforts in Zimbabwe, Cote D'Ivoire, Egypt and South Sudan were less effective.

A number of considerations explain the successful outcome of AU's preventive diplomacy in Kenya and Madagascar. These include the personality of the chief negotiator, the successful attempt to forestall parallel negotiation processes, and the ability of the mediators to manage an intricate balance between international expectations and local realities

With respect to peacekeeping, the study shows that African leaders' appetite for peace support operations grew from the 1990s. It was in the 1990s that the OAU deployed its peace operations in Rwanda (1991–1993), Burundi (1993–1996), the Comoros (1998–2002), the Democratic Republic of the Congo (1999–2000) and Eritrea and Ethiopia (2000–2008). The African Union undertook nine peace support operations between 2002 and 2012. These ranged from small operations to complex large-scale peacekeeping operations such as those in Darfur and Somalia. My assessment of these operations shows that AU interventions brought the conflict in Burundi under control, helped installed a transitional government in Somalia and provided security to a large section of the population in Darfur. They also paved the way for UN takeover and for greater international support for AU peace initiatives. However, AU's peace support operations brought to the fore a number of pitfalls. These range from the *problematic application of the principle of subsidiarity to limited agency autonomy.*

AU's peace support operations were undertaken on the basis of *subsidiarity*, which governs the Union's relations not only with the United Nations but also with the regional economic communities. As a principle, subsidiarity is meant to foster efficiency through division of labour between the United Nations and the regional organizations and between the regional organizations and sub-regional entities. But for some observers, subsidiarity fostered a onesided relations between the African Union and the United Nations. It led to the African Union designing peace support operations only as interim measures until the United Nations could take over. It also encouraged the AU to be overly ambitious by taking on peace support operations in extremely difficult circumstances before building the relevant security architecture. A reverse argument is that by encouraging regional entities to lead in finding solutions to regional conflicts, subsidiarity served as an instrument of passing the responsibility of regional peace to regional entities even when these have no capacity to assume such responsibility. AU's peace support operations substantiate both charges. The Union took on operations that it had no capacity to sustain; it was also forced to take leadership responsibility in instances (such as Somalia) at a time when the United Nations Security Council was reluctant to deploy UN peace-keepers.

Although subsidiarity was implied in the frameworks that govern AU's relations with the RECs/RMs, the principle appeared to lack legal clarity, especially with respect to preventive diplomacy and peacekeeping. As a result, AU and the RECs maintained different views of the application of the principle. For the AU just as the Union was to seek UN endorsement for its peace support operations, so would the RECs need to obtain AU's endorsement for their enforcement actions and peace support operations. For the REC's the subsidiarity principle implied that AU should only assume a coordinating role and leave actual implementation of peace support operations to the region.

The study shows that limited agency autonomy characterizes AU's operations in various areas. In the area of peace and security, weak early warning capacity, limited enforcement capability, and limited financial and human resources epitomized AU's limited autonomy. Although AU had a strong appetite for peacekeeping operations, the Union's capacity to maintain such operations remained weak. Operations were therefore either transitioned into United Nations operations or became totally dependent on the United Nations and other partners for funding. The result was that the implementation of the continental peace and security agenda suffered from "ambition-capacity gap," a disjuncture between what the AU wanted to do and what it had capacity to implement

GOOD GOVERNANCE AND RESPECT FOR HUMAN RIGHTS

My assessment of the OAU/AU role in the promotion of democracy and human rights protection shows that during the period under consideration a number of legal instruments were adopted.[1] These were integrated in the African Governance Architecture that came into effect in 2012. Alongside the continental frameworks were good governance norms and institutions developed at regional and national levels across Africa. The role of these frameworks and institutions (constitutions, laws and parliaments) in enhancing human rights protection must be recognized. If not for anything, they remained hanging over the heads of policy makers who could not afford to ignore them completely, especially as the African Commission on Human and Peoples' Rights and the regional human rights bodies continued to hear human rights cases. To that extent therefore the continental human rights norms substantiates the argument of the constructivist students that institutions have transformative effects on national elites. But the number of challenges that these institutions faced reduced their effectiveness considerably. The institutions were for the most part not sufficiently empowered to enforce human rights protection at the national level. And although approved by member states, most national institutions were invariably seen as agents with foreign agenda or being outright hostile. Moreover, most of them remained scattered and largely uncoordinated.

Regarding constitutional governance, there is clear evidence to suggest that African Union governance frameworks and institutions also had some transformational effects on African civilian and military elites. The African Union regime on unconstitutional change of government played a decisive role in reducing the incidence of military coups on the continent, and had been an enhancing factor in the continent's experiment with democratic pluralism. For example, between 1952 and 2012, 88 successful military coups took place in Africa. Of these, 63 took place before 1990 and only 10 occurred after the adoption of the Lomé Declaration in 2000.[2] Several factors may have accounted for the reduction of the number of coups d'états on the continent, but the Lomé Declaration undoubtedly played a decisive role. Since the adoption of the declaration, the AU systematically suspended all governments that came to power through unconstitutional means from participating in the activities of the African Union. Countries suspended included Central African Republic (March 2003–June 2005); Togo (February 2005–May 2005); Mauritania (August 2005–April 2007); Mauritania (August 2008–June 2009); Guinea (December 2008–December 2010); Niger (August 2009–March 2011); Madagascar (March 2009–today); Côte d'Ivoire (December 2010–April 2011); Egypt, Tunisia and Libya (2011–2012).[3]

Parallel to the establishment of continent-wide frameworks for democratic governance was the direct involvement of the OAU/AU as election observer during elections in member states. However, AU's engagement in elections observation and monitoring produced mixed results. In most instances, AU's association, just like the participation of other regional and global observers, enhanced the integrity, transparency and credibility of the elections and thereby reduced the risks of election-related violence. Therefore, by observing and monitoring elections, the AU was not only fostering democracy on the continent, the Union was also engaged in preventive diplomacy. But the AU continued to face a number of challenges including inadequate financial and human resources. Member states were reluctant to allocate sufficient resources for election monitoring, and the general scepticism about elections in Africa accounted for the Union's inability to raise extra-budgetary resources from non-African sources.[4] The result was that AU teams had often been too small to cover national territories or other important activities such as the voter registration, campaign and ballot counting. What is more, election observers at times went to mission areas without appropriate insurance despite the inherent risks.[5]

AU involvement in elections on the continent also came under strong criticism especially from outside the African continent.[6] The charges include the fact that the number of regular multiparty elections did not make these elections contributory factors to building and sustaining democracy.[7] And the spate of election observation activities did not correspond to improvement of electoral processes and democracy as a whole.[8] What is more, the AU and the RECs may have developed important frameworks that established benchmarks for credible elections, but the experience in Africa had shown that different missions had arrived at divergent conclusion on the same elections under assessment.[9]

SOCIO-ECONOMIC DEVELOPMENT

With respect to socio-economic development, the study has explored continental efforts at regional integration and the development and implementation of collective development plans. My findings are that various welfare effects such as greater peace and security, deeper economic linkages, and expansion of trade, that integration potentially has on community members, made regional integration a major preference of African states. This accounts for the fact that by 2002 Africa had 14 regional groupings, with two or more in each of the five regions.[10] But if the advantages of regional integration attracted African countries to regional arrangements, the proliferation of these institutions constituted major challenges too. Not only did blocs have overlapping membership, they also pursued identical mandates and objectives. The overlap in particular added to the burden of member states, who faced multiple financial obligations, and had to cope with different meetings, policy decisions, instruments, procedures and schedules. In addition, it was member states that were required to implement at the national level the various protocols, decisions and agreements relating to economic integration. While a number of countries had established appropriate mechanisms at the national level to meet the various obligations including ministries responsible for integration issues, others did not do so. And even where they existed, such mechanisms were often too loosely defined or insufficiently equipped with human, material and financial resources to make the necessary impact at the national level. The result was that most governments failed to translate their commitment at the regional level into substantive policy at the national level. In various instances, the national governments were unwilling to subordinate immediate national political interests to longterm regional economic goals.

Regional communities were also plagued by problems of inadequate financial resources. During the period under consideration, external funding accounted for the bulk of the funding requirements of most regional economic communities. Although recurrent budgets were based on contributions assessed to member states, actual payments of contributions had declined in such a way that the majority of the communities found themselves in serious financial difficulties, as many governments did not have a specific budget for activities and programmes on the topic.[11]

The African Union was not only faced with the difficulty of coordination and harmonization of the policies of the RECS; the Union also had to rationalize and streamline the RECs in order to make them more responsive to the exigencies of African integration.[12] This requirement led to the adoption of two important measures. The first was the Assembly's decision to reduce the number of groupings recognized as regional economic community from 14 to eight and not to recognize any new grouping as being a regional economic community.[13] The second measure consisted in the AU Commission strengthening its relations with the RECs.

For a long time, relations between AU and RECs were characterized by mistrust,[14] which led to duplications, lack of cooperation, lack of experience sharing and lack of information exchange between the commission in Addis Ababa and the communities.[15] In order to address this particular problem, AU Commission and the RECs undertook within the framework of a joint protocol[16] to cooperate in various areas including peace and security. They also jointly drew up a Minimum Integration Programme (MIP) that comprised a set of activities, projects and programmes to be implemented by the RECs in order to accelerate the regional and continental integration processes.[17] Despite the progress registered, a number of challenges remained. The MIP action plan did not receive adequate funding; as a result, the action plan could not be implemented for many years. Another challenge was AUC's weak capacity to coordinate the activities of the RECs. While the RECs recognized and accepted the principle of subsidiarity in their relations with the AUC, there was less clarity on the application of this principle. Some RECs were of the view that the AUC should not view itself as an implementing agency, rather it should play a coordinating role.

With respect to collective development plans, the study has paid particular attention to the New Partnership for Africa's Development (NEPAD). Adopted in 2001, NEPAD added a new dimension to Africa's development strategy by charting a programme of action in the areas of infrastructure, health, education, environment, agriculture and governance. The NEPAD programme estimated that for Africa to achieve 7 per cent of annual economic growth, which was needed to reduce by half the number of people living in poverty by the year 2015, the continent would need to fill an annual resources gap of about 64 billion.[18] Proponents maintained that Africa could meet much of the funding requirement through increased export earnings, and foreign investment and by reversing the flow of capital flight. However, they also conceded that Africa would hope to receive 10–12 billion more a year in aid[19] to achieve the established targets of expenditure.

By and large, NEPAD was well received by Africa's development partners including the G8, the European Union, the UN and the Brettonwoods Institutions. In 2003, the G8 made a set of pledges within the framework of the Africa Action Plan (AAP) that required each G8 country to establish "enhanced partnership with African Countries whose performance reflects the NEPAD Commitment".[20] The G8 also welcomed the APRM, which it considered to be an innovative and potentially decisive element in NEPAD.

However, the considerable moral support that NEPAD initially received did not translate into effective material support. The volume of aid to the continent might have doubled in real terms between 2000 and 2010, but a massive delivery gap of 0.39 per cent of DAC donor Gross National Index (GNI) remained.[21] And most donors failed to deliver on the 0.7 per cent of GDP aid target (0.15–0.20 for LDCs) and the Gleneagles G8 Commitment towards Africa. The lack of complementarities in debt, aid and trade policies towards Africa also militated against policy coherence, and this was found to be as much of a challenge as increasing the volume of aid was. For much of the past 20 years, ODA to Africa was offset by debt service. Furthermore, the sharp decline of Africa's market share during the 30 years before the turn of the century amounted to an estimated income loss of US$70 billion per year almost five times the average annual amount of ODA to Africa.[22]

Support from the UN did not fare any better. According to the Secretary General, increased financial commitment by the United Nations system for NEPAD was dependent on the United Nations and the agencies receiving additional financial resources for these programmes. And while the organizations of the United Nations system were required to initiate an increasing amount of joint programming and new initiatives, the lack of additional financial resources limited the scope and prospects of joint activities.[23]

These difficulties, together with the economic and financial constraints African states themselves faced, underlined the main pitfall of the NEPAD programme: making the implementation of major strategies such as PIDA, CAADP and CARMMA contingent upon the goodwill of the development partners. The Chief Executive Officer of NEPAD Planning and Coordination Agency himself admitted this pitfall in the following manner: "Africa's own limited resources … and the difficulties and unpredictability of external support have inevitably affected the pace at which NEPAD's ambitious programmes have been implemented."[24]

Limited success also characterized AU's human development programmes. No doubt the Union developed and adopted frameworks in health, education, gender mainstreaming, as well as population control and migration. More significantly, the African Union established the Pan African University and launched the Mwalimu Nyerere scholarship programme for African students in African universities outside their home countries. The importance of both the PAU and the scholarship programme is indisputable. But apart from these two facilities, there is hardly any other human development area where the impact of the African Union can be measured in concrete terms. For example, under various AU frameworks, African states undertook to increase their health budget and to commit a minimum of 10 per cent of their national budgets to agriculture. In 2010, only three countries allocated more than 15 per cent of government budget to health;[25] an equally low number of countries had passed the Maputo threshold of allocating 10 per cent of national budget to Agriculture.[26] Thus, for the most part, AU human development activities were limited to the development and adoption of agreements and charters that took several years to implement on the ground. I attribute the organization's ineffectiveness in these areas to its limited autonomy or lack of enforcement and implementation capacity at the country and regional level. This goes to demonstrate the argument of the Institutionalists that integration involves the creation of institutions that are empowered to a varying degree, depending on the preferences of the principals.

THE AFRICAN UNION AFTER THE FIRST TEN YEARS

Clearly, the African Union offers clear insights into integration as a multi-dimensional process that no single theoretical tradition can explain in a comprehensive manner. This limitation accounts for my proposal for *fusionism*, an integrated approach that combines the views of the various schools of thought. Throughout this study, I have shown that the African Union was an intergovernmental institution that involved intergovernmental processes at various levels. The Union also represented a rational choice of its member states, who saw it as a means to advancing their individual and collective preferences for liberation, peace and security, good governance and socio-economic development. The Union did not only make marked progress in a number of areas; it also established norms that had transformational effects on military and political elites at country and regional levels. But like in most agent–principal relations, the autonomy of the Union was limited by member states, and this affected the Union's achievements in many other areas, especial in human and socio-economic development, as well as in sustaining peace support operations.

Ten years after its inception, the African Union remained as relevant as it was in 2002. Although the steady economic growth that many African states registered over the years offered the continental body the opportunity to foster development across the continent, the Union continued to face a number of challenges. But the most serious challenge and one that constituted a major risk for Africa's development was fragility. Nowhere was this risk more acute than in governance as well as in peace and security. An assessment by the African Development Bank shows that conflict and political fragility constituted the most serious constraints to Africa's development by 2011. Although the number of fragile states dropped from 20 in 2007 to 17 in 2011, the number of conflict situations rose from 29 in 2005 to 40 in 2010.[27] While on average 39 per cent of the population of sub-Saharan Africa lived below the poverty line of US$1.25, 51 per cent of the population in fragile states and countries in conflict lived below the poverty line. These countries also had 50 per cent higher rates of malnutrition, 20 per cent higher child mortality rates and 18 per cent low primary completion rates.[28]

The gains made in governance also remained fragile. Only a handful of African countries had reached a point where the peaceful transfer of power through elections was routine. For many, elections posed considerable risks for election-related violence; for the others, the playing field was not only unlevelled, it was also stacked in favour of the incumbent.[29] Thus, in addition to new issues, the efforts that African leaders deployed to consolidate the fragile gains made in peace, security and governance must necessarily form a central piece in any further research into the history of the African Union after the first ten years.

NOTES

1. These include the Cairo Agenda for Action on Relaunching of the Economic and Social development of Africa, Declaration on the Framework for an OAU Response to Unconstitutional Change of Government, Solemn Declaration on the Conference on Security, Stability, Development and Cooperation in Africa (CSSDCA), The Africa Peer Review Mechanism of NEPAD, Declaration on the Principles Governing Democratic Election in Africa, the African Charter on Democracy, Election and Governance.
2. For more on this see, Issaka K Souaré, "The African Union as a "Norm Entrepreneur," pp. 69–94.
3. Konstantinos D. Magliveras: The Sanctioning System of the African Union.
4. Ibid.
5. Ibid.
6. For more on this see, Judith Kelley, "Watching the Watchmen: The Role of Election Observers in Africa."
7. D.K Leonard, Election and Conflict in Africa: "An Introduction", *Journal of Elections*, Vol. 8, 1 (2009), pp.1–15; D Kadim, "An Overview" Compendium of Elections in Southern Africa 1989–2009.
8. EISA "Two Decades of Elections Observation in Africa."
9. H. Ogune, Appraising Election Monitoring and Observation in Africa.
10. See Table 5.1 above.
11. African Development Bank et al., *African Economic Outlook 2013*, p. 14.
12. Commission of the African Union, *Strategic Plan of the Commission of the African Union Vol.1: Vision and Mission*, p. 31.
13. Decision Assembly/AU/Dec.112(VII) 2006
14. Commission of the African Union, *Solidarity Budget for the Financial Year 2005, Part X, Department of Economic Affairs* (2004), p. 13.

15. Ibid.

16. African Union, protocol on relations between the African Union Commission and the regional economic communities (RECs).

17 Commission of the African Union, *Strategic Plan of the Commission of the African Union Vol. 2: 2004–2007 Strategic Framework,* pp. 29–30.

18. The New Partnership for Africa's development, C1, paragraph 144.

19. United Nations, "Funding for NEPAD," p. 5

20. Ibid.

21. United Nations Economic Commission for Africa, *Issue Paper, Partnerships and Financing for Development in the Post-2015 Development Agenda,* (Feb 2013) p. 5.

22. World Bank, "Africa Region Trade Progress Note," cited in Secretary General of the United Nation, "The New Partnership for Africa's Development," p. 17.

23. Ibid., p. 22.

24. Cited in Baffour Ankomah, "NEPAD, 10 Years on."

25. Botswana, Rwanda, and Zambia. See WHO, *State of Health Spending in Africa, January 2013,* available at www.afro.who.int/.../8698-state-of-health-financing-in-the-african-region/.

26. The countries are Burkina Faso, Ethiopia, Malawi and Mali, See Shenggen Fan, Tewodaj Mogues, and Sam Benin "Setting Priorities for Public Spending for Agricultural and Rural Development in Africa" *IPFRI Policy Brief No.12 April 2009;* available at http://www.ifpri.org/sites/default/files/publications/bp012.pdf.

27. African Development Bank, *Annual Development Effectiveness Review 2012,* p. 20.

28. Ibid.

29. Ibid.

References

Abass, Ademola, Mashood A. Baderin, "Towards Effective Collective Security and Human Rights Protections in Africa: An Assessment of the Constitutive Act of the New African Union," *Netherlands International Law Review*, Vol. 49 (2002) pp. 1–38.

Abdullah, Ibrahim "Bush Path to Destruction: the Origin and Character of the Revolutionary United Front/ Sierra Leone," *Journal of Modern African Studies*, 36, 2 (1998), pp. 203–235.

Africa Risk Capacity – *Sovereign Disaster Risk Solutions,* Concept Note (March 2012).

Africa Union, Protocol to the Treaty Establishing the Abuja Treaty Relating to the Pan African Parliament, Addis Ababa, 14 November 2003.

Africa Union, Protocol to the Treaty Establishing the African Economic Community, Abuja 1991.

Africa Union, Report of the First Meeting of African Ministers of Defence and Security on the Establishment of the African Standby force and the Common African Defence and Security Policy MIN/Def.&Sec/RPt (1) Original: English January 2004.

African Development Bank and OECD: *African Economic Outlook 2002/2003*, Paris: OECD Development Centre, 2003.

African Development Bank et al., *African Economic Outlook 2013.*

African Development Bank: *International Investment in Africa: Trends and Opportunities,* Private Sector Department Working Paper Series No. 1, Abidjan: ADB, 2001.

African Leadership Forum, *The Kampala Documents: Towards a Conference on Security, Stability, Development and Cooperation in Africa,* Lagos: 1991.

African Union Commission, "Peace and Security Department at a Glance" available at http://www.peaceau.org/uploads/au-booklet.pdf

African Union Mission in Sudan (AMIS). Experiences and Lessons Learnt", *FOI Report*, August 2008.

African Union Treaty and the New Partnership for Africa's Development," *Indiana International and Comparative Law Review*, Vol. 13, 1 (2002): pp.185–236;
African Union, A Joint Africa-EU Strategy 2007;
African Union, "Declaration on the Framework for an OAU Response to Unconstitutional Changes of Government" Document AHG/Decl.5. (XXXVI).
African Union, "Protocol to the African Charter on Human and People's Right's on the Rights of Women in Africa" Doc Min/Wom.rts/Prot II Rev.5 Article 2.
African Union, "Talking Points on Burundi" Document presented to the Second Ordinary Session of the Peace and Security Council, Addis Ababa, 25 March 2004, PSC/PR/Comm/II.
African Union, African Union Commission Consultation with African Member-states on Transitional Justice, December 2011;
African Union, African-EU Action Plan 2011–2013;
African Union, *Amisom Review*, Issue No 6, Jan 2012;
African Union, Approved Structure of the Commission as of July 2011;
African Union, Declaration on the African Union Border Development Programme and the Modalities for the Pursuit and Acceleration of its Implementation 2010;
African Union, Framework for Action and Recommendations on Harmful Traditional Practices;
African Union, Framework for Common African Defence and Security Policy, 2003;
African Union, Human Rights Strategy for Africa, 2011;
African Union, Mid-Term Monitoring and Evaluation, 2011;
African Union, Operational Budget, 2009, 2010, 2011, 2012;
African Union, Ouagadougou Action Plan to Combat Trafficking in Human Beings Especially Women and Children 2006;
African Union, Peace and Security News, No 04. Vol 3, September 2011;
African Union, *Priority Plan of Action, Horizon 2007* Vol.1 (2004).
African Union, Programme Budget 2009, 2010, 2011, 2012;
African Union, Project Document on the Establishment of the Pan African University;
African Union, Protocol Relating to the Establishment of the Peace and Security Council of the African Union, 2002;
African Union, Report of the 13th Ordinary Session of the PRC (PRC/Rpt XII/Jan 2007;
African Union, Report of the 18th Ordinary Session of the PRC (PRC/Rpt XVIII) June 2009;
African Union, Report of the 20th Ordinary Session of the PRC (PRC/Rpt XX) July 2010
African Union, Report of the 21st Ordinary Session of the PRC (PRC/Rpt XXI) Jan 2011;
African Union, Report of the 22nd Ordinary Session of the PRC (PRC/Rpt XXII/ June 2011;
African Union, Report of the African Union on the 10th AGOA Forum held in Lusaka Zambia June 2011;
African Union, Report of the Chairperson on the Activities of the Commission Covering the Period January – June 2010, Document Ex Cl/579/XVII, July 2010;

African Union, Report of the Chairperson on the Activities of the Commission Covering the Period July to December 2009, Document Ex Cl/565/XVII Jan 2010;

African Union, Report of the Second Ministerial Conference on Disaster Risk Reduction, Nairobi April 2010;

African Union, Strategic Plan 2009–2012;

African Union, "Concept Paper on the Establishment of a Common African Defence and Security Policy," (2003);

African Union, "Concept Paper on the Establishment of a Common African Defence and Security Policy," (2003);

African Union, "Policy Framework for the Establishment of the African Standby Force and the Military Staff Committee (Part 1), (exp/ASF-MSC/2(1)," 2003.

African Union, "Report of the First Meeting of African Ministers of Defence and Security on the Establishment of African Standby Force and the Common African Defence and Security Policy," MIN/Def.&Sec/Rpt(1) Original: English, 2003.

African Union, "Report on the Conference on Security, Stability, development and Cooperation in Africa," EX.CL/74 (IV), March 2004.

African Union, "Resource Mobilization for the OAU/AU Peace Fund" Background Paper presented to the Third African Peace and Security Agenda Brainstorming Retreat, Cape Town, 1–5 May 2004;

African Union, "The Report of the First Meeting of African Ministers of Defence and Security on the Establishment of African Standby Force and the Common African Defence and Security Policy," MIN/Def.&Sec/Rpt(1) Original: English.

African Union, "Concept Paper on the Establishment of a Common African Defence and Security Policy," 2003.

African Union, "Decade of Education in Africa (1997–2006) An Assessment," Document AU/Educ/2/(1), submitted to the conference of Ministers of Education of the African Union 8–11 April 2005.

African Union, "Draft Migration Policy Framework for Africa," Document EX.CL/176/(VII) June 2005. p. 3.

African Union, "Introductory Note to the Report of the Interim Chairperson of the Commission of the African Union," Report Presented to the 2nd Ordinary Session of the Executive Council, Njamena, Chad, 3–4 March 2003.

African Union, "Report of the Chairperson of the Commission on Follow-Up Steps on the Common African Position on the Review of United Nations Peace Operations," PSC/AHG/3.(DXLVII), 26 September 2015.

African Union, "Report of the Chairperson on the African Union-United Nations Partnership: The Need for Greater Coherence," 24 September 2013 available at www.peaceau.org /en/article/Report of the Chairperson.

African Union, *Africa Integration Review*, Vol 4, 2 , 2011;

African Union, Africa-EU High Level Policy Dialogue on Science, Technology and Innovation – First Meeting of Senior Officials October 2011;

African Union, *African Charter for Popular Participation in Development and Transformation* 1990.

African Union, *African Peace and Security Architecture 2010 Assessment Report.*

African Union, Algiers Declaration of the Ministers of Education of the Member-States of the African Union, Document AU/EDUc/4(1) Rev 1. April 2005.

African Union, AU-COMMIT Campaign on Combating Human Trafficking 2009–2012;

African Union, *Chairperson's Progress Report on the Implementation of the Solemn Declaration on Gender Equality in Africa,* Document EX.CL/170/(VII).

African Union, Concept Note on African ICT Week 2010;

African Union, Concept Note on the Commemoration of the International Human Rights Day, December 2010;

African Union, Concept Note on World Aids Day 2010;

African Union, Conference for the Horn of Africa – A Joint AUC-FAO-IFAD-WFP Paper. August 2011;

African Union, Declaration on the Principles Governing Democratic Elections in Africa AHG/Decl.1 (XXXVIII) July 2002.

African Union, Ezulwini Framework for the Enhancement of the Implementation of the Measures of African Union in Situations of Unconstitutional Changes of Government in Africa, September 2009;

African Union, Framework for the Operationalization of the Continental Early Warning System Document PSD/EW/EXP Framework 2006;

African Union, Heads of State Resolution on the Recommendation of the African Commission on Human and People's Rights to elaborate a Protocol on the Rights of Women in Africa Doc. AHG/Res.240(XXXI),

African Union, Memorandum of Understanding on Cooperation in the Area of Peace and Security between the African Union, Regional Economic Communities and the Coordinating Mechanisms of the Regional Standby Brigades of Eastern and Northern Africa 2008;

African Union, Memorandum of Understanding on Cooperation in the Area of Peace and Security Between the African Union and the Regional Economic Communities and the Coordinating Mechanisms of the Regional Standby Brigades of Eastern and Northern Africa (2008)

African Union, Mid-term Review of the Chairman's Mandate 2008–2010, May 2010;

African Union, Monitoring and Evaluation Report: Mid-Term Report 2009 Programme Budget, 2009;

African Union, *Our Common Interest: Report of the Commission for Africa* (May 2005).

African Union, Policy Framework for the Establishment of the African Standby Force and the Military Staff Committee, Part I, 2003;

African Union, Policy Framework for the Establishment of the African Standby Force and the Military Staff Committee (Part I) Exp/ASF-MSC/2 (1) May 2003.

African Union, *Progress Report on the Maputo Decision on Recruitment* EX.CL/207 (VIII), January 2006.

African Union, *Rapport intérimaire sur la création d'une cour Africaine des droits de l'homme et des peuples* MIN/CONF/HRA/9 (11), May 2003.

African Union, *Rapport intérimaire sur la création d'une cour Africaine des droits de l'homme et des peuples* MIN/CONF/HRA/9 (11), May 2003.

African Union, Report of the 17th Ordinary Session of the PRC (PRC/Rpt XVII) Jan 2009;

African Union, Report of the 19th Ordinary Session of the PRC (PRC/Rpt XIV/) Jan 2010;

African Union, Report of the 23th Ordinary Session of the PRC (PRC/Rpt XXIII/ Jan 2012;

African Union, Report of the 5th Ordinary Session of the African Populations Commission (APC) Document EX.CL/ 187 (VII) June 2005.

African Union, Report of the Chairperson on the Activities of the Commission Covering the Period July to December 2010, Document Ex Cl/621/XVIII Jan 2011;

African Union, Report of the Chairperson on the Activities of the Commission Covering the Period January to June 2009, Document Ex Cl/520/XVI) June 2009;

African Union, Report of the Chairperson on the Activities of the Commission Covering the Period July to December 2008 Document Ex Cl/621/XIV Jan 2009;

African Union, Report of the Meeting of (African) Ministers of Finance on the G8 Meeting in Gleneagles, Scotland, Libya, 29 June 2005.

African Union, Report of the Secretary General on Strengthening the Role of the OAU/AU in Elections, Observations and Monitoring and the Advancement of the Democratization Process in Africa, CM/ 2257 (LXXVI) July 2002.

African Union, Report of the Third Ordinary Session of the Executive Council, Doc. EX/CL/Rpt (III).Maputo July 2003.

African Union, Review of the Millennium Declaration and Millennium Development Goals (MDGs): An African Common Position Doc. EX.CL/181 (VII), June 2005.

African Union, *Road Map for the Operationalization of the African Standby Force*, 2005.

African Union, Social Policy Framework, 2008.

African Union, Solemn Declaration on Gender Equality in Africa, Addis Ababa, Doc. Assembly/AU/Dec.1(III), Rev.1 July 2004.

African Union, SPPMERM, Departmental Reports 2009–2011.

African Union, Strategic Plan 2004–2007.

African Union, *Strategic Plan of the Commission of the African Union Vol. 1: Vission and Mission of the African Union,* (May 2004),

African Union, *Strategic Plan of the Commission of the African Union Vol. 2: 2004–2007 Strategic Framework of the Commission of the African Union*, (May 2004).

African Union, *Strategic Plan of the Commission African Union*, Volume 2: 2004–2007 Strategic Framework of the Commission of the African Union,

African Union, Strategic Plan of the Commission of the African Union, Vol 2: 2004-2007 Strategic Framework of the Commission of the African Union, May 2002,

African Union, Tentative Lessons Learnt: AUC-AUPG Coordination in the Framework of the AUC 2011 Budget Planning Exercise;

African Union, *The* 2nd *Decade of Education for Africa 2006–2015: Plan of Action* (Addis Ababa: 2006),

African Union, *The Rules of Procedure of the Peace and Security Council of the African Union.*

African Union, *The Rules of Procedure of the Peace and Security Council of the African Union (2003)*

African Union, The State of the African Population 2006, Addis Ababa, 2006.

African Union, UNECA, UNAIDS, WHO, Scoring African Leadership for Better Health, Addis Ababa, 2004.

African Union, *Solidarity Budget for the Financial Year 2005, Part X, Department of Economic Affairs* (2004),

African Union. *Fourth Quarter Budget Execution Report for 2010* Document Adv.S/Cttee/1 (May 2011).

African Union. *Mid-Term Report on the Budget Performance of the AU Commission for the Period 01 January to 30 June 2006*

African Union. *A Plan of Action, Programmes to speed up Integration of the Continent,* (May 2004).

Agoagye Festus, "The African Mission in Burundi: Lessons Learned for the First African Union Peace-Keeping Operation," (2004) available at https://www.issafrica.org/uploads/CT2_2004.PDF

Akokpari, John "Policing and Preventing Human Rights Abuses in Africa: the OAU, the AU and the NEPAD Peer Review," *International Journal of Legal Information*, Vol 32, 2, (2004): 461–473.

Akokpari, John K. "The AU, NEPAD and the Promotion of Good Governance in Africa," *Nordic Journal of African Studies* Vol. 13, 3 (2004): 243–263;

Amate, C.O.C. *Inside the OAU: Pan Africanism in Practice,* London: Macmillan 1986.

Amjadi, Azita and Alexander J. Yeats, "Have Transport Costs Contributed to the Relative Decline of African Exports?" Policy Research Working Paper 1559, Washington DC: World Bank, 1995.

Annan Kofi, Address to the Central Organ of the OAU Mechanism for Conflict Prevention, Management and Resolution, (SG/SM/6192), Lomé 26 March 1997

Annan, Kofi, "The Causes of Conflict and Promotion of Durable Peace and Sustainable Development in Africa," Report of the Secretary General to the UN Security Council 1998 (A/52/871-5 1998/318).

Artinano, Mauricio Peace Operations Partnerships: The UN Security Council and (Sub)-Regional Organizations, Policy Briefing (Berlin Centre for International Peace Operations (ZIF) March 2012).

AU, Report of the Secretary General on Strengthening the Role of the OAU/AU in Elections, Observations and Monitoring and the Advancement of the Democratization Process in Africa, CM/ 2257 (LXXVI) July 2002 Annex I.

Ayouti, Yassin and William I. Zartman eds. *The OAU after Twenty Years,* New York Praeger 1984.

Ayouty, Yassin, editor, *The Organization of African Unity After Ten Years: Comparative Perspectives*, New York: Praeger Publishers, 1975.

Bah, Alhaji Sarjoh, Elizabeth Choge-Nyangoro, Solomon Dersso, Brenda Mofya and Tim Murithi, *The African Peace and Security Architecture: A Handbook* , Addis Ababa: Friedrich-Ebert-Stiftung, 2013.

Baimu, Evarist "The African Union: Hope for Better Protection of Human Rights in Africa," *African Human Rights Law Journal*, Vol.1, 2 (2001), pp. 299–314;

Bainbridge, Timothy *The Penguin Companion to the European Union*, London: Penguin Books, 1998.

Bangura, Dominique "Les nouvelles institutions africaines en matière de sécurité," in Pierre Pascallon, *La Politique de sécurité de la France en Afrique* Paris: Harmattan, 2004.

Barnes Cedric and Harun Hassan "The Rise and Fall of Mogadishu's Islamic Courts" available at https://www.chathamhouse.org/sites/files/chathamhouse/public/Research/Africa/bpsomalia0407.pdf

Berman, Eric G. and Katie E. Sams, *Peacekeeping in Africa: Capabilities and Culpabilities,* Geneva UNIDIR and Prestoria: ISS 1999.

Bernman Eric G. and Sams, Katie E. *Constructive Disengagement: Western Efforts to develop African Peace Keeping*, Institute of Security Studies Monograph Series No. 33, Pretoria: ISS 1998.

Bigombe, Betty, Paul Collier and Nicholas Sambanis, "Policies for Building Post Conflict Peace," *Journal of African Economies*, Vol.9, 3 (2000), pp. 323–347.

Boutellis, Arthur and Paul Williams, "Peace Operation, the African Union and the United Nations: Toward More Effective Partnerships," New York: International Peace Institute, April 2013.

Brownlie Ian, editor, *Basic Documents on Human Rights*, 2nd Edition, Oxford: Clarendon Press 1981.

Bujra, Abdalla and Said Adejumob, *Breaking Barriers, Creating New Hopes: Democracy, Civil Society and Good Governance in Africa*, New Jersey: Africa World Press 2004.

Bula-Bula, Suleyman, "Les fondements de l'union africaine," *African Yearbook of International Law*, vol.9 (2001), 39–74.

Cervenka Zdenek and Colin Legum, "The Organization of African Unity in 1978: The Challenge of Foreign Intervention," *Africa Contemporary Record*, Annual Survey and Documents, (1978–1979).

Cervenka Zdenek and Colin Legum, "The Organization of African Unity in 1979," in *Africa Contemporary Record* (1979–1980).

Cervenka, Zdenek "Major Policy Shift in the Organization of African Unity," in Ingram K. (ed) *Foreign Relations of African States*. London: Butterworth 1974.

Chabal, P. "The Quest for Good Governance and Development in Africa: Is NEPAD the Answer?", *International Affairs* 78, 3 (2002), pp. 447–462.

Chazan, Naomi Mortimer, Robert Hill, John Raven and Donald Rothchild, *Politics and Society in Contemporary Africa,* Boulder: Lynne Rienner, 1992.

Collier P. and J. Gunning, "Explaining African Economic Performance," *Journal of Economic Literature* 37 (1999), pp. 64–111.

Cornwell Richard, "Madagascar: First test for the African Union," *African Security Review* 12(1) (2003), pp. 41–53.

Cowling, Michael "The African Union: An Evaluation," in *South African Yearbook of International Law*, vol. 27 (2002), pp. 193–205;

Crawford Young, "The End of the Post-Colonial State? Reflections on Changing African Political Dynamics," *African Affairs* Vol. 103, 410 (2004), pp. 23–49,

De Real, Ricardo and P De Sousa, "The African Peace and Security Architecture (APSA): subsidiarity and the Horn of Africa: The Inter-Government Authority on Development (IGAD)" in Alexandra Magnolia Dias, editor, *State and Societal Challenges in the Horn of Africa*, Lisbon: Centre for African Studies 2013.

Deng Francis M. and William Zartman, *A Strategic Vision for Africa: The Kampala Movement,* Washington DC: Brookings Institution 2002.

Dersso, Solomon, "Egypt Vs African Union: A mutually Unhappy Ending" *Aljazeera* 14 July 2014, available at http://www.aljazeera.com/indepth/opinion/2014/07/egypt-vs-african-union-mutually-u-2014714687899839.html

Elbadawi, Ibrahim and Nicholas Sambanis, "Why Are There So Many Civil Wars in Africa? Understanding and Preventing Violent Conflict," *Journal of African Economies*, Vol.9, 3 (2000), pp. 244–269.

Election Institute of Southern Africa "Two Decades of Elections Observation in Africa: Lessons Learned, Role, Performance and Impact on Democracy Building," available at www.eisa.org/event/symposium 2.htm

Eric G. Bernman and Katie E. Sams, *Constructive Disengagement: Western Efforts to develop African Peace Keeping*, Institute of Security Studies Monograph Series No. 33 (Pretoria: ISS 1998).

Ernst and Young, Assessment of the African Union Commission, AIDCO C5 Debriefing Memorandum 12 Jan 2012.

European Union, 10th European Development Fund: The Africa Component of the ACP Research Programme for Sustainable Development, Ref EuropeAid/132-331/11/ACT/ACP;

European Union, Annex II: General Conditions Applicable to the European Union Financial Grant Contracts for External Action, March 2011;

Freear, M. and de Coning, C. Lessons from the African Union Mission for Somalia (AMISOM) for Peace Operations in Mali. *Stability: International Journal of Security and Development.* (2013). 2(2), p.Art. 23. DOI: http://doi.org/10.5334/sta.bj

Geert, La Porte and James Mackie, editors. *Building the African Union: An Assessment of Past Progress and Future Prospects for the African Union's Institutional Architecture,*" *Policy and Management Report 18*, Nordic Africa Institute and ECDPM, October 2010

Ghali, Boutros, *An Agenda for Peace: Preventive Diplomacy, Peacemaking and Peace-keeping*, Report of the Secretary-General Document A/47/277 – S/24111, 17 June 1992.

Gilpin, Raymond and Michelle Swearingen, "Financing and Refocusing the African Union Peace Fund," *International Network for Economics and Conflict,* (June 24 2013), available at https: //www.swp-berlin.org/ fileadmin /contents/products/comments/2012C29_vrr.pdf

Gottschalk Keith and Schmidt, Siegmar "The African Union and the New Partnership for Africa's Development: Strong Institutions for Weaker States," available at www.weltpolitik.net/attachment/international politik und gesellschaft 2004.

Harsch, Earnest, "Africa Builds its Own Security," *Africa Recovery*, Vol. 17, 3 (2003).

Harsch, Ernest, "Funding for NEPAD: Africa Still Waiting for Genuine Partnership," *Africa Renewal*, 2002.

Harsch, Ernest. "Africa Defends Democratic Rule," *African Renewal* , April 2010.

Herbest, Jeffrey. "Economic Incentives, Natural Resources and Conflicts in Africa," *Journal of African Economies,* Vol. 9, 3 (2000), pp. 270–294.

Hopkins, A.G. editor, *Globalization in World History*, London: Pimlico 2002.

Huliara, Asteris. "Qadhafi's Comeback: Libya and Sub-Saharan Africa in the 1990s," *African Affairs*, Vol: 100, 398 (2001), pp. 5–25

Imobighe, T.A. *The OAU (AU) and OAS in Regional Conflict Management: A Comparative Assessment*, Lagos: Spectrum 2003).

International Labour Office et al., "Issue Paper," Presented at the African Union Extraordinary Summit of Heads of State and Government on Employment and Poverty Alleviation in Africa, Ougadougou, 8–9 September 2004.

Johanson, Richard K *Implications of Globalization and Economic Restructuring for Skills Development in Sub-Saharan Africa*, Working Paper No. 29. Geneva: ILO, 2004.

Kabbaj, Omar. *The Challenge of African Development.* Supplement of the African Development Bank Report, Oxford: OUP, 2003.

Kadim, D. "An Overview" Compendium of Elections in Denis Kadim and Susan Boayse (editors) *Southern Africa 1989–2009: 20 Years of Multiparty Democracy (*Johannesburg*:* Electoral Institute of Southern Africa 2009.

Kagwanja, Peter, Patrick Mutahi, "Protection of Civilians in African Peace Missions. The Case of the African Union Mission in Sudan, Darfur" *ISS Paper 139*, May 2007.

Kagwanya Peter, and Roger Southall, editors, *Kenya's Uncertain Democracy: the Electoral Crises of 2008*, Oxford: Routledge 2010.

Kanyinga, Karuti and Sophie Walker "Building a Political Settlement: The International Approach to Kenya's 2008 Post-Election Crisis," *International Journal for Security and Development*, Vol: 2, 2 (2013), available at http://www.stabilityjournal.org/articles/

Karuma, Shubana and Eleanora Mura, "Reflections on African Union Election Assistance and Observations," in IDEA, The Integrity of Elections: The Role of Regional Organizations, IDEA 2012.

Keating, Tom and Andy W Knight, eds., *Building Sustainable Peace*, United Nations University Press 2004.

Kelley, Judith. "Watching the Watchmen: The Role of Election Observers in Africa," available at www.thinkafricapress.com May 2013.

Khadiagala, G. M. "Regionalism and Conflict Resolution: Lessons from the Kenyan Crises in Peter Kagwanya and Roger Southall, editors, *Kenya's Uncertain Democracy: the Electoral Crises of 2008.* Oxford: Routledge 2010.

Kioko, Ben "The Right of Intervention under the African Union Constitutive Act: from Non-interference to non-Intervention," *International Review of the Red Cross*, Vol 85 (2003), pp. 807–25.

Koehane R and Nye, J. "Transnational Relations and World Politics", *International Organization*, Vol: 25, 3 (1971), pp. 329–350.

Koehane Robert and Joseph Nye, *Power and Interdependence: World Politics in Transition*, Boston: Little Brown, 1977.

Koning, Niek *Should Africa Protect its Farmers to Revitalize its Economy*, Gatekeepers Series No, 105. London: International Institute for Environment and Development, 2002.

Konstantinos D. Magliveras: The Sanctioning System of the African Union: Part Success, Part Failure, 2011 available at /http://www.academia.edu/1103678.

Landsberg, Christopher "The Fifth Wave of Pan-Africanism," in Adekeye Adebajo and Rasheed, Ismail eds, *West Africa's Security Challenges: Building Peace in a Troubled Region* Boulder: Rienner 2004.

Langer Johannes, "The Responsibility to Protect: Kenya's Post – Electoral Crises" *Journal of International Service* (Fall 2011) available at www.american.educ/sis.

Le Vine, Victor T. "The Fall and Rise of the Constitutionalism in West Africa," *Journal of Modern African Studies*, Vol. 35, 2 (1997), pp. 207–229.

Legum Colin et.al., *Africa in the 1980s: A Continent in Crises* (New York: McGraw-Hill Book Company, 1979.

Legum, Colin "The OAU after Twenty Years: The Record of Failures and Success," *Africa Contemporary Records* Annual Survey and Documents (1983–1984).

Legum, Colin "The Role of the Organization of African Unity in Dealing with Violent Conflicts," in Colin Legum et.al. *Africa in the 1980s: A Continent in Crises,* New York: McGraw-Hill Book Company, 1979.

Legum, Colin *Africa since Independence*, Bloomington and Indianapolis: Indiana University Press 1999

Legum, Colin et al, *Africa in the 1980s: A Continent in Crises*, New York: McGraw Hill Book Co. 1979.

Legum, Colin *Pan Africanism: A Short Political Guide*, Revised Edition, New York: Praeger 1965.

Leonard, D.K. Election and Conflict in Africa: An Introduction, *Journal of Elections*, Vol. 8, (2009), pp. 1–15.

Leonce, Ndikumana, Jeffrey "Towards a Solution to Violence in Burundi: A Case for Political and Economic Liberalization," *Journal of Modern African Studies*, Vol. 38, 3 (2005), pp. 431–459.

Levitt, Jeremy I. "The Peace and Security Council of the African Union: the Known Unknowns," *Transnational Law and Contemporary Problems*, Vol.13, 1 (2003): 109–137.

Lonsdale, John "Globalization, Ethnicity and Democracy: A View from the Hopeless Continent," in A.G. Hopkins, editor, *Globalization in World History* (London: Pimlico 2002).

Makinda, Samuel M., F. Wafula Okumu, David Mickler, *The African Union: Addressing the challenges of peace, security, and governance*, London: Routledge 2016.

Malan, Mark "Conflict Prevention in Africa: Theoretical Construct or Plan of Action," *KAIPTC Paper No. 3 February 2005,* available at http://www.kaiptc.org/Publications/Occasional-Papers/Documents/no_3.aspx.

Maluwa, Tiyanjana "Re-imaging African Unity: Some Preliminary Reflections on the Constitutive Act of the African Union," *African Yearbook of International Law,* Vol. 9 (2001), pp. 3–38.

Maluwa, Tuyanjana "The Constitutive Act of the Africa Union and Institution-building in Post-Colonial Africa," *Leiden Journal of International Law,* Vol. 16, 1 (2003), pp. 157–170.

Marshal, Monty G *Conflict Trends in Africa, 1946–2004: A Macro-Comparative Perspective, October 2005*, available at http://www.systemicpeace.org/africa/ Africa Conflict Trends MGM2005us.pdf

Mbeki, Thabo, Speech delivered on the Occasion of the Launch of the African Renaissance Institute, Pretoria, 11 October 1999.

McGowan, Patrick J. "African Military Coups D'Etat, 1956–2001: Frequency, Trends and Distribution," *Journal of Modern African Studies,* Vol. 41, 3 (2003), pp. 339–370.

Memorandum of Understanding on Security, Stability, Development and Cooperation in Africa, annexed to The Report of the Secretary General on the Implementation of the CSSDCA.

Mingst, Karen *Essentials of International Relations,* New York: W W Norton and Company, 1999.

Mohammed, Abdul; Testagiorgis Paulos and de Waal, Alex "Peace and Security Dimension of the African Union", Document Presented at the African Development Forum III. Addis Ababa: ECA 2003)

Morgenthau, Hans *Politics among Nations*, 5th ed. rev, New York: Knopf, 1978.

Murithi, Tim, "The African Union's Evolving Role in Peace Operations: The African Union Mission in Burundi, the African Union Mission in Sudan and the African Union Mission in Somalia", *African Security Review* Vol. 17,1 (2008), pp. 70–82.

Murray, Rachel *Human Rights in Africa, From the OAU to the African Union,* Cambridge University Press, 2004.

Naldi, Gino "The African Union: A New Dawn for Africa?", *The International and Comparative Law Quarterly*, Vol.51 (2002), pp. 415–425;

Naldi, Gino J. *The Organization of African Unity: An Analysis of its Role*, London: Mansell, 1989.

Nathan Laurie, "Mediating in Madagascar by Bypassing the AU Ban on Coup Legitimization," *Kujega Amani,* 5 November 2013, available at www.ssrc.org.

Ndlovu-Gatsheni, Sabelo J. *Coloniality of Power in Post-Colonial Africa: Myth of Decolonization*, Dakar, CODESRIA, 2013.

New Partnership for Africa's Development, *Basic Documents*.

OAU Report of the Secretary General on the Implementation of the CSSDCA C/2255 (LXXVI), Rev. 1 Original English.

OAU, *The Organization of African Unity: A Short History*, Addis Ababa, OAU Secretariat, 1977.

OAU, "Inventory of African Conflicts since the Establishment of the Organization of African Unity in 1963," Addis Ababa, 1998.

OAU, African Charter on Human and People's Rights, 1987.

OAU, Declaration of the Assembly of Heads of State and Government of the Organization of African Unity on the Political and Socio-Economic Situation in Africa and the Fundamental Changes Taking Place in the World, July 1990.

OAU, Declaration of the Assembly of Heads of State and Government of the Organization of African Unity on the Political and Socio-Economic Situation in Africa and the Fundamental Changes Taking Place in the World, July 1990.

OAU, *Introductory Note to the Report of the Secretary General to the 38th Session of the Assembly of Heads of State and Government and the 76th Session of the Council of Ministers*, Durban 4–10 July 2002.

OAU, *Lagos Plan of Action for the Economic Development of Africa, 1980–2000*, Addis Ababa, 1988.

OAU, *Proceedings of the Conference of the Independent African States* Vol. I Addis Ababa: 1963.

OAU, Report of the Secretary General on Strengthening the Role of the OAU/AU in Elections, Observations and Monitoring and the Advancement of the Democratization Process in Africa, CM/ 2257 (LXXVI) July 2002.

OAU, Secretariat, *Resolving Conflicts in Africa: Implementation Option*, Addis Ababa, ND.

Obasanjo Olusegum and Mosha felix G.N. editors, *Africa: Rise to Challenge – Towards a CSSDCA*, Lagos: Africa Leadership Forum 1993.

Obasanjo, Olusegun and Mosha Felix G.N. editors, *Africa: rise to Challenge, Conference Report of the Kampala Forum*, Abeokuta, Nigeria: Africa Leadership Forum, 1992.

Ogune, H. "Appraising Election Monitoring and Observation in Africa: The Case of the Democratic Republic of Congo's 2011 Presidential Elections," sited in www.eisa.org.za

Ojo, Olatunde J.C.B; Orwa D.K. and Utete, C.M.B. *African International Relations,* London and Lagos: Longman 1985.

Olukoshi, Adebayo O. *Governing the African Developmental Process: The New Challenge of the New Partnership for Africa's development (NEPAD)*, Occasional Paper, Copenhagen: Centre of African Studies 2002.

Packer Corinne A.A and Rukare, Donald "The New African Union and Its Constitutive Act," *The American Journal of International Law*, Vol. 96, 2 (2002), pp. 365–379.

Pfister R. Gateway to International Victory: the Diplomacy of the African National Congress in Africa, 1960–1994, *The Journal of Modern African Studies*, Vol. 41, 1 (2003), pp. 51–73.

Polch Lauren and Nicolas Cook, "Madagascar's Political Crises," *Congressional Research Services*, June 18 2012, available at https://www.fas.org/sgp/crs/row/R40448.pdf;

Prosser, Gifford and Roger-Louis, WM editors, *Decolonization and African Independence: The Transfer of Power, 1960–1980*, Connecticut: Yale University Press 1988.

Ramsbotham, Alex, Alhaji M.S Bah and Fanny Calder, "Enhancing African Peace and Security Capacity: A Useful Role for the UK and the G8," *International Affairs*, Vol. 81, 2 (2005), pp. 325–339.

Report of the Secretary General on the Implementation of the CSSDCA C/2255 (LXXVI), Rev. 1 Original English.

Rimmer Douglas, editor, *Action in Africa*, London, The Royal African Society 1993.

Roggio, Bill J. The Rise and Fall of the Islamic Courts: An Online History January 4, 2007, *The Long War Journal*, available at http://www.longwarjournal.org/archives/2007/01/

Rupiya Martin, A review of the African Union's experience in facilitating peaceful power transfers: Zimbabwe, Ivory Coast, Libya and Sudan: Are there Prospects for Reform, *Africa Journal of Conflict Prevention*, Vol. 12, 2 (2012), pp.161–183.

Sachs, Jeffrey "Helping the Poorest of the Poor," *The Economist,* 14 August 1999;

Schnabel Albrecht and David Carment, editors. *Conflict Prevention: From Rhetoric to Reality* London, Lexington Books 2004.

Secretary General of the United Nations. "The Causes of Conflict and Promotion of Durable Peace and Sustainable Development in Africa," report to the UN Security Council 1998.

Sharamo, R, The African Union's Peacekeeping Experience in Darfur, Sudan, *Conflict Trends*, 3 (2006), pp. 50–55.

Shaw Timothy M. and Nyang'oro, Julius E. "Conclusion: African Foreign Policies and the Next Millennium – Alternative Perspectives, Practices and Possibilities," in Wright Stephen (editor), *African Foreign Policy*, Boulder, Westview 1999.

Shinkaye, J.K. "Nigeria's role in shaping the African Union," in Nigerian Ministry of Cooperation and Integration in Africa, *African Union and the Challenges of Cooperation and Integration,* Proceedings of the National Seminar 15–15 May 2001, Abuja: Spectrum Books Ltd. 2002.

Singer, J. David "The Levels of Analysis Problem," in James Rosenau, editor, *International Politics and Foreign Policy*, rev ed, New York: Free Press, 1961.

SIPRI Year Book 2003, Appendix 10A, Tables 10A.1 and 10A.3.

Söderbaum, F and R. Tavares (eds), *Regional Organizations in African Security*, London: Routledge 2010.

Solomon Hussein and Maxi Van Aardt, *"Caring": Security in Africa,* Institute of Security Studies Monograph Series No. 20. Pretoria: ISS, 1998.

Souaré, Issaka K. "The African Union as a 'Norm Entrepreneur' on Coups D'Etat in Africa, 1952–2012: An Empirical Assessment," *Journal of Modern African Studies*, Vol 52, 1 (2014), pp. 69–94.

"South Africa Opposes US War on Iraq," www.africacrisis.org 19 December 2002;

"South Africa Regrets Iraq War", www.bbc.co.uk 20 March 2003.

"South Africa Tries to Avert War in Iraq." *Mercury*, 27 January 2003.

Sow, Ahmed Iyane. "L'Union Africaine," *Revue Internationale de Droit Africain*, 49 (2001), pp. 7–28;

Sturman, Kathryn "The Rise of Libya as a Regional Player" *African Security Review* Vol. 12, 2 (2003), pp. 109–112.

Susungi, N.N. "The Origins of the Debt Crises and its Aftermath in Africa," in Rimmer Douglas (editor), *Action in Africa*, London: The Royal African Society, 1993.

Swigert, James W. "Challenges of Peace Keeping in Africa," *The DISARM Journal* (Winter 2004–2005), pp. 37–39;

The African Leadership Forum, *The Kampala Documents: Towards a Conference on Security, Stability, Development and Cooperation in Africa,* Lagos: 1991.

'The Heart of the Matter', and 'Hopeless Africa' *The Economist*, 13 May 2000.

Thompson, Vincent B. *Africa and Unity: The Evolution of Pan Africanism*, London, Harlow 1969.

Thompson, W.S. *Ghana's Foreign Policy: Diplomacy, Ideology and the New State, 1957–1966* Princeton, Princeton University Press, 1969.

Tieku, Thomas Kwasi "Explaining the Clash and Accommodation of Interests of Major Actors in the Creation of the African Union," *African Affairs,* 103 (2004), pp. 246–247.

Touray, Omar A. "The Common African Defence and Security Policy," *African Affairs*, Vol. 104, 417 (2005), pp. 635–654;

Touray, Omar A. *The Gambia and the World: A History of the Foreign Policy of Africa's Smallest State, 1965–1995,* Hamburg African Studies Series Vol. 9, Hamburg: Institute of African Affairs, 2000.

Udombaba, Nsongurua J. "A Harmony or Cacophony?: The Music of Integration in the African Union Treaty and the New Partnership for Africa's Development, *Indiana International and Comparative Law Review*, Vol. 13, 6 (2002), pp. 185.

Udombana, Nsongurua J. "Can the Leopard Change its Spots?: The African Union Treaty and Human Rights," *American University International Law Review*, Vol. 17 (2002), pp. 1177–1195;

Udombana, Nsongurua J. "The Institutional Structure of the African Union: a Legal Analysis," *California Western International Law Journal,* Vol. 33 (2002), pp. 49–135;

UN Economic and Social Council and UNECA, *What NEPAD Implies for African Policy Makers*, Document of the 21st Meeting of the Committee of Experts of the Conference of African Ministers of Finance, Planning and Economic Development, Document E/ECA/CM.1/2, Johannesburg, South Africa, 16–18 October 2002.

UN Security Council, "Special Research Report No. 2: Working Together for Peace and Security in Africa: The Security Council and the AU Peace and Security Council" available at http://www.securitycouncilreport.org/special-research-report/lookup-c-glKWLeMTIsG-b 6769467.php

UN Security Council, "Special Research Report No. 2: Working Together for Peace and Security in Africa: The Security Council and the AU Peace and Security Council" available at http://www.securitycouncilreport.org/special-research-report/lookup-c-glKWLeMTIsG-b 6769467.php.

UNCTAD, *Commodity Yearbook, 1995*; Geneva: UNCTAD 1995;

UNDP *Human Development Report* Several Years from 2002–2012.

UNDP, Knowing the What and the How, RBM in the UNDP: Technical Note 2010

UNECA, *Assessing Regional Integration in Africa*, ECA Policy Research Report, Addis Ababa: ECA 2004.

UNECA, *Economic Report on Africa 1999: the Challenges of Poverty Reduction and Sustainability*, Addis Ababa, ECA, 1999.

UNECA, *Economic Report on Africa 2004,* Addis Ababa: ECA 2004.

UNECA, *Economic Report on Africa, 2002:Traking Performance and Progress*, Addis Ababa 2003.

UNECA, *Harnessing Technologies for Sustainable Development*, ECA Policy Research Report, Addis Ababa, ECA 2002.

UNECA, *Millennium Development Goals in Africa: Progress and Challenges*, Addis Ababa, 2005.

UNECA, *The ECA and Africa: Accelerating a Continents Development.* Addis Ababa, ECA, 1999.

UNECA, *Transforming Africa's Economies*, Addis Ababa: UNECA, 2001.

UNECA, *Transforming Africa's Economies*, Addis Ababa: UNECA, 2001.

UNEP, *Development of an Action Plan for the Environment Initiative of NEPAD,* UNEP 2003. Available at www.environment-directory.org/nepad/content

UNESCO, *World Science Report*, Paris, 1998.

United Nations Conference on Trade and Development, *Foreign Direct Investment in Africa: Performance and Potential*, UNCTAD, 1999.

United Nations Development Programme, "Conflict Prevention Thematic Guidance Note," *NHDR Occasional Paper No 3, 2004 a*vailable at http://hdr.undp.org/sites/default/files/nhdr _conflict _gn.pdf.

United Nations Population Division, *International Migration Report* 2002.

United Nations Security Council, "Support for AU peace keeping," *Updated Report* No. 3, 22 October 2009, available at www.securitycouncilreport.org.

United Nations, Security Council Presidential Statement (S/PRST/2009) March 2009.

United Nations, "Report of the African Union – United Nations on Modalities for Support to African Union Peace Keeping Operations," (A/63/666; S2008/813) December 2008.

United Nations, "Report of the Secretary-General on the Causes of Conflict and the Promotion of Durable Peace and Sustainable Development in Africa," A/52/871-S/1998/318, (1998).

United Nations, Address of the Secretary General address to the Central Organ of the OAU Mechanism for Conflict Prevention, Management and Resolution, Lome 26 March 1997 (SG/SM/6192).

United Nations, New Partnership for Africa's Development: Report of the Secretary General on Progress in Implementation and International Support" June 2004, Doc. E/AC.50/2004/6 and Doc. A/59/150.

United Nations, Security Council Report, Monthly Forecast March 2015 available at www.securitycouncilreport.org.

United Nations, Ten Year Capacity Building Programme for the African Union, First Triennial Review (2006–2009), Final Report November 2010.

United Nations' *In Larger Freedom: Towards Development, Security and Human Rights for All*, Report of the Secretary General 2005.

United States Department of Defense, "African Union,' Summary of the 2005–2006 *Quadrennial Defense Review* (May 2006), pp. 1–9;

Villalon, Leonardo A. and Peter Von Doepp, editors, *The Fate of Africa's Democratic Experiment: Elites and Institutions,* Bloomington: Indiana University Press, 2005.

Walraven, Klaas van. "From Union of Tyrants to Power to People? The Significance of the Pan-African Parliament for the African Union," *Afrika Spectrum*, Vol. 39, 2 (2004), pp.197–221.

Walreven, K. Van. *Dreams of Power: The Role of the Organization of African Unity in the Politics of Africa, 1963–1993*, Research Series 13/1999, Lieden: African Studies Centre 1999.

Waltz, Kenneth N. "Realist Thoughts and Neo-Realist Theory," *Journal of International Affairs*, Vol. 44, 1 (1990), pp. 21–37

Waltz, Kenneth *Theory of International Politics*, Reading Mass: Addison-Wesley, 1979;

Wiklund, Cecilia Hull, *The Role of the African Union Mission in Somalia*, Stockholm, Ministry of Defence 2013.

Williams, Paul D, The African Union's Conflict Management Capabilities, Working Paper , Council on Foreign Relations (October 2011).

Wing, Adrien Katherine and Smith, Tyler Murray "The New African Union and the Women's Right," *Transnational Law and Contemporary Problems* Vol. 13 (2003), pp. 33–81;

World Bank, "Africa Region Trade Progress Note," available at www.worldbank.org/afr/trade/wb-assistance_2003-03

World Bank, "Recent Trade Performance of Sub-Saharan African Countries: Causes for Hope or More of the Same?" in *http://www.worldbank.org/afr/findings/english/find176.htm* p.1–3.

World Bank, *Can Africa Claim the 21st Century*, Washington: World Bank, 2000.

World Bank, *Can Africa Claim the 21stCentury*, Washington DC 2000.

World Bank, *Intensifying Action against HIV/AIDS in Africa: Responding to a Development Crises*, Washington DC: World Bank, 1999.

World Bank, *Trade Blocks* Washington DC: World Bank, 2000.

World Health Organization, *Health Life*, Geneva: WHO, 2002, available at (ww.who.int/whr).

Wright, Stephan "The Changing Context of African Foreign Policies," in Stephen Wright, editor, *African Foreign Policies*, Boulder, Westview 1999.

Young, Crawford "The End of the Post-Colonial State? Reflections on Changing African Political Dynamics," *African Affairs* Vol. 103, 410 (2004), pp. 23–49,

Zuma, N.C. Dlamini Opening Statement Foreign Minister of South Africa, at the meeting of Experts on Common African Defence and Security Policy, Randburg, South Africa, 27 March 2003.

Index

About the Author

Omar Alieu Touray is a Gambian diplomat and development professional. For several years, he was Permanent Representative of The Gambia to the African Union and Ambassador to Ethiopia with concurrent accreditation as High Commissioner to Kenya and South Africa. He had been Permanent Representative Designate to the United Nations in New York before he was appointed Minister of Foreign Affairs and International Cooperation. He also worked as Regional Policy Adviser at the Regional Bureau for East and Central Africa (ODN) of the United Nations World Food Programme, and as consultant for the United Nations Economic Commission for Africa, United Nations Development Programme Gambia Country Office and the Commission of the African Union. He presently works at the Islamic Development Bank in Jeddah, Saudi Arabia. Dr Touray holds a PhD in International Relations from the Graduate Institute of International Studies, University of Geneva, Switzerland. He also studied Finance and Islamic Finance at the IE Business School in Madrid. He is the author of *The Gambia and the World* and several papers on international development and African affairs.

Lightning Source UK Ltd.
Milton Keynes UK
UKOW01n0622091017
310573UK00011BA/382/P

9 781442 268975